ETHICS,
THE SOCIAL SCIENCES,
AND POLICY ANALYSIS

THE HASTINGS CENTER SERIES IN ETHICS

A Continuation Order Plan is available for this series. A continuation order will bring delivery of each new volume immediately upon publication. Volumes are billed only upon actual shipment. For further information please contact the publisher.

ETHICS, THE SOCIAL SCIENCES, AND POLICY ANALYSIS

Edited by
DANIEL CALLAHAN and
BRUCE JENNINGS

The Hastings Center
Institute of Society, Ethics and the Life Sciences
Hastings-on-Hudson, New York

PLENUM PRESS • NEW YORK AND LONDON

Library of Congress Cataloging in Publication Data

Main entry under title:

Ethics, the social sciences, and policy analysis.

(The Hastings Center series in ethics)
Includes bibliographical references and index.
1. Policy sciences—Addresses, essays, lectures. 2. Social ethics—Addresses, essays, lectures. 3. Social values—Addresses, essays, lectures. I. Callahan, Daniel,
1930– . II. Jennings, Bruce, 1949– . III. Series.
H97.E835 1983   361.6′1   82-22277
ISBN 0-306-41143-1

© 1983 The Hastings Center
Institute of Society, Ethics and the Life Sciences
360 Broadway
Hastings-on-Hudson, New York 10706

Plenum Press, New York
A Division of Plenum Publishing Corporation
233 Spring Street, New York, N.Y. 10013

Printed in the United States of America

CONTRIBUTORS

JAMES M. BANNER, JR., formerly a professor in the History Department at Princeton University, is Chairman of the American Association for the Advancement of the Humanities in Washington, D.C.

ROBERT N. BELLAH is Ford Professor of Sociology and Comparative Studies and Chairman, Department of Sociology, at the University of California, Berkeley. His most recent book (with Philip E. Hammond) is *Varieties of Civil Religion*.

MARTIN BULMER is Lecturer in Social Administration at the London School of Economics and Political Science. His main teaching and research interests are in the methodology of social research and the applications of social research to public policymaking. His publications include *Social Policy Research, Social Research and Royal Commissions*, and *Social Research Ethics*.

DANIEL CALLAHAN, a philosopher by training, is Director of The Hastings Center. He has published a number of articles on ethics and public policy and is the author of *Abortion: Law, Choice and Morality* and *The Tyranny of Survival*.

JEANNE GUILLEMIN is Associate Professor of Sociology at Boston College. Her publications include *Urban Renegades: The Cultural Strategy of American Indians* and *Anthropological Realities: Readings in the Science of Culture*. She is a former Congressional Fellow of the American Anthropological Association.

RUTH S. HANFT is Senior Research Associate at the Association of Academic Health Centers in Washington, D.C. She was formerly Deputy Assistant Secretary for Health Research Statistics and Technology, Department of Health and Human Services.

IRVING LOUIS HOROWITZ is Distinguished Professor of Sociology and Political Science at Rutgers University, holder of the Hannah Arendt Chair, and Director of Studies in Comparative International Development. He is also editor in chief of *Transaction/SOCIETY*. He has written a trilogy of volumes on policy: *Social Science and Public Policy in the United States, Equity, Income, and Policy,* and *Constructing Policy.*

BRUCE JENNINGS is Research Associate for Policy Studies at The Hastings Center. His publications include several articles on the history of political theory and he is coeditor of *Darwin, Marx, and Freud* (forthcoming).

MICHAEL S. MCPHERSON is Associate Professor of Economics at Williams College and a member of the School of Social Science, Institute for Advanced Study, Princeton, N.J. He has done work on the relation between economics and morality and on policy problems in higher education.

MARK H. MOORE is Daniel and Florence Guggenheim Professor of Criminal Justice Policy and Management at Harvard

University. A policy analyst concerned with crime control policy and the regulation of dangerous substances, he is author of *Buy or Bust: The Effective Regulation of an Illicit Market in Heroin* and coeditor of *Public Duties: The Moral Obligations of Public Officials.*

THOMAS H. MURRAY is Associate for Social and Behavioral Studies at The Hastings Center. He was trained as an experimental social psychologist and has since worked on the epistemology and ethics of social science knowledge and research. He has written on the ethics of deception research and is coeditor of *Doing Well and Feeling Better: Ethics and Pleasure and Performance Enhancing Drugs* (forthcoming).

KAI NIELSEN is Professor of Philosophy at the University of Calgary, Alberta, Canada. He is author of *Reason and Practice, Skepticism,* and *Contemporary Critiques of Religion.*

THOMAS F. PETTIGREW is Professor of Social Psychology at the University of California, Santa Cruz. He is a specialist in race relations as well as author of *A Profile of the Negro American,* and *Racially Separate or Together?* and editor of *The Sociology of Race Relations: Redefinition and Reform.*

KENNETH PREWITT is President of the Social Science Research Council and has taught political science at Washington University, Stanford University, Columbia University, and the University of Chicago. Before joining the SSRC he was Director of the National Opinion Research Center in Chicago. His books in the field of American politics include *The Recruitment of Political Leaders, Labyrinths of Democracy,* and *Introduction to American Government.*

MARTIN REIN is Professor of Social Policy at Massachusetts Institute of Technology. He is author of *Social Policy, Dilemmas of Social Reform* (with Peter Marris), *Social Science and Public Policy, From Policy to Practice*, and other books. He is currently preparing a book with Lee Rainwater on the welfare state in Britain, Sweden, and the United States.

DONALD P. WARWICK is an Institute Fellow at the Harvard Institute for International Development and a Lecturer on Education and on Sociology at Harvard. He is author of *A Theory of Public Bureaucracy* and coauthor of *The Sample Survey: Theory and Practice*, among other works.

CAROL H. WEISS is a sociologist at the Harvard Graduate School of Education. She has been conducting research on the influence of the social sciences on government policy, which has led to two books on the subject—*Social Science Research and Decision-Making* and *Using Social Research in Public Policy Making*.

CONTENTS

ix

INTRODUCTION

The social sciences play a variety of multifaceted roles in the policymaking process. So varied are these roles, indeed, that it is futile to talk in the singular about the use of social science in policymaking, as if there were one constant relationship between two fixed and stable entities. Instead, to address this issue sensibly one must talk in the plural about uses of different modes of social scientific inquiry for different kinds of policies under various circumstances.

In some cases, the influence of social scientific research is direct and tangible, and the connection between the findings and the policy is easy to see. In other cases, perhaps most, its influence is indirect—one small piece in a larger mosaic of politics, bargaining, and compromise. Occasionally the findings of social scientific studies are explicitly drawn upon by policymakers in the formation, implementation, or evaluation of particular policies. More often, the categories and theoretical models of social science provide a general background orientation within which policymakers conceptualize problems and frame policy options. At times, the influence of social scientific work is cognitive and informational in nature; in other instances, policymakers use social science primarily for symbolic and political purposes in order to legitimate preestablished goals and strategies.

Nonetheless, amid this diversity and variety, troubling general questions persistently arise. They concern the epis-

temological validity of social scientific knowledge and its appl-
icability, the proper relationship between the social scientist
and the policymaker, and the balance that must be struck
between the empirical and the normative components of political decision making in a democratic society. These questions are not new. For three centuries, beginning with Thomas
Hobbes, they have been central to the strand of modern political thought that predicated stable, effective government on
the application of a science of human behavior. But in recent
years these questions have once again come to the fore, following a period in the 1960s and 1970s when it began to look
as if Hobbes's dream of a scientifically based governance was
finally becoming a practical possibility.

There are several reasons why such fundamental questions about the use of social scientific knowledge in public
policymaking are being raised today, but before turning to
them it will be helpful to recall briefly the context from which
these questions have emerged.

Though there has been a persistent interest in the application of social scientific knowledge throughout the twentieth century, the early and mid-1960s were halcyon years for
applied social science. Social scientific data, theories, and
methodologies began, rather suddenly, to be called upon for
policy-related purposes with a new sense of urgency and
purpose. Their contribution took two principal forms: policy
analysis and aggregate social survey studies. Administrative
reforms undertaken first in the Department of Defense during
the McNamara years and then directives mandating planning,
programming, and budgeting systems (PPBS) swept across
the entire federal bureaucracy, creating new openings for policy analysis. Social scientists armed with sophisticated microeconomic theories and models, systems theory, decision
theory, cost–benefit analysis, and the like quickly responded
to this opportunity. The creation of new graduate programs

of policy analysis at major universities helped to institution-alize policy analysis as a principal channel through which particular components of social scientific research flowed—and continue to flow—into the policy arena. Concomitantly, the civil rights movement, antipoverty programs, and concern with urban problems created a second opening for applied social science, this time in the form of large-scale empirical studies.

Looking back on this period, one is struck by the speed with which the social sciences—principally economics but also psychology, sociology, and political science—rose to a prom-inent place in the policy process. Even more striking are the largely unexamined and unchallenged presuppositions upon which this development rested, presuppositions that had ac-tually been questioned by earlier social scientists. Included among them were a particular understanding of the nature and purpose of policymaking in contemporary American so-ciety, a conception of the proper function of the social scientist in a policymaking process so understood, and an underlying positivistic account of the nature of social science itself. These three presuppositions were, for a time, interlocking and mu-tually reinforcing. When their interconnection began to un-ravel and when each began to come under critical scrutiny from various quarters, many lingering or submerged ques-tions about policy analysis and the political role of the social sciences could no longer be held in abeyance.

Speaking to the White House Economic Conference in 1962, President John F. Kennedy articulated a then widely held view of the challenge facing government in the United States:

> The fact of the matter is that most of the problems, or at least many of them that we now face, are technical problems, are administrative problems. They are very sophisticated judgments which do not lend themselves

> to the great sort of "passionate movements" which have
> stirred this country so often in the past. Now they deal
> with questions which are beyond the comprehension of
> most men.

These remarks succinctly express the first two presuppositions mentioned above, and they convey as well the climate of opinion that came to dominate the attitude of American policymakers in the 1960s and 1970s. Underlying the President's formulation here—which, by the way, reflected views being expressed by many prominent social scientists during this period as part of the so-called "end of ideology" thesis—was the belief that a stable normative or ideological consensus had finally been achieved in the United States. That consensus assumed an era of unlimited economic growth and centered on the basic tenets of welfare state liberalism: the extension of civil liberties to previously disenfranchised groups, equality of opportunity, and the provision of a minimum floor of social welfare entitlements. Under these conditions, political "issues" gave way to or became administrative "problems" amenable to technical "solutions." Normative debates about ends could be put aside in favor of purportedly much more rational and manageable factual debates about means. Freed from the perturbations of the great passionate movements of the past, governmental decision making could concern itself with questions of efficiency and the fitting of means to ends. Knowing where we wanted to go , our only problem was how to get there.

Moreover, once policymaking was taken to be primarily an administrative, technical activity, cut off from broadly normative or ideological considerations and concerned solely with the efficient fitting of means to ends already given, a particular conception of the relationship between the social scientist (or policy analyst) and the policymaker became appropriate. The social scientist was cast in a normatively passive—objective or value-neutral—role. Having been assigned a particular goal by the policymaker (who, in turn, was acting on authority delegated by democratically elected representatives), the social scientist was to analyze particular policy options which, on the basis of empirically confirmed generalizations about human behavior, could be evaluated in terms of their potential consequences, the relationship between costs and benefits, and their likely effectiveness.

Here the final presupposition mentioned above came into play. A broadly positivistic conception of the nature of social science dovetailed quite nicely with the notion of policymaking as technical problem solving and with the normatively passive role of the social scientist vis-à-vis the policymaker. Indeed, on this conception social scientists could hardly play any role but this if their activities were to be intellectually honest and politically legitimate. To claim special expertise and authoritative knowledge regarding matters of fact was precisely what the social scientist *qua* scientist was supposed to do and could do now that the social sciences had reached a certain stage of intellectual maturity. But to claim expertise and authority regarding matters of value was unwarranted. Thus, during this period, the belief that policy questions were technical questions and the positivist belief that the social sciences, by emulating the empirical methodologies of the natural sciences, could provide expert factual and instrumental knowledge needed for the solution to these problems converged to create a powerful intellectual rationale for the rapid rise of applied social science.

Within the confines of these presuppositions, the ethical questions pertinent to the use of social science in policymaking are quite limited and tend to merge with the canons of professional scientific methodology. Intellectual honesty, the suppression of personal bias, careful collection and accurate reporting of data, and candid admission of the limits of the scientific reliability of studies—these were essentially the only ethical questions that could arise, given this general understanding of the situation. And, since these ethical responsibilities are not particularly controversial at least in principle, it is not surprising that during this period neither philosophers nor social scientists themselves devoted much time to analyzing or discussing them. Simultaneously, ethical questions in a broader sense, like the disturbingly antidemocratic implications of the view that governance had become something to be left to technical experts—because, in President Kennedy's words, it dealt with "questions which are beyond the comprehension of most men"—were largely neglected as well.

Now, to be sure, this brief account of the climate of opinion that prevailed while policy analysis and applied social science rose to prominence in American government is drastically oversimplified. But it is not, we believe, fundamentally misleading. The presuppositions we have mentioned are still to be found, albeit in more sophisticated forms, in a good deal of the current literature on policy analysis. However, in the last few years there have begun to appear discussions of policy analysis which challenge many of these presuppositions and which raise once again some long neglected epistemological, political, and ethical questions concerning the use of social scientific inquiry in public policymaking. This volume is intended as a contribution to the discussion of these questions.

There are two principal reasons why these sorts of questions have been receiving increasing attention recently. First, the positivistic account of the nature of social scientific knowledge has come under sustained attack. In particular, the positivist account of objectivity and its insistence on a sharp separation of facts and values has been rendered problematic by recent philosophical analysis of science. It is also now becoming clear, and widely recognized, that even the most quantitative and formalistic policy-analytic techniques contain concealed value choices and inextricable normative implications. Second, and equally important, historical and sociological studies of the interaction between social scientists and policymakers—and of the ways social scientific studies have actually been used in policy settings—have shown that this interaction is a good deal more complex and problematic than had previously been thought. These studies have indicated that the direct impact of social science on policy outcomes is usually very slight, that the indirect influence of generally circulated social scientific theories and concepts may be the social sciences' most telling contribution, and that actual dynamics of policymaking render it anything but a merely administrative or technical undertaking.

This book represents an effort to see what these wide-ranging reassessments of policy analysis mean for the ethics of applied social science. If the social sciences are not able to deliver the objective knowledge positivism promised, what kind of knowledge do they have to offer? What kind of validity does this knowledge possess? What kinds of questions can the social sciences ask? What kinds of answers can they provide? How can social scientists work effectively in the policymaking process? How direct a role ought they play? The essays collected here are intended to suggest that the ethical responsibilities of social scientists as policy advisers can neither be well defined nor clearly understood apart from the context of these broader epistemological, political, and organizational concerns.

The essays are grouped into four parts. Part I raises basic ethical and political questions about the nature of social scientific knowledge and its proper use in a democratic society.

The essays by Jennings, Bellah, Rein, and Nielsen detail various aspects of contemporary critiques of positivistic social science and explore new modes of policy analysis that might follow from these critiques.

Bruce Jennings analyzes the philosophical bases of "interpretive" social science and argues that this important stream of contemporary social inquiry could make a significant contribution to policy analysis. He contrasts interpretive modes of analysis with the methodological tenets of positivism and explores the political implications of these methodological differences. He concludes that the development of interpretive policy analysis would contribute to a revival of the communitarian tradition of American political thought and considers the possibility that such a revival would lead to a more democratically participatory form of policymaking.

In the next essay, Robert N. Bellah sets up a contrast similar to the one Jennings made, distinguishing between what he calls "technological" and "practical" social science. Placing himself in both an Aristotelian and radical democratic tradition, Bellah attacks the elitism and purported value neutrality of technological social science and its instrumental conception of knowledge and rationality. Against this he argues that, in a democratic society, social inquiry should be a part of a larger, participatory form of life based on the exercise of practical reason and moral judgment. Bellah insists that the relationship between the social scientist and the persons studied should be one of mutual learning and respect rather than of calculated manipulation and control. Critically commenting on Bellah's position, James M. Banner, Jr., worries that even Bellah's preferred conception of social science is not immune to antidemocratic ideological manipulation. Michael S. McPherson, while generally sympathetic to Bellah's position, argues that his stark antithesis between technological and practical social science leads him to overlook the need for, and the constructive possibilities of, a dialogue between these two dimensions of social science.

In his essay, Martin Rein emphasizes the value-laden character of policy analysis, particularly in the ways policy problems are identified and conceptualized. Arguing that relative perspectives or "frames" are an inextricable feature of social scientific knowledge (and, indeed, of all human knowledge), he suggests that one of the most important contributions that social science can make to policymaking is to clarify the nature and working of these frames. He concludes with a discussion of what this kind of value-critical social science would look like and how it could be applied.

Finally, Kai Nielsen analyzes Jürgen Habermas's critique of positivistic social science and, in turn, raises some critical questions of his own about the adequacy of Habermas's attempt to get beyond both mainstream social science and Marxism to a new, synthetic "critical theory." Raising a general point that bears on earlier essays in this section as well as on Habermas, Nielsen suggests that all attempts to apply nonpositivistic modes of social science to policymaking in a liberal capitalist state face severe, perhaps insurmountable dangers of cooptation and ideological distortion.

Turning from philosophical and metatheoretical discussions of the foundations of social science, Part II is devoted to a historical assessment of the political contributions that have been made by works coming out of various traditions of social inquiry. Martin Bulmer reflects upon the British tradition of social administration, a mode of social science self-consciously devoted to a normative program of social reform. After outlining the basic components of this tradition, Bulmer discusses the reasons why American policy studies in the postwar period have gone in a different direction. He concludes that the British and American orientations each have characteristic strengths and weaknesses and that future developments in policy studies ought to combine the empirical rigor of the American approach with the moral sensitivity of the British one.

Looking at a different tradition of twentieth-century social science—the ethnographic studies that grew out of the Chicago school of sociology—Jeanne Guillemin and Irving Louis Horowitz trace the use of research on marginal, deviant, or oppressed groups as the basis for policy advocacy on behalf of these groups. Their essay stresses a danger of cooptation different from that which worries Nielsen: namely, the fact that as these groups become politically self-conscious and organized, the social scientist's access to them is dependent upon ideological sympathy and favorable reporting and that this compromises the ideal of scientific objectivity.

Concluding this part, the essay by Carol H. Weiss provides a survey of recent sociological studies of the role of social scientific advisers in the policymaking process. She points out that the influence of social science is mainly indirect and that the relationship between social scientists and policymakers is beset by mutual misunderstandings and cross-purposes. In order to understand why this is so and develop realistic expectations about the roles that social science can play, she argues that the complexity of the policy process must be fully appreciated. To this end she proposes a model of policymaking in which three factors—information, ideology, and interests—each shape policy, and she suggests ways that social science might affect each of these variables.

Part III focuses on the differences between disciplinary social science and policy analysis and begins to explore the ethical implications that these differences hold for those engaged in policy analysis. Drawing examples from the area of health services data and health policy, Ruth S. Hanft reflects on the various ideological pressures that shape the design of studies and the interpretation of data. Generally, she concludes that greater care must be taken when policy analysts use limited and ambiguous data to draw policy conclusions.

Mark H. Moore's essay contrasts social science and policy analysis in terms of the methodological criteria appropriate to each. The exacting methods and standards of disciplinary social science cannot and should not be carried over into the domain of policy analysis, he argues, because the purposes served by these standards in academic inquiry—the advance of general and social knowledge and the refinement of existing paradigmatic theories—are not pertinent to the policy analyst's task. The policy analyst must make specific recommendations about particular problems; his or her function is to enhance the rationality of the policymaker's choice rather than to advance general theoretical knowledge of society. Hence, the studies conducted by a policy analyst must be accommodated to the constraints of the policy setting, even if this means that they fail to live up to the currently prevailing canons of disciplinary rigor. In his rejoinder to Moore, Kenneth Prewitt questions Moore's sharp distinction between disciplinary and policy research. Moreover, he maintains that it is precisely because disciplinary standards do not easily fit into the policymaker's work that policy analysis should not be thought of as an autonomous enterprise with its own rules. By remaining faithful to the canons of disciplinary rigor, policy analysts can make their greatest contribution by questioning the policymaker's preconceptions. Policy analysts, in Prewitt's view, should challenge the constraints and premises of the policy process so as to make it more open to new considerations and perspectives.

Returning to issues raised by Weiss and Hanft, Thomas H. Murray's essay discusses the ways in which the relationship between the policy analyst and the policymaker is influenced by the partial, incomplete knowledge social science provides. Drawing on the insight that neither social science nor the policy process are single, undifferentiated entities, he argues that cooperation could be improved if it were recognized that different aspects of social science are relevant to different stages of the policy process. Even with this more refined notion of application, however, the fact remains that social scientific knowledge is partial knowledge in a double sense: it is incomplete and in any particular instance it is tilted in a certain moral or normative direction. This situation creates special ethical responsibilities both for individual policy analysts and for the profession of policy analysis as a whole. Murray concludes by outlining some of these ethical responsibilities.

The fourth and concluding part is devoted to a fuller elaboration of the ethical guidelines pertinent to the practice of policy analysis and the use of applied social research. Donald P. Warwick and Thomas F. Pettigrew undertake to define key ethical problems raised by the relationships between social science and public policy; they present suggested ethical guidelines designed to alert applied researchers to the morally sensitive aspects of their work.

Each of the essays in this volume was originally commissioned for a research project on the ethics of social inquiry conducted by the Hastings Center from 1979 to 1981. The project involved a number of working meetings and independent research efforts as well as a great deal of consultation with a variety of people concerned with the social sciences and public policy. We think it fair to say that the project was one of the most difficult we have had to manage in recent years. While disputes and disagreements are common with most issues of any seriousness and are certainly present in these papers, that in itself was not the main difficulty. More critically, it soon became evident not only that there are many schools of thought, perspectives, and methodologies in the social sciences but also that they do not easily communicate with each other. To some extent, the same is true of the policy sciences (and whether policy analysis ought to be thought of as an art or a science is itself a lively question). An economist interested in "the social sciences and public policy" can share that same general interest with a political theorist. But if the former is concerned only with the generation of better data and a better use of data and the latter is solely interested in the critiques of social science generated, say, by Jürgen Habermas or Richard Bernstein, useful common discussion can be very difficult. What an academic sociologist may find interesting and important may be of little concern to a working policy analyst. There are, then, not only competing paradigms of a very fundamental kind concerning the relationship between the social sciences and public policy but also a wide range of differences in interest between academics and non-academics in the field.

Nonetheless, after two years, the group did learn to talk together and to make greater sense of each other's perspectives and interests. As a result, many if not most of the papers are different in their final form from what they were in earlier draft versions. We want to thank the authors for their willingness to listen to their critics and for their efforts to try to understand and accommodate the perspectives of others who approach the same issues very differently; we have also appreciated the general goodwill of all in trying to sort out what, at times, seemed a hopeless muddle. This book, we hope, will be seen as a way station on an intellectual journey that is by no means finished.

The project was supported by a grant from the Ford Foundation, and we would like to acknowledge their generous support gratefully. In particular, Richard Sharpe, then Program Officer for the Committee on Public Policy and Social

Organization, was both a prodding and substantively helpful grant officer. Thanks are also due to Mary Ann Fordyce, Mary Gualandi, and Eva Mannheimer for their skillful and good-humored assistance in the typing and preparation of this volume.

DANIEL CALLAHAN

Director
The Hastings Center

BRUCE JENNINGS

Research Associate for Policy Studies
The Hastings Center

I

POLICY ANALYSIS IN A NEW KEY

Exploring Alternatives to Positivism

1

INTERPRETIVE SOCIAL SCIENCE AND POLICY ANALYSIS

BRUCE JENNINGS

I

The last ten years have been a period of remarkable theoretical and methodological diversity in the social sciences. In one sense, there is nothing unusual about this. The social sciences have never had the kind of standardized textbook education and puzzle-solving, normal research that Thomas Kuhn describes as characteristic of the mature natural sciences.[1] But, at least until recently, most social scientists did share a common view of what scientific inquiry ought, in principle, to be like. So, in spite of the fact that social scientists were divided among a plethora of various theoretical "approaches," methodologically and epistemologically they enjoyed a relatively secure set of common aspirations and regulative ideals: de-

[1]Thomas S. Kuhn, *The Structure of Scientific Revolutions* (2nd ed., enlarged; Chicago: University of Chicago Press, 1970), chaps. 2–4.

BRUCE JENNINGS ☐ Research Associate, The Hastings Center, Institute of Society, Ethics and the Life Sciences, 360 Broadway, Hastings-on-Hudson, New York 10706.

ductive–nomological explanation, the experimental testability of proposed theoretical and empirical laws, the operationalization of concepts, formal modeling, and the like.[2] What is new about the course that discussions of these matters has taken in the 1970s is that, while substantive theoretical diversity continues to be the rule, the epistemological consensus centering around the tenets of logical positivism and empiricism has itself been shaken almost to the point of nervous collapse. The principal reason for this is that recent work in the history and philosophy of science has persuasively called into question the validity of these tenets, showing that they do not provide an adequate conception of the nature of inquiry within the natural sciences themselves.[3] This thoroughgoing philosophical reassessment of the natural sciences has created, in turn, an opening for a parallel reconsideration of the nature of social scientific inquiry. As a result, the theoretical situation in the social sciences has become a good deal more difficult and complex than it used to be, because now each "approach" must not only defend itself on substantive and conceptual grounds but also cast about for its own epistemological justification.

[2]For fairly typical accounts, see Quentin Gibson, *The Logic of Social Enquiry* (New York: Humanities Press, 1960); Walter L. Wallace, *The Logic of Science in Sociology* (Chicago: Aldine–Atherton, 1971); and George C. Homans, *The Nature of Social Science* (New York: Harcourt Brace & World, 1967). The principal philosophical writings upon which these accounts are based are Carl G. Hempel, *Aspects of Scientific Explanation* (New York: The Free Press, 1965); and Ernest Nagel, *The Structure of Science* (New York: Harcourt Brace & World, 1961).

[3]For a thorough and insightful overview of recent developments in the philosophy of science, see Frederick Suppe, "The Search for Philosophic Understanding of Scientific Theories" and "Afterward—1977," in *The Structure of Scientific Theories*, ed. by F. Suppe (2nd ed.; Urbana, Ill., University of Illinois Press, 1977), pp. 3–241, 617–730. Cf. also Harold I. Brown, *Perception, Theory, and Commitment: The New Philosophy of Science* (Chicago: University of Chicago Press, 1977).

The import of the new philosophy of science for the philosophy of social science cuts two ways. For the proponents of positivistic social science, steadfast in their belief that eventually their "young" disciplines will mature into analogues of physics with the arrival of their Newton and their paradigm, it means that their received image of science is, at least in some fundamental respects, an illusion. As one commentator has aptly remarked, positivistic social scientists "are not only waiting for a train that won't arrive, they're in the wrong station altogether."[4] At the other end of the spectrum, the new philosophy of science has dealt a body blow to social scientists who continue to insist on a categorical distinction between the social and the natural sciences roughly along the lines formulated by the late-nineteenth-century German philosopher Wilhelm Dilthey. Much of their opposition to the positivist conception of social science now appears to have been based upon an uncritical acceptance of the positivist conception of natural science; once the latter is rejected along with the former, their claim about the logical uniqueness of the social sciences collapses. If the positivists are in the wrong station, their erstwhile humanistic colleagues have been left in a no less embarrassing posture. "Old guard Diltheyans," Charles Taylor notes, "their shoulders hunched from years-long resistance against the encroaching pressure of positivist natural science, suddenly pitch forward on their faces as all opposition ceases to the reign of universal hermeneutics."[5]

---

[4]Anthony Giddens, *New Rules of Sociological Method* (New York: Basic Books, 1976), p. 13.

[5]Charles Taylor, "Understanding in Human Science," *Review of Metaphysics*, 34 (September, 1980), 26. It should be noted that Taylor does not hold the view described in the quotation. He maintains in the remainder of the article that the natural and the human sciences are fundamentally different in terms of the basic criteria of validity that accounts in them must meet. One of the leading spokesmen for the "universal hermeneutics" position is Richard Rorty, *Philosophy and the Mirror of Nature* (Princeton, N.J.: Princeton University Press, 1979).

Taylor's recourse to the term *hermeneutics* in this context, a word long familiar to theologians and literary critics but quite alien to the idiom of philosophers and social scientists until very recently, suggests the irony of the present situation. Many of the purported characteristics of the natural sciences that the new philosophers of science have been emphasizing—the theory-ladenness of observation, the inherently metaphorical, nonformalizable character of scientific languages, the imaginative dimension of scientific discovery, the nonreferential meaning of scientific terms—are precisely the same characteristics that opponents of positivism have underscored as the distinguishing features of the social and human sciences.[6] Thus, at the cutting edge of contemporary philosophy of science, a new link is being forged between the *Naturwissenschaften* and the *Geisteswissenschaften*—a link reminiscent of the logical positivists' original program of a unified science, now constituted not by a logic of deductive–nomological explanation but by a common hermeneutic of nature and of culture.

In short, there is a newly emerging epistemological landscape facing social scientists today, a landscape in which many of the familiar methodological and metatheoretical stances are no longer secure. However, it would be a mistake either to expect drastic transformations in the conduct of social scientific inquiry or to expect social scientists suddenly to begin thinking about the nature of their activity in radically new ways. In the first place, the philosophers themselves are a long way from completing their reassessment of the nature of scientific knowledge. Although the traditional versions of logical positivism and empiricism have been pretty thoroughly discredited, there is little agreement concerning what

[6]Cf. Mary Hesse, *Revolutions and Reconstructions in the Philosophy of Science* (Bloomington, Ind.: Indiana University Press, 1980), esp. chapter 7.

other doctrines, if any, can be put in their place. Moreover, if positivism and empiricism are now on the wane as epistemologies, the research procedures and protocols that have grown out of them remain firmly institutionalized in legislative and administrative requirements, funding structures, graduate curricula, and professional reward systems. Positivism is the basic methodological orientation of the social sciences and will surely remain so for some time, even though it has now lost the secure philosophical warrant it once enjoyed.

Nonetheless, the recent frontal assault on the epistemological foundations of mainstream social science has taken its toll. It, together with the growing list of unanswered questions and unsolved problems generated by corporate capitalism and welfare-state liberalism, has left the social sciences, with their promise of comprehension and control, vulnerable and confused. Not since they first appeared upon the scene as an institutionalized, professional status group in American life some fifty years ago have social scientists been quite so self-reflective and so deeply perplexed about the philosophical status of their work, the proper standards with which to assess the competing theories and approaches they offer, and their own proper social and political roles as intellectuals.

Moreover, if recent philosophical analyses have left the epistemological status of social scientific inquiry problematic, in the last decade there have been two major trends within the social sciences themselves that have complicated the situation still further. The first trend has been the emergence of policy analysis as an institutionalized specialty in American higher education and the growing shift toward an applied or policy orientation within the disciplinary frameworks of the traditional social science curricula. Thus far, the development of policy analysis as a separate discipline and as a profession has enjoyed only limited success, to be sure. Many within the academic community remain skeptical of both its intellectual merits and its political benefits. And, as several of the contributions to this volume point out, the relationship between policy analysts and government policymakers has been marked by tension and mutual distrust. Nonetheless, policy analysis has become a force to be reckoned with in contemporary social inquiry and—as social scientists renew their connection with the immediate, practical concerns of the larger society through the mediation of the state—policy analysis provides a setting in which the ethical and epistemological questions inherent in the relationships among knowledge, action, and power cannot be ignored.

Alongside the rise of policy analysis, but so far largely unconnected to it, a second trend transforming the shape of the social sciences in the United States has appeared: namely, the rapid development of what is now generally referred to as "interpretive" social inquiry.[7] The current interest in interpretive social science can be explained in part by the widespread dissatisfaction, especially among younger social scientists, with the established forms of positivism and behavioralism. But the interpretive approach is not simply a negative stance; it has an affirmative intellectual tradition of its own, with variants drawing on such diverse sources as phenomenology, analytic philosophy of action, historiogra-

[7]Cf. Paul Rabinow and William M. Sullivan, eds., *Interpretive Social Science: A Reader* (Berkeley, Calif.: University of California Press, 1979); and Fred R. Dallmayr and Thomas A. McCarthy, eds., *Understanding and Social Inquiry* (Notre Dame, Ind., University of Notre Dame Press, 1977). For general discussions of this approach and its relationship to positivism, see Richard Bernstein, *The Restructuring of Social and Political Theory* (New York: Harcourt Brace Jovanovich, 1976); J. Donald Moon, "The Logic of Political Inquiry: A Synthesis of Opposed Perspectives," in *Handbook of Political Science*, ed. by Fred I. Greenstein and Nelson W. Polsby, I (Reading, Mass.: Addison-Wesley Publishing Co. Inc., 1975), pp. 131–228; and Brian Fay, *Social Theory and Political Practice* (London: George Allen & Unwin, 1975).

phy, and literary criticism. The common thread that runs through this approach is the emphasis on the meaningfulness of human action, and the *explications* (a more appropriate term in this context, perhaps, than *explanations*) of human activity constructed by interpretive social science are typically, and deliberately, designed to reproduce the purposive, intentional character of the practical reasoning carried out by the agents themselves in the given situations under examination. In this way, interpretive analysis attempts to account for an action by making sense of it in the same way that the participating agents did make—or could in principle have made—sense of it themselves. Thus, the general aim of interpretive social inquiry is to enable us to see events through the eyes of those who lived in and through them. Armed with this point of view, we come to conceive of the human beings studied as acting subjects rather than as behaving objects—as persons in situations, as agents acting within a public world of understandable norms, conventions, and rules. This aim gives interpretive social science a powerful thematic focus, but, beyond that, it generates certain important methodological prescriptions as well. For example, it requires a careful attentiveness to the agents' own self-understandings, hence its common recourse to open-ended interview techniques and other sources of "qualitative" data. And, as one important test of the validity of a proposed interpretation, it requires that that interpretation be persuasive to the agents themselves, at least in principle or under certain hypothetical conditions.[8]

While each of these trends has been the subject of considerable attention and commentary, their possible relation-

---

[8]Cf. Peter Winch, *The Idea of a Social Science and Its Relation to Philos phy* (London: Routledge & Kegan Paul, 1958); and Hanna F. Pitkin, *Wittgenstein and Justice* (Berkeley, Calif.: University of California Press, 1975), chap. 11.

ship has not been explored adequately. Accordingly, my purpose in this chapter is to examine whether and to what extent the interpretive approach to social inquiry can and should become a component of public policy analysis.

At the present time, interpretive social science and policy analysis tend to be seen as fundamentally antithetical enterprises inasmuch as the latter has drawn exclusively upon, and served to reinforce, a strongly positivistic conception of social science, while the former has been committed to a rejection of positivism both as a philosophical metatheory and as a mode of social scientific practice. Certainly, very little constructive dialogue has taken place between these two camps; each side has tended to look upon the other with indifference or outright hostility. Nonetheless, this division can be overcome, and I think that each movement would benefit from a creative engagement with the other's concerns. There is nothing inherent in the potential uses and purposes of policy analysis that makes only social scientific inquiry in the positivist mode pertinent to it; in fact, there are good reasons for thinking that the interpretive approach is better suited to the goals of policy analysis than are the more mainstream, positivistic approaches, especially in certain areas of social welfare policy and foreign policy where a subtle and sympathetic appraisal of the intentions and self-understandings of the agents involved is crucial to the policy's effectiveness and justice. And there is nothing inherent in the type of knowledge offered by interpretive social science that limits it to purely academic or pedagogical settings or undermines its relevance to the broader political arena in which public policy is formulated, debated, and assessed.

In general, then, I propose that practitioners of interpretive social science turn their attention to concrete policy issues and not limit themselves exclusively to metatheoretical discourse or general ethnographic studies; further, I suggest that policy analysts should pay close attention to the insights and techniques that the interpretive approach has to offer. If the relationship between social scientific knowledge and public policy is to be a more progressive and constructive one than it has been in the past, it is important that the prospects and possibilities of what might be called interpretive policy analysis be fully explored. At the same time, it is equally important to recognize the limitations and weaknesses of the interpretive approach. As a number of critics have pointed out, the interpretive approach's emphasis on subjective meaning and intentional agency tend to make it weak in explaining social change, analyzing the role of structural forces, and reckoning with the patterns of unintended consequences and the effects of ideologically distorted self-understanding among social actors.[9] Moreover, these same emphases tend to give interpretive social inquiry a basically conservative cast in the classical or Burkean sense; that is, they lend an abiding respect for coherent, well-established, ongoing forms of cultural life and a profound suspicion of externally imposed, rationalistically conceived programs of institutional reform.[10] While I agree with these criticisms, I would still argue that for some purposes this same emphasis—on community, traditions of shared meaning and belief, and intentional agency—contains a very important contribution that interpretive social science can make to policy analysis. Too often it has been precisely these con-

[9] Cf. Giddens, chaps. 3–4; and Fay, pp. 83ff.

[10] The contemporary thinker who most clearly exemplifies the affinity between the interpretive approach and classical conservatism is Michael Oakeshott. Cf. *Experience and Its Modes* [1933] (Cambridge: Cambridge University Press, 1978) and *On Human Conduct* (Oxford, England: Clarendon Press, 1975). For a discussion of Oakeshott, see Hanna F. Pitkin, "The Roots of Conservatism: Michael Oakeshott and the Denial of Politics," *The New Conservatives: A Critique From the Left*, ed. by Lewis A. Coser and Irving Howe (New York: Meridian, rev. ed., 1977), pp. 243–88.

cepts and aspects of human social life that policy analysts and policymakers have neglected in the past. And while I am more than a little uneasy about some of the conservative implications of the interpretive approach, that aspect of it too can be redeeming if it lends supporting grounds (as other varieties of conservatism certainly have not) to a measure of renewed democratic participation in political life and in the process of governance in our society.

II

In assessing the relevance of interpretive social science for policy analysis, there are several features of this mode of inquiry that merit special attention. In this section I shall discuss first what I take to be the central methodological characteristics of the interpretive approach and then take up three of its more general features. These features will surely make interpretive social science more difficult to integrate practically into the currently institutionalized settings of policy analysis. Still, they do not provide any compelling epistemic warrant for denying its potential policy relevance.

Throughout this chapter I refer to interpretive social science in a very broad and general way. In doing so, I do not intend to give the misleading impression that the interpretive approach constitutes a unified or fully developed movement or to suggest that it provides an alternative "method" that can be applied mechanistically to grind out policy options. Nonetheless, there is, I think, a common orientation or style of inquiry that constitutes interpretive social science and cuts across the different forms that this approach takes in various fields. The basic features of that orientation are easy enough to specify.

First, interpretive social science construes human behaviors, social relationships, and cultural artifacts as texts (or dramas or rituals) and then seeks to uncover the meaning that those texts have to the agents who constitute them and to others located spatially or temporally outside them.

Second, interpretive social science focuses on three key concepts: action, intention, and convention. It aims to make sense of (elucidate or explicate) individual actions in terms of the agent's intentions in (or reasons for) the action. And these intentions, in turn, are explicated in terms of the cultural context of conventions, rules, and norms within which they are formed.

This second step in the explicative analysis is crucial, and it is important to understand how the notion of intention is typically construed in these studies. Intentions are not construed as internal mental events or private wants but rather as the purposes that an agent constructs or might in principle have constructed using the publicly available concepts and meanings of his or her culture. Thus, in some instances, we might want to say that an agent's intentions are conscious self-interpretations and conscious interpretations of the culture's judgment of the appropriateness of a given action. In other instances, however, it may be necessary to hold that the "intentions" ascribed to the agent in order to elucidate the action are not those of which he or she was (fully) aware at the time, but are rather the constructs of the social scientists, formulated on the basis of an assessment, broader than the agent was able to make, of the overall cultural context within which the action took place. This is a perfectly legitimate move, and it suggests two additional points worth noting.

Interpretive social science does not rely, as has sometimes been charged, on some mysterious imaginative process whereby the social scientist (or historian) sees into the mind of the persons being studied. The categories of an interpretive analysis are publicly available concepts, drawn from the stock of intersubjective social knowledge. Concomitantly, interpretive analysis is not imprisoned in "the native's point of view"; it may—and usually must—go beyond the agent's own limited comprehension of this situation, filling out and correcting that comprehension with a broader, more critical perspective.

Moreover, and this is the second point, the logical form of the accounts given in interpretive social science is teleological rather than deductive–nomological. Another way of putting this is to say that interpretive explications offer an account that purports to make sense of the action by reconstructing the reasoning process leading up to it in terms of a practical syllogism.[11] In order to do this, the analysis must contain: (1) an empirically accurate description of the factual circumstances surrounding the action and (2) an understanding of the norms and values operating in the cultural context to make the action "appropriate." Thus, interpretive analysis is committed, by the internal logic of its method, to treating both facts and values as rationally comprehensible entities with specifiable public, intersubjective meanings.

Accounting for an action by reconstructing the practical reasoning it instantiates is particularly instructive when the action in question is atypical and for that reason especially puzzling. The fact that interpretive social science provides a way of comprehending these cases of what J. W. N. Watkins has called "imperfect rationality"[12] suggests one of the most important ways in which it can contribute to policy analysis. Policy analysis is often motivated in the first place by policy failures, and these failures, in turn, are usually a function of

[11]Cf. George H. von Wright, *Explanation and Understanding* (Ithaca, N.Y.: Cornell University Press, 1971); and Charles Taylor, "The Explanation of Purposive Behavior," *Explanation in the Behavioral Sciences*, ed. by Robert Borger and Frank Cioffi (Cambridge, England: Cambridge University Press, 1970), pp. 49–79.

[12]J. W. N. Watkins, "Imperfect Rationality," in Borger and Cioffi, eds., pp. 167–217.

the fact that some significant actors did not respond as it was assumed they would. Ideally, a good policy analysis must identify these anomalous responses, explain them in some coherent way, and provide policymakers with more realistic expectations about the behavior of those with whom they must deal and to whom the policy will apply. The question of whether positivistic or interpretive social science provides a more useful basis for policy analysis is really the question of whether a deductive–nomological causal explanation/prediction or a reconstruction of processes of practical reasoning can most adequately perform these tasks. In many instances, at least, it seems clear that the latter is a more promising approach than the former. Indeed, the interpretive reconstruction of practical reasoning also seems to be closer to the kinds of political, psychological, and sociological judgments that policymakers and most experienced policy analysts actually make. Like so many *bourgeois gentilhommes* who speak prose without knowing it, policymakers think in interpretive social scientific terms without calling their thoughts by that name.[13]

The third and final basic feature of interpretive social science is that it stresses the notion of coherence in the explications it offers. Its aim is to demonstrate the interconnections among the various conventions that make up the cultural context within which actions take place and to show how the agent's intentions in any particular action are related to the overall pattern of projects and roles that make up his or her self-identity. In this respect as well, the structure of an interpretive analysis differs from that typically found in

[13]Cf. Charles E. Lindblom and David K. Cohen, *Usable Knowledge: Social Science and Social Problem Solving* (New Haven, Conn.: Yale University Press, 1979); and Aaron Wildavsky, *Speaking Truth to Power: The Art and Craft of Policy Analysis* (Boston: Little, Brown and Company, 1979), pp. 1–19; 109–41; 385–406.

positivistic social science. In the connections it looks for, positivistic social science moves from the specific to the general, the aim being the subsumption of particular events under general laws. In interpretive social science, the analysis does not move up and down a ladder; it spins a web. That is, it seeks to place a particular event in an ever-widening network of relationships; it seeks to transform thin particularity into thick particularity.

With these methodological orientations in mind, I now want to consider three broader points about the interpretive approach. First, interpretations are inherently value-laden and essentially contestable. The evaluative criteria for selecting among competing interpretations are much more imprecise than those proposed in the positivistic conception of science and are more closely akin to the evaluative criteria operative in certain disciplines in the humanities. Second, success in interpretive social analysis depends heavily on the personal, intellectual characteristics of the analyst, his or her insight and creativity. Third, interpretive social analysis is largely a rhetorical or persuasive medium. Literary, figurative, and stylistic considerations and skills play a much more important role in this genre than in positivistic social analysis. This will inevitably affect the dynamics of the interaction between the interpretive policy analyst and the policymaker and will require a reorientation in the latter's expectations and capabilities if the material supplied by the interpretive policy analyst is to be useful.

Each of these three points raises serious questions about the practical arrangements and accommodations that will have to be made if interpretive social science is to be used in public policymaking and policy analysis, especially in agency settings. Unfortunately, since the use of interpretive social science in policy settings has been so little discussed in the sociological literature on policy analysis, questions about the feasibility of these practical arrangements remain unanswered. In what follows my purpose is merely to raise these issues so that the feasibility questions can begin to be addressed.

Essential Contestability

When discussing positivistically inspired social science, it seems both possible and appropriate to use the logical reconstructions of modal scientific reasoning developed by philosophers of science as the standard with which to assess the adequacy of a particular analysis. With interpretive social science, however, it is much more difficult to specify a regulative ideal for a complete interpretation. Even putting the issue in these terms misstates the problem. General philosophical analyses of the logic of the interpretive process and the problems of verification it poses are certainly useful, but more for the purpose of distinguishing interpretation from other forms of inquiry than for the purpose of setting out a method or a set of epistemological rules that must be followed if an interpretation is to be judged competent and complete.

Recall my preceding formulation of the three components of the interpretive orientation and it will be clear why this is the case. Interpretations involve the placing of a given action in the cultural context within which the agent's intentions in acting are constituted. This requires the description of that context, and such a description can never, either in practice or in principle, be complete. In practice it cannot be complete because the sheer complexity of the phenomena makes this impossible. In principle it cannot be complete either, because the "description" in question here is not a simple enumeration of brute "facts" but rather is itself an interpretation. Thus, interpretation at one level presupposes interpretation at another level, and so on. This is what is commonly referred to as "the hermeneutic circle."[14] Thus, any interpretation of a given action/intention complex can always be challenged, and a rival interpretation adduced, either by a more complete description of the cultural context or by a different interpretation of the same features of that context originally put forward.

Similarly, any interpretation (or teleological explanation) of human action is inherently value-laden, not simply in terms of the personal beliefs and selectivity of the analyst but because the action concepts with which the analyst works refer to cultural conventions and "institutional facts"[15] that are themselves constituted by the particular traditions and norms of the people who live and act, so to speak, through them. Moreover, the activity of interpretive analysis is itself a conventional practice set within a particular cultural context. Perhaps the interpreter (here especially an anthropologist or historian) can successfully enter a cultural context different from his or her own, although this claim has been the topic of prolonged dispute.[16] But it is clear that no interpretation can be contextless and hence value-free. In interpretive social science there is no epistemological Archimedian point outside of language—except silence.

There are two things that all this does *not* entail. First, interpretive social science is not a nonempirical or antiempirical mode of analysis. The notion that it is rests on a simple

---

[14]Cf. David C. Hoy, *The Critical Circle: Literature, History, and Philosophical Hermeneutics* (Berkeley, Calif.: University of California Press, 1978); and Richard E. Palmer, *Hermeneutics* (Evanston, Ill.: Northwestern University Press, 1969).

[15]On the notion of an "institutional fact," cf. John Searle, *Speech Acts: An Essay in the Philosophy of Language* (Cambridge, England: Cambridge University Press, 1969), pp. 50–4; and Charles Taylor, "Interpretation and the Sciences of Man," in Dallmayr and McCarthy, eds., pp. 101–31.

[16]On this issue see the articles collected in Brian R. Wilson, ed., *Rationality* (New York: Harper & Row, Publishers, Incorporated, 1970).

confusion between empirical analysis and empiricism as an epistemological doctrine. Interpretive social science is incompatible with the latter but not with the former. The real question raised by interpretive social science is not whether empirical data are relevant to the analysis—that is taken for granted, without data there is nothing to interpret—but what kinds of data are useful and how they are to be interpreted.

Second, the essential contestability and value-laden character of interpretive analysis does not mean that there are no standards for judging the validity of an interpretation or that interpretive social science plunges us into irrationality and subjectivism. These features merely imply that in order to get clear on how a work of interpretive social science can be evaluated, we shall need to turn our attention away from the logical positivists' conception of natural science and, instead, look more closely at how standards of judgment operate and are developed in the humanistic disciplines, such as historical narrative, ethical argument, literary exegesis, and jurisprudential reasoning.

Insight and Creativity

Despite all the philosophical difficulties surrounding it— difficulties that have been made quite clear in recent years by Kuhn, Hesse, and other "postempiricist" philosophers of science—the notion that scientific investigation involves a precise, impersonal method has remained an almost unshakable article of faith. There are at least three reasons why this is the case. First, the existence of such a method permits the replication of experiments by different investigators and hence provides the basis for intersubjective agreement. Second, the existence of such a method provides the basis for the development of standards of professional competence and facilitates the bureaucratic management and regulation of scientific research. Third, and perhaps most important for our purposes in this discussion, the existence of such a method ensures that normal scientific research will not have to rely on the availability of large numbers of especially gifted individuals. Scientific discovery and the formulation of revolutionary new theories may require persons of extraordinary intelligence, but the more mundane tasks of experimentation, testing, and controlled observation can be carried out by reasonably intelligent persons capable of mastering the standardized training techniques made possible by a determinate methodological framework. From Bacon and Descartes on, it has been argued that what has made natural science such a cumulative, progressive, and powerful form of knowledge is the fact that within the confines of its method large numbers of quite ordinary people can achieve extraordinary things.

One of the most striking things about the interpretive approach to social science is that it does not fit into this image at all. To many, the increasing popularity of this approach in recent years seems to be a regressive step, a sign that the social sciences remain in their preparadigm phase. If the Baconian image of science were correct and if it were possible for social science to have a method in the sense that image demands, then these fears would be well taken. Interpretive studies are not, in fact, replicable and cumulative. Interpretations do not provide the same grounds for intersubjective agreement that empirical test results can produce (at least in some cases). And finally, there seems to be no room in interpretive social science for the plodding technician, the unexceptional "normal scientist." Each interpretive analysis bears the mark of the personal, intellectual qualities of its author. To be successful, an interpretation must capture the imagination of its readers; it must lead them to see themselves and their social world in new ways. The capacity of an interpretive analysis to do this is always a function of the creativity, insight, and judgment of the social scientist. This, in turn, has some important implications for the content of graduate education in the social sciences. The educational background required by interpretive social science is less the mastery of a set of methodological "tools" and research techniques than the cultivation of imagination and sympathy; that is, the ability to understand others as they understand themselves and the ability to grasp the diversity, particularity, and complexity of the cultural and social contexts within which human actions take place.

Rhetoric and Persuasion

Finally, if the habits of mind and the creative demands requisite to interpretive social inquiry differ from those that have generally been emphasized by the positivistic approach, the presentational or "performative" requirements of the interpretive approach differ as well. The objective of interpretive analyses is to explicate human activities by reference to what Clifford Geertz has called "thick descriptions"[17] of the symbolically mediated cultural contexts within which intentions are formed, interpersonal relationships are negotiated, and human projects are carried out. If these contextualizing descriptions are to capture the meaning of the action and communicate that meaning to the reader, they must go beyond the mere enumeration of facts or the mere cataloguing of information. They must draw connections, assign emphases, tease out the nuances of style and the ambivalence of intention, recapture the emotional tone and ambiance of a situation—in short, these descriptions must make situations come alive once more in the medium of the social scientist's language. Moreover, since interpretive accounts are principally concerned with instances of practical reasoning and offer te-

[17]Clifford Geertz, *The Interpretation of Cultures* (New York: Basic Books, 1973), chap. 1.

leological or purposive explanations of action, they must include coherent narrative sequences. Therefore, the validity
and persuasiveness of interpretive analyses depend, to a much
greater extent than with other modes of social science, on the
literary skills of the social scientist. What is said in this genre
cannot be separated from the way it is said. Matters of style,
the use of figurative discourse, the play of metaphor and
analogy, and the construction of narrative sequences linking
conventional meaning, intention, and action: these are not
mere decorative trappings, they are constitutive of the kind
of understanding that interpretive social inquiry is uniquely
suited to offer.

III

The preceding discussion has gone, I hope, some way
toward setting an agenda of the kinds of issues that need far
more elucidation if the possibilities for the use of interpretive
social science are to be seriously assessed. I have covered a
lot of ground very briskly, littering the trail with unanswered
questions and unsettled disputes. None of the aspects of interpretive social science mentioned suggest, in my estimation,
an epistemic warrant for holding that the kind of social knowledge provided by this approach has no cognitively valid role
to play in policy analysis. To be sure, there are formidable
practical, attitudinal, and political obstacles to be overcome
before interpretive inquiry can inform the policy process in
any but the most sporadic and ad hoc ways. This is not the
place to formulate specific strategies for overcoming these
obstacles, but I would like to suggest some reasons why it
might be worth the effort to try.

In my judgment, there are at least three promises offered
by the potential incorporation of interpretive social science—
understood in the generic, ideal-typical form I have adum-

brated—into policy analysis. The first promise has to do with the nature of our expectations about social scientific knowledge, the second concerns our definition of what counts as a policy issue, and the third involves what is essentially a moral question about the relationship between policymakers and citizens. In each instance, I shall argue, interpretive policy analysis has the potential to improve upon the existing relationship between social science and policy analysis.

I want to underscore the qualification contained in this last assertion. It is not my intention to suggest that interpretive policy analysis will *necessarily* lead to these improvements, nor that any single policy analyst drawing upon interpretive social science can bring them about, nor finally that interpretive policy analysis by itself can produce them without other changes in the policymaking process or, indeed, in the political system as a whole. Clearly, no type of social science and no mode of policy analysis provides a panacea for the shortcomings of the governance of our society or a "quick fix" for deep troubles facing us. It is essential that we do not reproduce, on behalf of the interpretive approach, the extravagant claims of the early proponents of positivistic policy analysis. It is with a certain diffidence then, and without believing that it is free from problems and limitations of its own, that I propose the following brief for interpretive policy analysis.

Defining the Limits of Social Inquiry. In the preceding pages I have deliberately focused on the epistemological and methodological aspects of interpretive social science, treating it as a particular approach to the study of human activity definable in terms of certain specific procedures and requirements. At that level, I have highlighted the contrasts between the interpretive approach and social scientific inquiry conceived along positivist lines. This was done in order to bring out as clearly as possible the difference between what that positivist conception has led us to expect of social scientific policy analysis and what we should expect of the kind of social science the interpretive approach produces. Positivistic social science aspires to a type of nomothetic social knowledge that is incontrovertable, impersonal, and objective; interpretive social science does not claim to produce this type of knowledge more surely or efficiently than the positivistic approach—it rejects this as a viable epistemological ideal. For understandable political and historical reasons, social scientists have used the positivist promise to legitimate their vocation to policymakers and to the general public. But if this gambit is understandable, and even though it has been successful to a certain extent, it is a regrettable and unfortunate move nonetheless. For once this promise is shown to be philosophically false, the credibility of the entire social scientific enterprise is threatened. Need I point out what an ironic and regressive development for policymaking it would be if, with the passing of its positivist reputation, social science were to become as cut off from and as irrelevant to political decision making in our society as the humanities now are? The problem is not, as has sometimes been suggested, that the social sciences have been oversold. Rather, it is that they have been sold in an altogether misleading way; heretofore the nature and value of social scientific knowledge for policymaking have not been defined in metatheoretical categories that accurately reflect the kind of knowledge social science has offered in the past and can offer in the future. The responsibility for this only partially falls upon those social scientists and philosophical spokespersons who have systematically misunderstood the epistemological conditions of social inquiry; equally instrumental in producing this situation have been the bureaucratic administrative policy processes themselves, which tend to impose exceedingly narrow and unimaginative criteria for what counts as "useful" knowledge.

To the extent that interpretive social science—by dint of its essential contestability, its creative demands, and the rhetorical dimensions of its discourse—presents a type of knowledge that cannot readily be subsumed under the false promise of positivism, its growth and extension into areas of policy analysis ought to provide us with an occasion to reexamine our assumptions about the kind of knowledge social science has to offer and to revise our notions about what it means to use or to apply that knowledge.[18] Only in this fashion, I think, can we begin to build a new, less vulnerable case for the policy relevance of social scientific knowledge; only thus can we legitimate the public use of social science on solid ground so that the genuinely valuable insights, achievements, and wisdom contained in this body of knowledge will not be swept away in a general wave of skepticism following the inevitable debunking of positivism.

The first promise offered by interpretive policy analysis, then, is that it might stimulate a more realistic set of expectations about the "limitations" of social scientific knowledge and might lead to the development of more appropriate modes of criticism and assessment. Once these limitations have been

---

[18]In particular, much more work needs to be done on the question of how plausible interpretations get constructed and how conflicts among rival interpretations can rationally be adjudicated. Here, for example, two distinct avenues of investigation might converge: (1) what might be called interpretive sociological studies of the policymaking process and (2) interpretive policy analysis proper. To the extent that an understanding of the policy process leading up to and governing the implementation of a given policy is an integral part of the "policy analysis" of that policy, 1 is always a subset of 2. At the same time, 1 is distinct from and in a sense logically prior to 2 inasmuch as it is only from a better understanding of the interpersonal perceptions and relationships that constitute the policy process as a specific practice that we can begin to see how interpretive policy analysis can play a constructive role in that practice and how the present conduct of policymaking would have to be changed in order to accommodate interpretive policy analysis.

acknowledged and the epistemological or indeed ontological reasons for them have been clarified, misguided attempts to overcome them can give way to the more productive and pertinent enterprise of explicitly clarifying the ways in which the contestable, value- and theory-laden knowledge offered by the social sciences can be used most intelligently to inform public policy.

Concomitant with this promise, there is a corresponding danger. This is that the negative message carried by the interpretive approach will be conveyed without its positive response. As an example of the danger to which I refer, consider the one area where the critique of positivism has had its greatest impact outside academic circles: namely, the question of value neutrality. The notion that all social scientific inquiry contains certain normative or ideological "biases" is now virtually universally acknowledged.[19] But for all that, we have barely begun to make progress on an account of how differing value claims can be rationally assessed or how normative and descriptive claims function and reciprocally interact in social and political discourse. To a large extent, policy analysts still conceptualize the "values" inherent in their work as personal preferences or private psychological dispositions and fail to recognize the normative commitments embedded in the purportedly "descriptive" concepts and categories of the various social scientific idioms they employ.[20] As a direct consequence of this peculiar way of assimilating the recent philosophical bad news that the older ideal of value neutrality is an illusion—not in the cards for creatures who think and talk as human beings do—we are advised to make these value biases explicit, not by a careful and thoroughgoing scrutiny of the

[19]Frank Fischer, *Politics, Values and Public Policy: The Problem of Methodology* (Boulder, Colo.: Westview Press, 1980).
[20]For an example of the kind of analysis that is needed see Steven Lukes, *Power: A Radical View* (London: The Macmillan Company, 1974).

underlying theories and presuppositions contained in the analysis but by an exercise of sincere introspection followed by a confessional statement attached to the first paragraph of the policy memorandum or research report. Meanwhile, policymakers continue to make their own difficult judgments and choices, with very little significant guidance from policy analysts about how to assess the normative dimensions of those judgments and choices.

Seeing Policy Objectives in New Ways. The second promise of interpretive policy analysis is that it might lead to the formulation of new objectives and social goals for public policy and to a deeper, more sensitive comprehension of the sociological, cultural, and psychological ramifications of governmental actions. This promise does not grow so much out of the epistemological or methodological aspects of the interpretive approach as out of its characteristic themes and emphases and, more fundamentally, out of its underlying conception of the nature of human beings. For interpretive social inquiry, human beings are essentially makers of meaning; they are purposive agents who inhabit symbolically constituted cultural orders, who engage in rule-governed social practices, and whose self-identities are formed in those orders and through those practices. These are the reasons why the interpretive approach maintains that a social scientific explanation of human action must involve the placement of that action in its specific cultural context. And although it does not always come out explicitly in the work of interpretive social scientists, a certain ethical commitment is entailed by this underlying philosophical anthropology as well. On this view, the well-being—indeed the very personhood and humanness—of human beings depends on the integrity and coherence of these cultural orders and social practices; the structures of social life provide the context for moral agency and for human self-realization.

Even on the basis of these highly abbreviated formulations, which hardly do justice to the complexity of the issues evoked, it is possible to discern some of the policy implications to which the characteristic themes of the interpretive approach might lead. With its stress on purposive agency and the transformation of self-identity through practical activity, the interpretive approach would provide policy analysis with an impetus to investigate the effect that a given (or contemplated) policy had (or would have) on such things as the vitality of civic life in a particular area, opportunities for participation, the creation and preservation of neighborhood organizations, incentives for the establishment of cooperative projects of mutual aid, the encouragement of voluntary social service provision, and, finally, the delegation of authority and the distribution of decision-making power under the programs implemented by the policy. Similarly, given its stress on both the functional and the normative importance of stable social practices and cultural traditions (i.e., they provide a sense of meaning and belonging, the experience of which is an intrinsic human good), the interpretive approach would raise the question of a policy's effect on community and would take the fostering of community and the mitigation of alienation and anomie to be fundamentally legitimate and important policy considerations.

To be sure, the notions of decentralization, civic voluntarism, empowerment, and community are perennial concerns, but they have never played a central role in our thinking about public policy; often, in the past, they have been totally eclipsed by other values and considerations. The history of American political and social thought is composed of two major and largely antithetical traditions: (1) a dominant liberal, individualistic tradition that views society as a field of separate, conflicting interests and human beings as essentially egoistic monads caught up in a competitive struggle for material resources and personal gratification and (2) a communitarian tradition that stresses the organic linkages between the individual and society.[21] Many of the intellectual forerunners of contemporary interpretive social science were theorists who rejected the abstract individualism of nineteenth-century liberalism, and it seems clear that, in the American context, interpretive policy analysis would occasion a revitalization of the older communitarian tradition.

It also seems that the time is ripe for just such a development. During the past few years many policy analysts have begun to reassess the record of the major policy strategies of the sixties and early-seventies, a period of unprecedented federal activism and centralization. While these programs were surely not without merit and laudable effect, neither were they without many serious shortcomings.[22] In any event, the outlines of what will probably be the dominant policy strategy in the next decade are already becoming clear: block-grant federal funding, a shift away from the direct provision of social services in favor of various indirect approaches like voucher schemes, and many other similar programs, all of which add up to a movement away from the received vision of welfare-state liberalism in which the federal government is the guarantor of individual entitlements and the enforcer of certain uniform standards and universal principles of social justice and equality of opportunity. Presumably, these new policies are intended to reverse this quest for uniformity and centralization and would redistribute decision-making power downward to lower-level governmental units and outward to

---

[21]Here I have relied on the discussion in David E. Price, *The "Quest for Community" and Public Policy* (Bloomington, Ind.: The Poynter Center, 1977). For a history of American communitarian thought, see Wilson Carey McWilliams, *The Idea of Fraternity in America* (Berkeley, Calif.: University of California Press, 1973).

[22]Cf. Eli Ginzberg and Robert M. Solow, eds., *The Great Society: Lessons for the Future* (New York: Basic Books, 1974).

institutions in the private sector. This, in turn, would presumably mean that the operative standards of justice and
equality would, within limits, be determined by the give and
take of social life in various localities.

Many things need to be said about all this, but one observation is especially pertinent to our present concerns. In
order to assess the merits of this new policy strategy and its
specific components, it will be particularly important to have
a far better understanding of the internal conditions of those
local institutions, "communities," and "mediating structures"
than social science, particularly positivistic social science, has
yet given us. For example, debates over voucher schemes,
like Alain Enthoven's plan for national health insurance, already abound with claims and counter claims about whether
the formative cultural experiences of low-income persons have
deprived them of the capacity to recognize and act rationally
upon their needs and interests.[23] Similar arguments are sure
to proliferate in other policy areas in the years ahead. These
are important arguments, and they deserve more than the
armchair intuitions of affluent analysts. Interpretive studies
of working-class and ghetto life surely have an important role
to play in the analysis of these policies.

If the promise of interpretive policy analysis is that it will
lead to a restoration of the communitarian tradition in American political thought, the danger is that it will fail to give
policymakers an accurate, critical understanding of the ways
in which these communitarian concerns can be addressed,
given the realities of the political economy of contemporary
America.

What I have in mind here may become clearer if we pause

[23]Cf. John D. Arras, "Health Care Vouchers and the Rhetoric of Equity" and
Loren E. Lomasky, "The Small But Crucial Role of Health Care Vouchers,"
The Hastings Center Report, 11 (August, 1981), 29–42.

to consider a particular example. One of the most noteworthy contributions to the communitarian revival in policy analysis to appear thus far is the brief monograph by Peter L. Berger and Richard John Neuhaus entitled *To Empower People: The Role of Mediating Structures in Public Policy*.[24] As interesting and suggestive as it is in places, their discussion is deeply flawed and exemplifies precisely the kinds of shortcomings I have just been discussing. Berger and Neuhaus are appropriately sensitive to the alienation and the sense of powerlessness that afflict our society. They quite properly remind us—à la interpretive social science—of the human importance of the communities in which individuals share a way of life and a meaningful cultural tradition, and they are cognizant of the fact that political economic forces—the operation of what they call "megastructures"—are rolling like a juggernaut over traditional forms of life. For all that, however, their description of practical activity inside the world of mediating structures (neighborhoods, families, churches, and voluntary associations) is remarkably thin and sentimental. Tocqueville would scarcely recognize his own concerns in the portrait of mediating structures they paint. Their mediating structures are self-encapsulated atoms struggling in a hostile world of bigness—principally big government, since the role of corporations as megastructures is never seriously addressed—to preserve their internal integrity. *To Empower People* has very few people in it; it provides no discussion of the dynamics of human interaction within mediating structures, no discussion of how the production and reproduction of selfhood that goes on there shapes these structures from within even as they condition it from without. Berger and Neuhaus call for the

[24]Washington: American Enterprise Institute, 1977. For an interesting critique of Berger and Neuhaus, see David E. Price, "Community, 'Mediating Structures,' and Public Policy," *Soundings*, LXII (Winter, 1979), 369–94.

reempowerment of mediating structures (not, as they say, "the people," but then not people either) in the name of community and democracy, but we are left with no idea of how internally egalitarian, fraternal, and democratic these structures are. Similarly, their analysis is oblivious to the way mediating structures and megastructures intertwine in the lives of individuals who shuttle back and forth between them. We are given no sense, that is, of the ways in which mega-structures have not simply threatened mediating structures with dissolution but have reshaped them in their own image. For these reasons, I would argue that the analytic task of interpretive policy analysis as I have been envisioning it in this chapter begins precisely where discussions like Berger's and Neuhaus's end.

One final question remains to be discussed before I turn to the third promise of interpretive policy analysis. If I am correct in maintaining that the interpretive approach is to be located broadly within the communitarian tradition, it seems clear that it will inevitably stand in some tension with liberalism on substantive grounds, in much the same way—and for many of the same reasons—that it conflicts with positivism on methodological grounds. What then are its ideological dimensions? I do not think that any unequivocal answer to this question can be given. Whether the import of interpretive social science is "conservative" or "radical" depends, it seems to me, less on its underlying philosophical anthropology or its thematic emphasis on cultural traditions and complex webs of symbolic meaning than on one's empirical judgments about the viability and workings of particular cultural contexts at particular times. If an interpretive analysis shows that these contexts do, in fact, provide the conditions necessary for the genuine exercise of moral agency and meaningful sociality, then its policy implications will be conservative in the sense

that, like Burke, it will counsel a respect for those "little pla-
toons" of community life. But there is no reason *a priori* why
an interpretive analysis must show this. True, as I pointed
out above, interpretive social science does look for coherence
in the situations it studies and it does insist upon the proposition that no human situation is devoid of agency and meaning, but this does not preclude it from making negative judgments in certain circumstances. Indeed, in those cases such
judgments are entailed by the interpretive approach's own
humanistic ethical commitments. One may "make sense of"
a despotic culture, but that does not make it any less despotic.
An interpretive analysis of institutionalized slavery may show
that the slaves are able to make a meaningful life for themselves even within this context; what follows from this, however, is not that slavery is justified and should not be eliminated but only that slaves are human beings doing what human
beings always do for better or worse.[25] In short, if the findings
of an interpretive analysis are of a certain sort, the policy
implications of that analysis can be quite radical and trans-
formative vis-à-vis the status quo.

Enhancing the Democratic Ethos. The third promise of interpretive policy analysis involves not the content or goals of
policy but the process by which policy decisions are made
and implemented. The characteristic concerns and perspectives of interpretive social inquiry would inject a new kind of
style or ethos into the policymaking process. Let me try to
spell out more fully what I mean by this. It has frequently
been argued, persuasively I think, that positivistic policy anal-

---

[25]Consider, for example, Terrence Des Pres, *The Survivor: An Anatomy of Life
in the Death Camps* (New York: Oxford University Press, 1976); and Eugene
D. Genovese, *Roll, Jordan, Roll: The World the Slaves Made* (New York: Random House, 1974).

ysis and highly bureaucratic and rationalistic forms of public administration tend mutually to reinforce one another.[26] There is a symbiotic relationship between a mode of social scientific explanation which defines human agents as objects whose behavior is determined by causal forces and a form of governance which relies on the instrumental manipulation of those forces for the achievement of social objectives and the maintenance of social order. Paradoxically, it is not clear that positivistic social science has actually done much to make this form of governance more powerful and effective (the sources of its power and success lie elsewhere), but it has helped to make this conception of governance seem legitimate and inevitable at least to many policymakers themselves if not to the public at large.

However, if interpretive social science were ever to gain a serious and institutionalized role in the policymaking process, one might dare to hope that, over time, policymakers would begin to look in different ways at the nature of the social problems they have to address. This, in turn, might prompt them to be more democratically responsive in conducting their political and administrative activities. The reasons for this are pragmatic rather than simply moral or ideological.

To see the force of these admittedly counterintuitive claims, consider the following argument. If there is one dominant leitmotiv of interpretive social inquiry, it is this: human beings are self-monitoring and self-directing agents who invariably seek to pursue life plans that they find subjectively meaningful. From this conception of the human being as an active, self-interpretive being, it follows that if the incentives used by a given policy to restructure activity in a certain way are

---

[26]Laurence H. Tribe, "Policy Science: Analysis or Ideology," *Philosophy and Public Affairs*, 2 (Fall, 1972), 66–110.

to function as the policymaker intends, these incentives will have to be construed by the individuals to whom they are directed as an integral part of their own sense of meaningful self-identity. If these incentives are not so construed, if they are perceived as alien constraints externally imposed, experience shows that they will be resisted and subverted in various ways so that either the policy will not have its intended effect or an unacceptable and impractical degree of coercion will have to be used to achieve the desired restructuring of activity. The question then becomes how to facilitate this acceptance and internalization of policy incentives. And the answer, again implied by the interpretive social science perspective, is that the individuals to whom the policy is directed must be actively brought into the deliberative process in which the goals and values of the policy are formulated; they must come to understand the connection between these goals and the incentives they are being asked to accept. Assuming that one effect of interpretive policy analysis would be to get policy makers to see their situation in something like these terms, I think it is reasonable to conclude that interpretive social science would tend to reorient the style and ethos of governance so that the relationship between policymakers and citizens would take a more participatory or dialogic form.

If interpretive social science can further this end, then it surely will have fulfilled the most important ethical responsibility facing the applied social sciences today: to ensure that public policy is not only realistic, effective, and efficient but also democratically legitimate.[27]

[27]I am grateful to Robert Bellah, Stephen Toulmin, and my colleagues at The Hastings Center for their comments on earlier drafts of this paper.

2

SOCIAL SCIENCE AS PRACTICAL REASON

ROBERT N. BELLAH

Kenneth Prewitt begins his 1979–80 annual report as president of the Social Science Research Council with the sentence: "As the social sciences enter the 1980s, they move from a decade in which purpose or relevance became the dominant metaphor into a new decade characterized by the themes of performance, productivity, and usefulness."[1] The issue of the "usefulness" of social science might be less salient at the moment did it not bear so directly on decisions about funding that may have far-reaching consequences for American social science. Russell R. Dynes, executive officer of the American Sociological Association, in a recent letter addressed to graduate departments of sociology, urged a variety of forms of action to protest cuts proposed by the Reagan administration

---

[1] I view the statements Prewitt has made in his representative role as president of the Social Science Research Council as expressive of the majority of American social scientists. It is only as such that I wish to discuss them.

ROBERT N. BELLAH □ Ford Professor of Sociology and Comparative Studies and Chairman, Department of Sociology, University of California, Berkeley, California 94720.

ROBERT N. BELLAH □ Ford Professor of Sociology and Comparative Studies and Chairman, Department of Sociology, University of California, Berkeley, California 94720.

in the National Science Foundation budget for the social sciences. In that letter he says, "Again, the case has to be made for the importance and usefulness of support for the social sciences. Many of the goals of the present administration are informed by the social sciences." Perhaps the goals of an administration that has embarked on programs profoundly different from any administration since 1932—programs that will have extraordinarily broad political, ethical, and human consequences—are indeed "informed by" social science. But does that thought not arrest us and move us to consider things entirely beyond the question of "usefulness?" Does it not raise questions about the ethical meaning of social science?

Dynes appends to his letter an editorial written by Prewitt and published in the February 13, 1981 issue of *Science*, which in turn is a highly condensed version of the annual report referred to above. The editorial addresses the question of "the productivity, the performance, and the profitability" of the social sciences. It consists in large part of a list of "substantial contributions to economic growth and the public welfare." These include technologies marketed by "well-established industries," such as, "demographic projections, programmed language instruction, standardized educational testing, behavior modification, man-machine system design, political polling, consumer research and market testing, management consulting." In addition, social science has "vastly extended the observational powers of contemporary societies." Observations collected systematically include "economic indicators, demographic trends, national statistical systems, historical research, time-series analysis, input–output matrices, developmental psychology, area studies, political geography." Social science has also provided useful concepts that are now widely disseminated. These include "human capital, gross national product, identity crisis, span of control, the unconscious, price elasticity, acculturation, political party identification reference group, externalities." Neither in the editorial nor in the report is there a recognition that many of these technologies, activities, and ideas are profoundly problematic in their human and ethical implications. Nowhere does Prewitt ask "useful for whom, for what purpose?" Indeed there is, on the whole, a striking neutrality with respect to questions of purpose or value with the exception of the highly general reference to "economic growth and the public welfare."

There is a passage in Prewitt's 1978–79 annual report that may help us understand the apparent neutrality in the usefulness argument. At first sight its defense of scientific autonomy almost seems to preclude any argument for usefulness at all:

> Is the research free of extrascientific considerations? Is it autonomous inquiry? This returns to a point made earlier: The Council does not exist to sponsor research in which priorities or methods are set by political, commercial, ideological, or social welfare considerations. Council-sponsored research is not designed to keep a particular set of interests in power; or to discover that which will realize a profit; or to confirm pre-established worldviews; or to do good, other than the good which is a corollary of a more profound explanation or of superior problem-solving capacities. Rather, the Council sponsors research in which the scholars are in charge, in which methods emerge from scientific needs, and in which extending knowledge, whether basic or applied, is the goal of inquiry. (p. 11)

Social scientific research is to be above "political, commercial, ideological, or social welfare considerations." Such research is not to serve power, profit, dogmatic views, or ethical good. There is one exception: "the good which is a corollary of a more profound explanation or of superior problem-solving capacities." "[E]xtending knowledge, whether basic or applied" is the aim; only the good that flows from that has anything to do with social science. This is a widely accepted view among American social scientists, undoubtedly the dominant view. It allows one to argue for the independence of social science from political, economic, and ethical interests and values at the same time that one claims an abstract usefulness for the technologies, practices, and concepts to which social science gives rise. But it is a view that can no longer be taken for granted.

Michel Foucault has been reminding us that knowledge and power are not so easily distinguished—they are two aspects of a single process.[2] Cognitive discovery is never free from "extrascientific considerations." No amount of high-minded devotion to pure cognition will let us escape the fact that we exist in society and are part of its political, social, and ethical texture. There is one point where even those most devoted to "autonomous inquiry" know the truth of that embeddedness. Social science is itself part of society to the extent that it must be funded. But the very fastidiousness about scientific autonomy prevents those currently criticizing the budget cuts for social science from linking those cuts in any way to the larger economic, social, and human implications of the Reagan budget.

But my quarrel with this position goes much deeper than my uneasiness about turning social science into one more interest group competing for the bag of goodies. My quarrel arises from my belief that precisely that science which thinks itself nonideological and free of extrascientific considerations is profoundly ideological and political. I believe it is not fortuitous that so many of the "useful" technologies, practices, and concepts cited by Prewitt turn out to be manipulative instruments in the hands of political and economic power. It

---

[2]Michel Foucault, *Power/Knowledge: Selected Interviews and other Writings, 1972–1977* (New York: Pantheon Books, 1980).

is precisely a science that imagines itself uninvolved in society, that sees itself as operating under no ethical norm other than the pursuit of knowledge, that will produce instruments of manipulation for anyone who can afford to put them into practice.

Edward Shils, in his critique of what he calls "scientific or technological" social science, shows us what is left out in a view of social science that emphasizes autonomous inquiry and contextless "usefulness" alone:

> In its purely cognitive respects, sociology could, in principle, be a science like any other science. Sociology is not, however, an exclusively cognitive undertaking. It is also a moral relationship between the human beings studied and the student of the human beings studied.[3]

If one does not see that moral interaction is not only what social scientists study but also constitutive of social science itself, then an inherently manipulative conception of social science almost inevitably emerges:

> The manipulative conception of man and society entails the perception of the object of manipulation as a discrete entity having no social relationship with the manipulator except with regard to the manipulative actions themselves. It denies the object's capacities for and claims for moral regard by the manipulating person, and it thus denies the mutuality which is implicit in the sociological theory which is based on the acknowledgement of the moral, cognitive, and rational capacities of human beings. . . .
>
> I do not wish to deny that the type of sociology derived from behaviorism or from a scientistic utilitarianism has some element of truth in it. But it is a mistake to think that those elements contain all that is important and can be known about human beings and the societies

[3]Edward Shils, *The Calling of Sociology and Other Essays on the Pursuit of Learning* (Chicago: University of Chicago Press, 1980), p.20.

they form. It should also be clear that not all sociologists who espouse this kind of sociology are in favor of manipulation or that they have sought to construct their kind of sociology so that it could be used as a technological instrument to some end which the manipulator does not share with those he manipulates. . . . They are not hostile towards other human beings but their conception of them prevents them from taking human beings seriously. . . .

The sociology formed and adapted to technology is probably not wholly incorrect: there are undoubtedly human situations which can be ameliorated only by manipulation, or coped with only by coercion; and the scientific improvement of sociology might well make these actions more efficacious. The technological application of sociology, quite apart from its distortion and partiality, can hardly claim to be fitting for a democratic liberal society which respects the dignity of individual existence.[4]

Shils sums up his critique of technological social science and suggests its alternative in the following:

The real deficiency of technological sociology, which would remain despite its scientific rigor, its moral naiveté, and its harmlessness (hitherto) is its failure to grasp that the true calling of sociology is to contribute to the self-understanding of society rather than to its manipulated improvement.[5]

Shils's contrast between the self-understanding of society and technological manipulation as the two rival ends of social science gets to the heart of the matter. It reminds us of the deepest tension in the history of social thought, one that runs right through the development of modern social science. To give it a properly classical location, we may turn to Aristotle's

[4]Ibid., pp. 36–7.
[5]Ibid., p. 76.

distinction between *praxis* and *techne* as it is developed in the *Nicomachean Ethics*.[6] *Techne* is essentially making or producing. The artisan has a preexisting idea of what he wants to make and then shapes and controls his material to produce the desired product. It is precisely the point about *praxis* that it has no extraneous product. It has an end, namely the good for human beings, but its end is attained through itself, that is, through action or practice that is ethical and political. For Aristotle, technical reason helps the artisan shape material into a desired product; practical reason (*phronesis*) is the ethical and political reflection (Shils's "self-understanding of society") that helps the citizens of a free society practice the ethically good life.

Jürgen Habermas makes the same distinction in ways more in consonance with contemporary usage:

> Technical questions are posed with a view to the rationally goal-directed organization of means and the rational selection of instrumental alternatives, once the goals (values and maxims) are given. Practical questions, on the other hand, are posed with a view to the acceptance or rejection of norms, especially norms for action, the claims to validity of which we can support or oppose with reasons. Theories which in their structure can serve the clarification of practical questions are designed to enter into communicative action.[7]

Habermas points out that while the distinction between the technical and the practical is clear in Aristotle, Hobbes—by

---

[6]*Nicomachean Ethics*, VI, 4. We may locate the beginning of this tension in the struggle between Socrates and the Sophists. The Sophists had a *techne* to teach: the manipulative means to attain political power. Socrates taught with his own *praxis*, his own ethical example, as well as with dialogue that seeks the truth—not merely to defeat the opponent. Thrasymachus (*Republic*, I) is an example of a Sophist with substantive views that remarkably anticipate Hobbes.

[7]Jürgen Habermas, *Theory and Practice* (Boston: Beacon Press, 1973), p.3.

attempting to turn practical questions into technical ones—
brought about a fundamentally new direction of thought, one
that has been enormously influential ever since. Habermas
quotes the opening of the twenty-ninth chapter of *Leviathan*:

> Though nothing can be immortal, which mortals make:
> yet, if men had the use of reason they pretend to, their
> Commonwealths might be secured, at least, from per-
> ishing by internal diseases. Therefore when they come
> to be dissolved, not by external violence, but intestine
> disorder, the fault is not in men, as they are the *Matter*
> but as they are the *Makers*, and orderers of them.

The language of *techne* has now entered the practical realm.
As Habermas says,

> human behavior is therefore to be now considered only
> as the material for science. The engineers of the correct
> order can disregard the categories of ethical social inter-
> course and confine themselves to the construction of
> conditions under which human beings, just like objects
> within nature, will necessarily behave in a calculable
> manner. This separation of politics from morality re-
> places instruction in leading a good and just life with
> making possible a life of well-being within a correctly
> instituted order.[8]

Nevertheless, among human beings, acting can never be wholly
subsumed by controlling just because the controlling must
itself take place "through the consciousness of the citizens
who discuss and act." Human "material" is never as inert as
natural matter: "The act of technical domination of matter is
in principle a solitary and silent act—free from any negotiated
agreement among active subjects who wish to control their
social relations practically."[9] Therefore the problem for a ma-

[8]Ibid., p. 43.
[9]Ibid., p. 75.

nipulative social science is to control the process of action itself.

The prospect of a genuine science of human behavior on the model of the enormously successful modern natural sciences, true in all times and all places, has proven dazzling and seductive. But the question of why the idea of such a social science should arise at a particular time and place—mid-seventeenth-century England—suggests relations between the story of modern society and the story of modern social science that would be instructive to follow. This is not the place to trace those stories, but their relation does not seem fortuitous.[10]

There has been, however, another conception of social science, and that is the chief concern of this chapter. This is a tradition, however far it has wandered from Aristotle, that thinks of social science in terms of practical rather than technological reason. Both Shils and Habermas belong in this tradition, whatever other differences they may have. In this tradition, which we might call "practical social science," even the word *science* must be used with hesitation. It cannot have the rigorous meaning that it has taken on from modern natural science, for the degree of certainty found in physics is not to be expected in the study of human action.[11] In this tradition *science* retains its older meaning of "disciplined knowing."

In order to sharpen distinctions, I will take a more explicitly Aristotelian position as to what practical social science entails than would Shils or Habermas.[12] I would, with Aris-

---

[10]See, among many possible references, C. B. MacPherson, *The Political Theroy of Possessive Individualism, Hobbes to Locke* (New York: Oxford University Press, 1962).

[11]*Nicomachean Ethics*, I, 3.

[12]Habermas takes exception to "neo-Aristotelianism" on the ground that one cannot take Aristotle's ethics and politics without his physics and metaphysics. This is not the place to argue the point. See Jürgen Habermas, *Communication and the Evolution of Society* (Boston: Beacon Press, 1979), p. 201.

totle, assert the primacy of moral practice over both social and moral theory. This is to give a certain priority to practical reason over theoretical reason, though that issue is complex.[13] In any case, we start from where we are, in the midst of society, observing persons and actions that are deemed good or bad, right or wrong. We attempt to clarify our ideas about action by rational reflection and discussion, but action itself is rooted in established practice (*hexis, habitus*) that is not caused by nor fully amenable to theory or theoretical reconstruction. This is one reason why interpretation (of potentially inexhaustible meanings) takes precedence over explanation (in principle without remainder) in the human studies. This sense of the primacy of moral action rooted in established practices that are not entirely amenable to theoretical elucidation does not mean, however, that practical social science is irrational, particularistic, or historicist. Rational reflection is a vital part of social and ethical life and has a particularly important critical function. But there is a sense in which the paradigmatic example of the ethically mature person[14] can never be transcended by a rationally constructed theory. The question of universality is to be gradually clarified by everwidening interpretive circles and not by the fiat of logical necessity.[15]

---

[13]For Aristotle it is *politike*, not *phronesis*, which is the master *episteme* (science? knowledge?). *Nicomachean Ethics*, I, 2. On the primacy of the practical over the theoretical in Plato, see John Wild, *Plato's Theory of Man* (Cambridge, Mass.: Harvard University Press, 1946), pp. 22–34. Hans-Georg Gadamer has a particularly helpful treatment of *phronesis* (practical reason) in Aristotle in *Truth and Method* (New York: Seabury Press, 1975), pp. 278–89.

[14]*Nicomachean Ethics*, III, 4.

[15]Major recent thinkers who have seen the relevance of Aristotle include Leo Strauss, *Natural Right and History* (Chicago: University of Chicago Press, 1953) and Hannah Arendt, *The Human Condition* (Chicago: University of Chicago Press, 1958). Younger scholars making significant contributions to this discussion include John W. Danforth, *Wittgenstein and Political Philosophy* (Chicago: University of Chicago Press, 1978) and William A. Galston, *Justice and the Human Good* (Chicago: University of Chicago Press, 1980).

   If practical reason (prudence in its classical meaning) is always ethically informed reflection relative to specific social and historical conditions, perhaps we should return to where we began—the present situation in American society—in order to explicate further the differences between our two types of social science and their relevance. Shils calls ours "a democratic liberal society" and suggests that a purely technological social science "can hardly claim to be fitting" for such a society. That is not such an obvious conclusion if we consider how complex an entity liberal democratic society is. Hobbes, as Habermas and others have held, is, though no democrat, the founder of modern liberalism. "Manipulated improvement" and technological social science have been part of liberalism and modern liberal society since their inception. Nonetheless, Shils is surely right when he considers the possibility that technological social science could "develop into a tool for technocrats to rule the human race"[16] and would therefore be wholly incompatible with democratic society. The relation of the two types of social science to our society is clearly not simple.

   The problem is only rendered more complex when we reflect on the degree to which our particular kind of society is in danger at present. It is in danger because of loss of belief in it and commitment to it on the part of its citizens, and it is in danger because of the growth of centralized and decentralized systems of control incompatible with a society ruled with democratic consent. In short, the fears for our future expressed by Alexis de Tocqueville in *Democracy in America* —namely that our citizens might ultimately withdraw their concern for the common good in pursuit of a purely private good and that structures of "soft despotism" would almost

---

[16]Shils, p. 37.

unnoticeably replace our free institutions—are coming true.[17]
Daniel Bell describes the failure of commitment as

> the loss of *civitas*, that spontaneous willingness to obey
> the law, to respect the rights of others, to forgo the
> temptations of private enrichment at the expense of the
> public weal—in short, to honor the "city" of which one
> is a member. Instead, each man goes his own way, pur-
> suing his private vices, which can be indulged only at
> the expense of public benefits.[18]

Our problems are not unique and many advanced societies
are at the moment undergoing a failure of commitment. There
is considerable evidence of such a failure in the Soviet Union,
so much so that we are told that the "new Soviet man" has
turned pessimist. But by late 1978, the average American had
turned pessimist too, if we are to believe national survey data.
A majority of Americans for the first time in recorded history
believed that their future would be worse than their past and
their children's lives worse than their own. It is under these
conditions that problems of control become acute and temp-
tations to resort to nondemocratic forms of control grow.

    If this analysis of our present situation is at all accurate,
then there is good reason to question the argument for the
"usefulness" of social science in the 1980s. Most of the useful
mechanisms, practices, and concepts have ambiguous, not to
say ominous, implications for a democratic liberal society,
particularly one that has begun to lose confidence in its own
project. Many of the inventions of social science are being
applied today in ways that are inimical to the political pro-

---

[17]*Democracy in America* is an almost archetypal example of practical reason.
It is rooted in a commitment to moral practice in a free society and is
primarily concerned with how, under specifically American conditions,
such practice could be maintained.

[18]Daniel Bell, *The Cultural Contradictions of Capitalism* (New York: Basic Books,
1976), p. 245.

cesses of a free society. "Cost-benefit analysis" is an administrative weapon of enormous power now being used from the federal government to the local community college to justify decisions made without any effort to reach informed consensus through discussion and collective decision making. David Stockman tells us that the costs of the Consumer Product Safety Commission outweigh its benefits and therefore it must be eliminated. This kind of argument, for which the justification is supplied by experts, short-circuits political discussion, not to mention participation. I believe that political polling—another contribution of social science—in tandem with the mass media, has, during the last thirty years, moved American presidential campaigns significantly away from being occasions for political education toward being occasions for political manipulation. Parts of that story are well known, but the full case remains to be made.

However, examples such as these, suggesting, as they rightly do, that technological social science presents a danger to the survival of our democratic institutions, only touch the surface of our problem. Manipulated improvement and technological social science are constituent elements in a modern liberal democratic society and a concerted attempt to eliminate them from our society would undoubtedly have disastrous moral and political consequences. Indeed, the present policies emanating from Washington indicate what some of those consequences may be. Joseph Gusfield, in his 1978 presidential address to the Pacific Sociological Association, links sociology to the rise of the welfare state and so suggests, from the point of view of 1981, why the current attack on the welfare state should also include an attack on social science:

> Sociology in America has been an offspring of the Welfare State. Its position in the educational marketplace, its role in the training of professions and occupations, and the demand for its research have largely

reflected the concerns of a society and a state wishing
to alleviate the inadequacies of a market economy. The
demand for new programs and personnel with skills in
influencing, manipulating, and understanding human
behavior has been the base of the immense expansion
of sociology in the post-war period. The loss of faith in
the market as a model of social and political action has
contributed, as well, to the intellectual rise of sociology
and to sociologists as progenitors of social vision and
political directions.[19]

The present effort to refurbish the market economy as an
answer to our problems, itself guided by technical arguments
put forward by social scientists, not surprisingly involves the
dismantling of the social scientific establishment devoted to
the construction of the welfare state. Yet one must wonder
whether, in late capitalist society at this moment of world
history, a return to laissez faire economics together with a
vast remilitarization will not cause such severe problems that
once again the manipulated improvements of the welfare state—
and its social scientific architects—will not be called for. If we
can learn, as Gusfield is concerned to, what went wrong in
the past, perhaps we will be better prepared to face the future.

Social science, says Gusfield, achieved its influence and
its access to power precisely because of the claim to be
scientific: "It is as a branch of science and as a user of scientific
method that sociology has staked its claim to intellectual authority, as an empirical and not as an analytical method, as
theory rather than as history."[20] But, according to Gusfield,
social science in fact carried a number of dubious functions
only indirectly related to its self-image as "science," and, what
is worse, the degree to which social science genuinely became

---

[19]Joseph Gusfield, " 'Buddy, Can You Paradigm?' The Crisis of Theory in
the Welfare State," *Pacific Sociological Review*, 22 (January, 1979), 7.
[20]Ibid.

scientific was not reflected in superior performance with respect to questions of policy.

One function of social science has been ideological. Habermas analyzes this phenomenon by pointing out that science in general and social science in particular provide legitimating conceptions for the modern state and even for individual power holders.[21] Whatever the reality may be, to argue that particular policies and even particular decisions are based on scientific knowledge has become more and more compelling in our political life. And in opposing a policy initiative, a politician would be inept indeed if he or she did not also present a full array of supporting experts and scientists.

A second function is what Gusfield calls "institutional." Here social science provides ideas, techniques and, again, legitimation to a variety of new professional groups who have arisen to implement the welfare state, to staff what Gusfield calls "the 'troubled persons' industries or 'human resources' occupations." It is precisely those casualties of the laissez faire economy who become the new focus for occupational specialization:

> The emergence of occupations in which knowledge is used to solve human problems is then a part of the "social problems" orientation of contemporary societies and their public politics. People viewed as "troubled" or "deviant" or "needing" are the object of others' activities. The "troubled persons" industries are a vital source of the new professionals. They have no clear designation but certainly include such people as social workers, counselors, community organizers, race relations specialists, clinical psychologists, psychiatrists, educational

---

[21]See particularly chap. 5, "The Scientization of Politics and Public Opinion," and chap. 6, "Technology and Science as 'Ideology, ' " in Jürgen Habermas, *Toward a Rational Society* (Boston: Beacon Press, 1970).

guidance personnel, medical health workers, alcohol treatment and prevention personnel, substance abuse specialists, and those who teach and train them. They claim a mandate to advise, plan, and treat on the basis of an expertise that rests on a "state of the art" or a body of fact and theory of ascertained and valid form. It is the source of their claim to skill and knowledge. The gerontologist, for example, purports to address a world in which there is a body of knowledge and skills making up gerontology and providing his or her source of professional claim to treat, plan, and advise; to create and evaluate policy about the aged.[22]

The authority and even power of these professionals—and we should not forget that at the microlevel they do exercise power—is guaranteed by the theoretical and methodological prestige of social science as science.

But, as Gusfield goes on to point out, in the heartland of disciplinary social science itself, as opposed to the bureaucrats and professionals who rely on it, there is growing doubt that scientific social science can indeed produce the expected results:

The more refined our techniques, the less we have to say. The depictions of pathways and analyses of variance have given us greatly advanced tools for analyzing the play and interplay of variables. At the same time they have frequently ended in the view that everything is relevant and everything causes everything else. . . .

The bright hope had been that sociology, by the logic of its theories and the power of its empirical findings, would provide the insights and generalizations enabling governments to frame policies and professionals to engineer programs that could solve the exigent problems of the society and helping intellectuals to direct understanding and criticism. Our record has not been very good. In area after area—gerontology, crime, mental

[22]Gusfield, p. 11.

health, race relations, poverty—we have become doubtful that the technology claimed is adequate to the demand. We are skeptical that the problems exist in the
direct fashion which policies and programs presuppose.
Posited as political issues, as matters of total system or
institutional change, we are unconvinced that a science
can point the way to a compelling conclusion on which
effective policies can be generated. It is not that conflicting interests lead groups to ignore social science. It is
rather that our belief in the legitimacy of our knowledge
is itself in doubt.[23]

These considerations give rise to doubts that the long-awaited
arrival of a social science true to the name may ever occur.
Gusfield quotes Anthony Giddens: "Those who still wait for
a Newton are not only waiting for a train that won't arrive,
they're in the wrong station altogether."

But Gusfield is not in despair:

At this point I will reveal my hidden agenda—not
a way out of the crisis of legitimating sociology as a
cultural enterprise but an avowal of it as a worthy activity
of human thought and creativity, part of social studies
rather than social science. One of the apocryphal sayings
of Robert Park was that, "sociology is at best a pedagogical exercise. . . ." The technical methods and the
formalized theories and propositions have had less impact than the specific works of sociologists that create
models, metaphors, and images for perceiving human
behavior and institutions. It is in the works that seek
significance and insight, that dare to ignore the demand
for closure and accuracy that sociology has made its
greatest effects. Would de Tocqueville have passed a
Ph.D. thesis committee's scrutiny of his methods? Works
like *The Gold Coast and the Slum, Street-corner Society, The
Power Elite, The Lonely Crowd, Asylums, Social Origins of
Dictatorship and Democracy* are deeply flawed when com-

---

[23]Ibid., pp. 17–18.

pared to any model of rigorous empirical science or a
grand, formal deductive theory. They do not tell us what
is absolutely there, but they make us aware of what is
possible and plausible. They do not avoid reflecting on
their limits by examining, testing, and learning from immersion into the confusion of an empirical world.[24]

Gusfield, it would seem, is calling for his own version of a
practical social science—in the face of the failure of a *technological* social science that is on the one hand misused and on
the other unable to fulfill the expectations it had aroused.
Gusfield is also suggesting that, among both the founders of
our disciplines and their most recent distinguished practitioners, a model of work that is communicative, practical, and
ethical rather than manipulative, technological, and scientific
is to be found that can give us courage for the future.

I am trying in this chapter to make a rather sharp distinction between two types of social science, a distinction that
remains rather indistinct even in the very helpful paper of
Joseph Gusfield. I am not trying, thereby, to deny the legitimacy of technological social science altogether. Neither do I
wish to argue for a banal "we need both kinds" position.
There is little doubt that social science today sees itself largely
in terms of the technological model. This is what it means to
be a science in the strong sense. Those who work in the
alternate tradition often do so with limited clarity about their
justification, with a bad conscience, and with a vague nod to
something called "humanistic." I am arguing that practical
social science not only exists as a vigorous enterprise but
should take precedence over technological social science rather
than the other way around.

I am suggesting that we reverse the priorities between
technical and practical interests, between *techne* and *praxis*,

[24]Ibid., pp. 18–19.

between control and action. The purpose of practice is not to produce or control anything but to discover through mutual discussion and reflection between free citizens the most appropriate ways, under present conditions, of living the ethically good life. To that end technological knowledge may be helpful provided that it is used in the context of a practical—that is, ethical and political—knowledge that has precedence over it. I am not foolish enough to imagine that this is going to happen any time soon. But I would like to devote the rest of this chapter to a consideration of that utopian possibility in hopes that such speculation may itself be instructive about our present condition.

I have already indicated that I believe a kind of technological social science will continue to be needed in a complex industrial society that requires the manipulated improvements of the welfare state if it is to be even minimally just. Hard data that will allow rough predictions about the economic and social consequences of various policies will certainly be required, and such analyses necessarily, to some extent, treat human action as "material" for administrative decision. But in a situation where we had a more effective and self-confident practical social science working together with a more chastened and modest technological social science, some of the negative consequences noted by Gusfield would be mitigated. For one thing, if the limitations of technological social science were clearly understood, neither politicians and administrators on the one hand nor "troubled persons" and "human resources" professionals on the other could claim the legitimating authority of science for their opinions or decisions. Technical knowledge would be viewed as only one rather uncertain input into a situation that also requires common sense, ethical insight, and a great deal of conversation with those affected before a policy can be formulated or a decision made. The important point is that technical knowledge does not necessitate anything. Decisions and commitments must emerge from the practical context of communicative action.

Such an understanding would move both administrators and professionals in a more democratic and less authoritatian direction. For bureaucrats, this would involve a much more vigorous exposure to a participatory political process, perhaps ultimately a democratic planning process such as Olaf Palme has advocated.[25] For "helping" professionals, this would involve toleration of high levels of uncertainty in trying to aid people to improve their own skills of practical autonomy, rather than categorizing them in terms of preconceived theories with resulting automatic formulas for treatment. I am aware that such a shift in the operation of the welfare state would require structural changes in the economy and polity that are not now likely.

Turning to the disciplines themselves, let us consider what a predominance of practical over technological social science would look like. Such a change here would meet fewer structural barriers, though entrenched attitudes and commitments do not make it very likely either. A shift in the predominance of the two kinds of social science would involve a shift in the dominance of two different paradigms for un-

---

[25]"Democratic control of the economy should not be confined to traditional Keynesian methods for stabilizing the economy. Instead one of the prerequisites of economic democracy is for civic influence to be effective at all levels of the economy. . . . It is therefore very important to find ways and means of having broad democratic participation in the planning. Planning is no act of mindless machinery. It should be founded in people's participation. Its purpose is to serve people. Since all political decisions are based on value judgments, they should not be left to experts or professionals. They must be reachable for ordinary people." Excerpts from the keynote address on economic democracy by Olaf Palme to the Eurosocialism and America conference, Dec. 5–7, 1980, Washington, D.C., reprinted in *Working Papers* (January, 8, 1981), 36.

derstanding human action. Technological social science was founded on and has always assumed what can be called a "strategic" paradigm of human action. Practical social science has worked with what can be called a "normative" paradigm. The strategic paradigm holds that human action is to be explained primarily in terms of the behavior of individual persons motivated by needs and drives, chief of which are self-interest and will to power. This conception is consistent with the natural science model of technological social science in its insistence on the sole validity of efficient causation. Individual drives seem to be just the right place to look if only efficient causes are scientifically respectable. In the strategic paradigm, morality tends to be viewed as secondary. It is either ideological false consciousness or a form of "side constraint" that utilitarian action must take into account. Those who defend the normative paradigm view the strategic paradigm as only a special case of their own more general conception. In the normative paradigm, human beings are seen as coming to be selves capable of interaction with others through a process of internalizing patterns of character and obligation that express what a good person in a good society ought to be. Among the norms learned in any society are the contexts in which rational self-interest can legitimately be pursued. In the view of the normative paradigm, the self-interest-maximizing individual of the strategic paradigm would never have come into existence in the first place without such a process of normative learning.

It is interesting that though the strategic paradigm originated with Hobbes in a primarily political context, it gained its greatest importance and influence as the central model of economics. Political science never wholly succumbed to the strategic paradigm because it kept touch with older conceptions of justice. Sociology was born in rebellion against the economic model and attempted, on modern scientific prin-

ciples, to work out a new defense of the normative model.
As technological social science has become dominant, the strategic paradigm has become powerful in all the social sciences,
notably in political science and sociology. Recently, in part
for reasons alluded to by Gusfield, the normative model has
undergone a modest revival, even in economics itself.[26]

The essential empirical question that this confrontation
of paradigms suggests is whether a society based on the articulation of self-interest alone is viable. The study of morality—the normative order or "the mores," to use Tocqueville's central term—suggests that strategic action always implies
a context of nonstrategic action. Even "the morality of the
market" can never be reduced to merely strategic agreements.
This is Émile Durkheim's point in arguing that there is always
a noncontractual element in contract. Some sociologists have
claimed that the project of a technological social science could
be carried out on the basis of the normative paradigm. This
is not the place to argue why this is not possible. Let me just
say that every attempt to do so has ended up in self-contra-
diction. Both Durkheim and Parsons finally sacrificed their
scientific ideal to their commitment to the normative paradigm. If I am right that only a practical social science is really
capable of understanding the problems involved in normative
order, then it is surely needed at a moment when the normative framework of action in our society is in such disarray.

The difference between technological and practical social
science has methodological as well as theoretical implications.
Here the linkages are in one way less tight. The practical social

[26]On this point, see Albert O. Hirschman, "Morality and the Social Sciences:
A Durable Tension," in *Social Science as Moral Inquiry*, ed. by Robert Bellah,
Norma Haan, Paul Rabinow, and William Sullivan, (New York: Columbia
University Press, 1983); and Michael S. McPherson, "Morality and the Use-
ful Economist," unpublished, 1981.

scientist can certainly use the quantitative data that the technological scientist prefers and the latter can use qualitative data and even hermeneutic interpretation. Yet there remains a deep methodological cleavage between them in that they have a different conception of the relation between the social scientist and those who are studied. It is in this context that Shils's term *consensual* can be used for practical social science. This is to say once again that social science is a moral as well as a cognitive enterprise and that the relations between the social scientist and those who are studied must be moral rather than manipulative. Not only must social scientists respect the "claims for moral regard" of those who are studied but they must also regard those who are studied as collaborators.

> The popularity of the interview is not simply a product of scientific necessity. It is not merely a technique of research; it is also an act of human conviviality and consensus. . . . The basic technique of sociological research—the interview—despite all its distortions and corruptions in market research and public opinion polls, is one of the ways in which this fellowship is expressed. The books which come forth from this kind of research are collaborative and in a sense much more important than that of the widely practiced team-research; they are collaborative of the investigator and those he studies.[27]

This collaborative process involves finally the sharing of research findings with those studied. If social science is essentially a form of social self-understanding, then it involves a mutual and reciprocal self-interpretation between the social scientist and the society that is studied.

But the practical social scientist is not, as this description so far might imply, simply a mirror for whatever he or she

[27]Shils, p. 14.

finds—a kind of populist reflector of existing social reality. Such scientists have commitments not only to the people they study but also to the tradition in which they stand, a tradition that has theoretical and methodological content but also substantive moral content. They believe, in continuity with that tradition, that democratic society is better than despotic society and that life is more complete, even in a sense more human, in such a society. They believe this not on "extrascientific" grounds but as part of their very understanding of human reality. In a democratic society, they presumably share such conceptions with those who are studied, but they are prepared to find many divergences from these views. Their work is not a mere passive reflection of what they study. Works of the greatest scientific value, such as *Democracy in America* or *The Division of Labor*, are simultaneously also designed to *persuade* the public of certain desirable policies.

All this implies a very different attitude toward the audience of social science as well as a different conception of the relation between social science and social policy from that found in technological sociology. Prewitt suggests one approach when he writes in his editorial: "Just as medicine draws upon biological research or electronics upon physics, government and management draw upon psychology, economics, demography, geography, and other social sciences." Here there is a clear analogy between the application of natural science to technology and the application of social science in the service of power.

It is not that practical social science is averse to conversation with "government and management." They are indeed part of the process of reciprocal self-interpretation. But practical social science does not provide useful applications. Michael Maccoby brought his profound commitment to democratic values to bear on his study of corporate management, and many of those he studied were interested in dialogue with him. But as he recounts in *The Gamesman*,[28] a book with an enormous general audience, the discussion provoked self-reflection, self-questioning, even dismay. His argument could not be applied to increase the effectiveness of existing forms, for it implied the need for a fundamentally different form of corporate organization—for the sake not of profitability but of human fulfillment.

The chief audience of practical social science is not "decision makers" but the public, and its chief impact on social policy is through influencing the climate of opinion rather than supplying discrete information for those in power. Of course in this new situation that I am envisioning, where practical social science has become predominant, the relation between the public and decision makers would undoubtedly be different. Furthermore, in such an atmosphere the technological social science that would still be necessary in government and industry would be more open to practical considerations.

But the premise of an informed and active public suggests just how utopian, under present conditions, my speculation

[28]Michael Maccoby, in *The Gamesman*, (New York: Bantam Books, 1978), pp. 32–33, discusses several elements of the psychoanalytic method that are clearly related to practical reason: "The psychoanalyst participates in a systematic self-exploration, different from any other specialization in the human sciences, where his goal is to develop himself as the instrument of investigation . . . unlike other forms of science, in psychoanalysis the object of study, the patient, ideally becomes the co-investigator, and in the process of dialogue and discovery, he increases his capacity for understanding . . . above discovering new knowledge, the goal of psychoanalysis is to improve the life of the person being studied, and it is solely for that reason that the individual takes part."

Maccoby underestimates the degree to which these points are all valid beyond psychoanalysis. He notes the particularly important contributions Aristotle made to the study of character.

is. In particular, the relation between social science and the public has become endangered at both ends. John Dewey, already in the 1920s, noted the decline of an effective public, and the tendencies he described have only grown worse in the half-century since. On the other hand, much of social science would be unintelligible to a public even if there were one. Technological social science is increasingly confined to a narrow circle of the esoterically informed. Yet in spite of that, much of what self-interpretation American society has had of late comes from those within the tradition of practical social science. Such names as Mills, Riesman, Bell, Sennett, Erikson, Heilbroner, and Galbraith come to mind. A revival of public life becomes a task for practical social science. Such a revival is a condition for its continued existence and indeed an imperative for the survival of democratic society.

Before summing up the relation between practical social science and social policy, I would like to attempt an experiment that might be instructive. I consulted with several friends in an effort to see whether I could construct a list of technologies, practices, and concepts from the tradition of practical social science that would parallel Prewitt's list, derived largely from technological social science. A number of things came to mind, but none of them were very new and snappy. *Voluntary association, citizen participation, republican virtue*, all at this point sound a little antique. Newer terms such as *public household* or *economic democracy* are merely combinations of older ideas, however helpful they may be today. Some terms, such as *public opinion* and *moral development*, are ambiguous because they have an older democratic and newer technological meaning. Finally, what struck us is that the vocabulary of practical social science is the common moral vocabulary of a free society. Among its basic terms are *justice, equality,* and *freedom*. Sometimes practical social scientists are tempted to use classical terms such as *civitas* or *pietas*. They may try to resurrect obsolete terms such as *virtue, courage, temperance, wisdom,* and *prudence.* It may be part of the task of practical social science to keep the common moral vocabulary alive— it is not only a vocabulary, it is a set of practices, of mores— in the face of the invasion of our vocabulary by technological social science. Terms of the latter origin seldom become part of common moral discourse, even when they drive out the older vocabulary. An impoverished moral vocabulary leaves an open field for the operation of calculating self-interest alone.

Practical social science, as I have said, is much more consciously related to ethics and social policy than is technological social science. Grounded in history and tradition, practical social science has a strong moral component in its very constitution, whereas technological social science is uneasy about "value judgments" other than cognitive validity and instrumental effectiveness. Practical social science overlaps with philosophy and shares many of its concerns. Practical social scientists are necessarily also philosophers, particularly moral philosophers, and should be familiar with the history of ethical thought. They are not technical specialists looking across a great gulf at other technical specialists calling themselves philosophers. Similarly, they are not purveyors of neutral information, the policy implications of which are of no concern to them. Ethical and policy concerns have determined their research interests from the beginning and they are acutely aware that the way data are presented always has policy implications.

Practical social scientists do not claim the degree of scientific precision to which technological social science aspires, partly because they do not think it possible in the study of human affairs. This means that there is a considerable humility in their claims. They do not offer definitive findings but only judgments informed by inquiry, quite fallible and containing many links that cannot be conclusively demonstrated. In this practical social scientists do not claim to be strikingly different from or superior to those who are addressed, whether ordinary citizens or decision makers. Such scientists see themselves precisely within the process of practical reason, where prudence and judgment must operate because scientific demonstration is not possible. They see their role, nonetheless, as a worthy part of the common life of a free society. If this kind of social science should become extinct, we may be reasonably sure that it will be replaced by a despotic social science in the service of a despotic society.

3

COMMENT ON ROBERT N. BELLAH, "SOCIAL SCIENCE AS PRACTICAL REASON"

JAMES M. BANNER, JR.

Professor Bellah's strictures against what he calls "technical social science" possess the authority of the grand tradition and of the increasing methodological self-consciousness of humanistic social science. As prescriptions of how practical social science might be pursued, however, his suggestions are less compelling.

That there is already a dated quality to Bellah's arguments should not blind us to their validity. It should not require the spur of recent radical critiques of academic social science nor of reductionist French theorizing for us to understand that knowledge, whether humanistic or social scientific, conveys power. Knowledge gives us power over the brute world and over the world of affairs, as it has always been understood to. Socrates, Erasmus, and the Founding Fathers knew this and were not abashed. Though they considered competing political ideologies to be the manifestations of ignorance, we

JAMES M. BANNER, JR. ☐ Chairman, American Association for the Advancement of the Humanities, Washington, D.C. 20006.

would rather say that those ideologies represent alternative kinds of knowledge and thought. Knowledge does not compete only with ignorance but also with other knowledge.

All knowledge, therefore, accepting Professor Bellah's own terms, is "profoundly problematic in [its] human and ethical implications." No knowledge, not even knowledge in the physical and natural sciences, is purely cognitive. The physical and natural sciences often involve moral relationships between the subjects and objects of investigation, and not merely animal objects. A case has been made for the standing of trees before the law.

Nevertheless, although no knowledge is neutral, its ideological implications are always extrinsic, applied by those who possess it. We cannot put an end to the creation of knowledge out of fear that someone may put it to a use which we did not intend or a use that we do not, and perhaps even cannot, conceive. That would place us in the obnoxious position of preventing the birth of knowledge, so that what might be known and thought may not or will not be known.

How then, and by what justification, using Shils's terms, are we to keep any knowledge gained for "the self-understanding of society" from being used for its "manipulative improvement"? One avenue open to practical social scientists would be for them to monopolize the application of their theories and findings. But that would risk ideological commitment and public obloquy, whose intensity even the hardiest social scientist would wish to avoid. The alternative is to encourage the creation of knowledge subjected always to the kind of evaluation that Bellah applies and to have confidence that criticism will play its sovereign role of advancing meritorious ideas and retiring others to their deserved fate.

In a free society the creation of knowledge is an act of moral faith. It is a civic act. Research and scholarship are justly considered to be engines of democracy, essential to the strength and vitality of a democratic republic and a liberal society. Surely, then, others besides scholars have the right to influence agendas for research. In that case, scholars then have a moral and civic obligation, in keeping with liberal principles, to supply knowledge that others seek, to provide information and reflection that others desire, in keeping with ethical standards.

That issue—ethical standards—is, for Bellah, the critical one. He correctly condemns the uses to which some social science has been put. Yet it is difficult to see how a social science that operates under his preferred ethical norms can be made secure from manipulation. A more empathetic, reciprocal, and communicative social science, one rooted in the tradition of Tocqueville, is surely desirable. We have too little of it. And yet such sociology—precisely because it is humane—is also ideological and therefore open to political exploitation. It can also as often be conservative as progressive in its intentions and implications.

Logically, the social sciences face an insoluble dilemma. If, in Professor Bellah's terms, "that science which thinks itself nonideological and free of extrascientific considerations is profoundly ideological and political," then how can any other science—that is, one that considers itself to be ideological and enmeshed in extrascientific considerations—be nonideological and nonpolitical? The problem is not that the social sciences delude themselves, which is what Professor Bellah thinks. It is rather that, even without illusions, the social sciences remain in the same fix.

Bellah's attack upon positivistic social science also overlooks the fact that positivistic inquiry, no matter what its outcome, originated in a scientistic attack on received opinion and in alliance with socialistic principles, which is one of the reasons "why the current attack on the welfare state should also include an attack on social sciences." Interpretive social science of the kind espoused by Bellah may have no necessary link with conservative social ideologies, a link hard to conceive today when it is a weapon against statist and "manipulative" public policies. Yet we would be foolish to ignore its earlier function or its potential.

Finally, practical social science possesses limitations that can be corrected only by what Bellah terms "technical social science." The former serves far less well in measuring social change and social structure, in discovering patterns of human and individual behavior, and in contributing to the design of specific public policies. Practical social science can move and persuade, cause us to understand matters of which we were ignorant—indeed, create a distinctive world view, as did Marx's sociology. But it does not yet meet the implacable requirements of policymaking nor the impulse—which, being rooted in modern thought itself, is not simply an emanation of the modern state—to count, measure, and compare. Social science as practical reason will carry the day only when it absorbs, rather than tries to vanquish, the methodological and conceptual advances of technical reason.

4

IMPERFECT DEMOCRACY AND THE MORAL RESPONSIBILITIES OF POLICY ADVISERS

MICHAEL S. McPHERSON

I

The idea of democracy plays an important role in reflection on the ethics of policy advising. Advisers to democratic governments are comforted by the thought that those whom they serve are in turn (at least at some remove) servants of "the people," chosen by the people, and that the values motivating the policies they help to shape are in some sense "society's values," expressed through the democratic process.

Used this way, the concept of democracy obviously bears quite a lot of normative freight. It is far from clear that the mere fact of electoral competition, often taken as the hallmark of democracy, has enough legitimating force to carry all that weight. Robert Bellah's contribution, as I see it, is to articulate

MICHAEL S. McPHERSON ☐ Associate Professor of Economics, Williams College, Williamstown, Massachusetts 01267 and member (1981–1982), School of Social Science, Institute for Advanced Study, Princeton, New Jersey 08540.

a conception of democracy that is rich and demanding enough to carry the normative significance we associate with that term. To Bellah, *democracy* describes not only a technique by which government officials are chosen but also a distinctive form of life. Democratic citizens display attitudes of mutual respect and a commitment to social equality; they participate widely and meaningfully in the decisions that shape their society. The "democratic process" is not mainly one of choosing leaders or expressing opinions; it is a process of reasoned deliberation and public conversation about the central issues of social life. By these standards, it is problematic whether and to what degree the United States is a democracy; more important, the very idea of a "fully democratic politics" becomes a kind of regulative ideal—a vision of social relations toward which societies can aim, knowing they may never fully achieve it.

This perspective on democracy is a welcome one, which puts questions about the ethics of policy in an appropriately large context. The question becomes: How can social science best contribute to the public life of a democratic society? A narrow conception of democracy encourages a narrow conception of the role of social science: just as "democracy" is simply a technical device for choosing leaders, so social science (in its public role) is simply a technical device for choosing policies. Bellah's larger conception of democracy opens our eyes to public roles for social science other than the purely technical: it can be a form of discourse that furthers social self-understanding and thereby part of the conversation among equals that, for Bellah, in an important sense *is* democracy.

It is interesting that Bellah does not, in his paper, make any particular attempt to use this rich conception of democracy to help guide the practice of social scientists who do work as policy advisers and analysts in our present society.

No doubt this is partly because he wants to focus our attention on modes of thinking and of public involvement other than "advising the prince," although I sense that there is also lurking in the background an ill-suppressed wish that technological social science could somehow just go away. But whatever the reason, Bellah doesn't say much directly about these issues. Since it seems to me that his framework does have some useful implications for the moral problems of policy advisers in our imperfectly democratic society, I will use the bulk of my space here trying to spell them out.

Before turning to that, however, I would like to pause to object to one aspect of Bellah's rhetorical strategy which I think is not helpful, and which turns out to bear on my other theme. This is his attempt to *oppose* "technological" to "practical" social science as two radically different forms of endeavor, an opposition that leads him to characterize the ethical problem as a sort of struggle for supremacy between these two ways of doing social science. I prefer, in what I think is a Deweyan spirit, to see the practical and the technological as two indispensable aspects or dimensions of the social scientist's activity rather than as two distinct and self-contained kinds of enterprise. Let me briefly explain why.

II

The dangers in forging a radical split between the "technological" and the "practical" in social science cut both ways. Such a split tends to make practical social scientists self-indulgent, freeing them from the need to meet the highest technical standards developed by the underlaborers in the discipline. The long quote from Joseph Gusfield on page 53 illustrates this danger nicely. Could it really be a virtue in sociological work, as he implies, that it "ignores the demand for . . .

accuracy" and is "deeply flawed when compared to any model of rigorous empirical science"? The works he cites may be great despite such defects but surely not because of them.

Richard Titmuss's book *The Gift Relationship*[1] further illustrates my point. Titmuss has provided an evocative and persuasive comparison of the blood supply systems in the United States and Great Britain, using that case as a vehicle for reflection on the roles and meanings of morality in advanced industrial societies. The work is an artful blend of interpretive and causal claims; stressing on one hand the special meaning of freely given blood as a symbol of human bonds and on the other the consequences for human health and for moral attitudes of tampering with that symbolic role. The book is good and important—an outstanding example of "practical" social science. But as Kenneth Arrow makes clear in a forceful but sympathetic review, it would be better if Titmuss had done his technical social science better.[2] The powerful insights and important hypotheses put forward by Titmuss are marred by uneven treatment of data, consistent neglect of possible extraneous factors influencing the comparison of the United States and Great Britain, and too much reliance on *post hoc ergo propter hoc* reasoning.

Why should we not expect good social science to give us, as Max Weber wanted, *both* causal explanation *and* interpretive understanding? And in assessing the adequacy of the causal stories told—which is, in general, essential to deciding on the worth of the interpretations—why should we not adhere to the best technical methods social scientists have

[1]Richard M. Titmuss, *The Gift Relationship: From Human Blood to Social Policy* (New York: Random House, Inc., 1971).

[2]Kenneth Arrow, "Gifts and Exchanges," *Philosophy and Public Affairs*, 1 (Summer 1972), 343–62. See also Peter Singer, "Altruism and Commerce: A Defense of Titmuss against Arrow," *Philosophy and Public Affairs*, 2 (1973), 312–20.

devised? Perhaps not much social science measures up very well to this dual standard, but so much the worse for most social science.

Looking the other way, the notion of a sharp split may give unintended aid and comfort to defenders of the myth of a purely technological social science, neutral ethically and in its presuppositions about human nature. The idea of a sharp divide suggests that there really is a self-subsistent entity on the other side of it. Bellah's paper as a whole is such an effective assault on that myth that it would be terribly ironic if his insistence on a rigid dichotomy worked to reinstate it.

It seems to me particularly useful to make the case against technological social science on its chosen ground, that is, in its claim to be able to predict and explain. There is a great deal about human behavior that a "strategic view" of the human being as self-interested calculator leaves out and which must be brought in to make explanations adequate. Bellah himself makes this case about sociology on pages 54–55; the same point is being (re)discovered by economists. As Albert Hirschman has said:

> The damage wrought by the "economic approach," based on the traditional self-interest model . . . extends to wide areas of analysis and is due to far too simplistic a model of human behavior *in general*. What is needed is for economists to incorporate into their analyses, whenever that is pertinent, such basic traits and emotions as the desire for power and for sacrifice, the fear of boredom, pleasure in both commitment and unpredictability, the search for meaning and community and so on.[3]

Such an expansion in the view of humanity, even if motivated in the first instance by the desire to account for the

---

[3]Albert O. Hirschman, "Morality and the Social Sciences: A Durable Tension," *Essays in Trespassing: Economics to Politics and Beyond* (Cambridge, England: Cambridge University Press, 1981), p. 303.

facts, would almost inevitably bring with it an opening of the interpretive and moral dimensions of inquiry that are stressed by practical social science.[4] This seems to me quite an appealing strategy for opening up the moral and human perspectives of economists and other social scientists.

It perhaps does not stretch the meaning of words too much to see the relationship between the practical and technological as itself a kind of dialogue—sometimes taking place within a single person. In this perspective, the language of "precedence"—and, by implication, subordination—that Bellah uses to characterize the ideal relation between these two aspects of social inquiry is somewhat out of step with the democratic commitments he generally displays.

III

As a contribution to this dialogue of the technological and the practical, I want now to explore a bit the implications of Bellah's notion of democracy as a form of life for the moral responsibilities of the policy adviser or analyst.

Sometimes, democracy serves as little more than an excuse for passing the moral buck. The responsibility of an adviser to an official in a democratic society, it might be said, is strictly a professional one—to provide clear and accurate technical analysis and information. What is done with the information, the moral responsibility for decision, rests squarely on the shoulders of the politically responsible officials who receive the advice. This clean and convenient division of labor

[4] I have expanded on this point in my paper "Want Formation, Morality, and some 'Interpretive' Aspects of the Economic Inquiry," in *Social Science as Moral Inquiry*, ed. by Robert Bellah, Norma Haan, Paul Rabinow, and William Sullivan (New York: Columbia University Press, 1983).

was articulated most clearly, perhaps, by some of the "new welfare economists" of the 1930s and 1940s who sought to put the role of the economic adviser in the policy process on a purely scientific footing.[5]

Bellah's discussion, I think, implies that this is a dubious picture of the role of the adviser, even in an ideal democracy, because it cuts the technician off so sharply from the dialogic and participatory aspects of democracy. But the problems with this picture become much more acute when we face up to the highly imperfect nature of existing democracies. In an ideal democracy—with a just distribution of income and power, fair representation of all groups, and adequate institutions for political debate and discussion—the adviser's moral problems would be considerably eased. He or she could confidently follow the lead of political authorities, feeling reasonably sure that their aims were a proper translation of public aims and that, if things did go astray, the basic strengths of the social organization would bring them back on course. (In fact, this view has some affinities with Bellah's portrait of the role of the technical adviser in a world where practical social science had become predominant and an active and informed public had been restored.)

As things stand, however, nobody could justify having that much faith in "the process." By any standard of democracy strong enough to support serious normative claims, it is plain that our democratic process is marred by severe inequalities of political voice and power and by important defects in the channels through which public opinion is formed and communicated. In these circumstances, advisers with serious democratic commitments can hardly lay their moral re-

[5]A lucid overview is Paul Streeten, "Recent Developments," an appendix to Gunnar Myrdal, *The Political Element in the Development of Economic Theory* (Cambridge, Mass.: Harvard University Press, 1954).

sponsibilities off onto the imperfect politicians and processes they serve. There is no escaping the need for the adviser to make an independent moral judgment about the consequences of his or her involvement and about the best way to proceed. (For that matter, even a decision that you lived in an ideal democracy would be an independent moral judgment.)[6]

This line of thought opens onto some treacherous and ill-explored moral ground, for we can hardly think that it is right for policy advisers simply to make up their own minds about what is the best policy and then do whatever is necessary by way of lying, scheming, and fudging the data to see that it gets adopted. The adviser's "independent moral judgment" has to show a proper concern for the integrity of the process he or she is involved in and for the democratic values he or she is obliged to serve. The trouble is that, in an imperfect democracy, the existing processes and institutions do not always adequately express those values. We can catch some of the complexities here by saying that the adviser really has a three-sided obligation: (1) to serve his or her superiors honestly, (2) to promote better policies, and (3) to respect and improve the democratic process by which decisions are made. These are all real moral obligations and, in a nonideal society, conflicts between every pair are likely. In particular, besides the obvious moral conflict raised when one's superiors pursue perverted ends, there is the perhaps less familiar difficulty that "good" policy and "good" process may conflict. Both Franklin Roosevelt and James Watt illustrate the impulse to

---

[6]The perspective on obligation outlined here is, I believe, consistent with that developed in Hanna Pitkin, "Obligation and Consent," in *Philosophy, Politics and Society*, ed. by P. Laslett, W. G. Runciman, and Q. Skinner (4th series; Oxford, England: Basil Blackwell & Mott, Ltd., 1972); and in John Rawls, *A Theory of Justice* (Cambridge, Mass.: Harvard University Press, 1971).

put results ahead of "due process"; the linking of their names suggests the moral ambiguities implied by this conflict. Wrestling with these various dilemmas defines a good portion of the moral life of a policy adviser. The dramatic extremes come, of course, when it's time to think about resigning in protest or leaking the Pentagon Papers. But the conflicts exist on the everyday level too, when you have a hand in shaping the alternatives your boss looks at, when you have the option to execute a bureaucratic end run around established procedures, when you can keep arguing or wait for a better time to fight.

I suppose in a way this is trivially obvious: we all make moral choices all the time if we choose to notice it. But the obvious is worth stressing here in order to lean against that very seductive notion of a neat division of labor between professionally responsible advisers and morally responsible politicians. This notion rests on an insupportable idealization of the political process and a drastic oversimplification of the moral issues.

Let me underline one aspect of this idealization. It is easy to characterize the morally self-conscious analyst as an arrogant sort who wants to substitute his or her own personal values for society's values, where a more humble individual might defer to the outcome of existing, presumptively legitimate processes. But the conflicts I have stressed arise because policy processes always fall short of the ideal; they cannot fully capture society's values. The adviser is not trying to substitute his or her own values for society's values but is rather trying to help to bring about socially desirable results from a flawed process. In doing this, advisers cannot escape exercising their own judgment about how to proceed, but the judgment is about what the underlying principles of the political order call for in this case rather than merely about what they personally would like.[7] Advisers who mindlessly defer to whatever the policy process grinds out are not putting society's values ahead of their own but are refusing to face up to flaws in that process, implicitly substituting an idealized democracy for the one that really exists.

This perspective reinforces and extends what I take to be a central point of Bellah's paper: the need to see the substantive criticism of social institutions as a central part of reflection about the ethical dilemmas of policy advisers and analysts. It is too easy to let discussions of "ethical codes" and the like take place in an institutional vacuum, as if the ethical responsibilities of advisers could somehow be detached from their real place in the world as it is. To cite an example, there is nothing *inherently* manipulative or antidemocratic about cost–benefit analysis. Imbedded in the right social context, it can be an extremely useful way to organize the information about certain aspects of a policy's effects. But when such a tool is employed to short-circuit the process of political discussion, or when its measures of cost and benefit are distorted by a highly skewed distribution of purchasing power, it becomes a potentially misleading and dangerous device. Thus, the moral significance of cost–benefit analysis can only be thought through in relation to the larger political–economic context in which it is employed. It is too simple either to write the technique off as inherently defective or to let economists off the moral hook by implying that misuse of the results is none of their business, even if that misuse is perfectly easy to foresee. Advisers, of course, are stuck in the middle: they didn't make this nonideal world, and all they can do (short of deciding

---

[7]This point is rather like Ronald Dworkin's view that judges in hard cases, rather than making law or following a personal view, try to figure out what the law is in light of their understanding of political theory. See Ronald Dworkin, *Taking Rights Seriously* (Cambridge, Mass.: Harvard University Press, 1977), especially the essay "Hard Cases."

there is no alternative but to resign) is try by whatever means they can find to ward off the misuse of their results. We, however, are not so stuck in the middle as the adviser. We can step back—as Bellah has done in his paper—and try to see how the sometimes unfortunate results of policy analysis as practiced are rooted in more basic defects of our social order. This substantive social criticism is a necessary part of (not a separate subject from) the study of the ethics of policy advising.

And yet a deeper understanding of the roots of the dilemma still leaves the policy adviser (or policymaker, for that matter) on the hook, trying (we hope) to make the best of it in a nonideal world. Ethical theory, as it stands, doesn't offer much help. The bulk of modern ethical theory, from Kant to Rawls, has been concerned mainly with "ideal" theory—what maxims of conduct would it be best for us all to adopt, assuming we would all follow them. The peculiar complexities that arise when other people or institutions don't perform as they ought to do have received much less systematic attention; when they are looked at, they seem frustratingly resistant to theoretical generalization.[8] This, however, may be a point where we can get some help from Bellah's Aristotelian notion of the priority of practice over theory.

While ethical theory can do more than it has done to shed light on the complexities of nonideal morality, it is probably a mistake to look to theory for a detailed casuistry or moral code to tell the policy adviser what to do next. As Bellah says (p. 46), "there is a sense in which the paradigmatic example

[8]For systematic work on these issues of "non-ideal theory," see Joel Feinberg, "Duty and Obligation in the Non-Ideal World," *Journal of Philosophy*, 70 (May 10, 1973), 263–75; C. D. Broad, "On the Function of False Hypotheses in Ethics," *International Journal of Ethics*, 26 (1916), 377–97; and John Rawls, *A Theory of Justice*, chap. 4.

of the ethically mature person can never be transcended by a rationally constructed theory." What we can hope to do is to encourage social scientists who serve governments to be morally serious people who are willing to face up to the moral ambiguities of their situation. I worry less about an adviser thinking through a moral dilemma and coming up with the "wrong" answer than about his or her failure to grasp the moral import of the situation in the first place. There is, of course, no magic by which such moral consciousness any more than any other desirable change can be achieved. But surely one thing that matters for this purpose is the character of the education social scientists get and the conception of their own discipline that they carry.

And here we come full circle, for it seems to me that there is nothing more important in this regard than to break down the idea of a sharp distinction between the technological and the practical. Much social science education is still informed by the positivist view that morality and values are simply a matter of emotion and personal preference. It is hard to imagine a view more destructive of moral seriousness or more discouraging of the idea that there is anything to be thought through in a moral dilemma. (In fact, the moral seriousness of most social scientists and policy advisers is testimony to their disbelief in their own education.) Social scientists ought to get in the habit of reflecting on the moral and human consequences of their work; they ought to understand better the deep intertwining of the moral and technical presuppositions of their work. Most of all, they ought to leave behind the positivist idea of a purely neutral social science which somehow has policy implications. This won't and shouldn't stop them from being technological social scientists: a complex society needs forecasters, public health specialists, and macroeconomic planners. But it will affect the spirit in which they approach their work and, in some measure, the results.

For these reasons it is worthwhile to open and maintain a dialogue between the "technological" and "practical" dimensions of social science. Changing the way social scientists think about their work is hardly a sufficient condition for a better society, but it just might be a necessary one.[9]

[9] I am grateful to Albert O. Hirschman for several especially helpful suggestions.

5

VALUE-CRITICAL POLICY ANALYSIS

MARTIN REIN

The task of policy analysis is to bring evidence and interpretation to bear on decision making and social practice. This task involves not only the presentation of evidence about the consequences of pursuing alternative actions but also an interpretation of what it is we are doing in society, why we are doing what we do, and what we might do differently given our puzzlement and worry about what we do.

When we consider the way we think when we analyze policy, we need to examine the interplay between theory, fact, and value. This examination into the life of the mind is perhaps special because thought about policy more than other streams of mental life is grounded in action, not as an afterthought but as an essential feature of policy. When we think about the limits of what we do or about what we ought to do (policy analysis), we work from examples of policies in action. Our thought is thus a concrete expression of our experience in acting. This essay reviews the theory–fact–value relationship, proposes an approach called "framing" to show how

MARTIN REIN ☐ Professor of Social Policy, Massachusetts Institute of Technology, Cambridge, Massachusetts 02139.

they are internally related, and explores the implication of a theory of frames for a value-critical policy analysis and for discourse across competing and conflicting frames.

THE THEORY–FACT–VALUE DILEMMA

At the center of this epistemological controversy is the question of the integration or segregation of fact, value, and theory. Conventional thought holds that knowledge should involve the separation of fact and value. This is thought to be a way that reason can understand reality without distortion. The view of facts and values as totally disjoint realms is so pervasive that it has led Hillary Putnam to conclude that the acceptance of an absolute dichotomy between fact and value

> has assumed the status of a cultural institution. By calling the dichotomy a cultural institution, I mean to suggest that it is an unfortunate fact that the received answer will go on being the received answer for quite some time regardless of what philosophers may say about it, and regardless of whether or not the received answer is right. Even if I could convince you that the fact/value dichotomy is without rational basis . . . still . . . the next time you had a discussion at some deliberative body of which you happen to be a member, you would find someone saying to you, "Is that supposed to be a statement of fact or a value judgment?" This way of thinking has become institutionalized.[1]

But it is something of a paradox that just at the point where the fact/value dilemma has become culturally institutionalized it has been repudiated by many who teach and carry out policy analysis. A review of leading journals—such

---

[1] Hillary Putnam, *Reason, Truth, and History* (Cambridge: Cambridge University Press, 1981), chap. 6.

as *Policy Review, Policy Science,* and *Public Policy*—suggests that while not all mainstream policy analysts have abandoned the ideal of value neutrality, there are signs of considerable discontent and disillusionment with this concept as a realizable ideal.

Haywood Alker has summarized the view of the sophisticated analyst:

> But the haloed value-neutrality of Weberian objectivistic hermeneutics (descriptive *Verstehen*) needs critically to be superseded through realizations that a) the scholar is always engaged with the society or text he or she is trying to understand; b) his or her individual knowledge-seeking reflects, often unconsciously, mixes of social domination and emancipatory interests; c) "values" themselves, however one tries to realize, exchange, or neutralize them, are as scientific concepts partially distorted, occluded conceptions of full human dignity.[2]

This disagreement between the thought of analysts and the conventional thought of policymakers has important consequences for the way in which policy analysis is carried out, presented, and discussed in the public arena. The credibility of an analysis depends upon its capacity to reinforce the illusion that theory, fact, and value are disjoint realms.

Policy analysts are, by and large, not self-consciously aware of this latent tension. There is a conventionally accepted social form of discourse in which findings are presented "as if" social life could be described in value-neutral terms. While a sophisticated postempiricist epistemology of reality rejects the validity of this social form, no overt confrontation occurs—largely, I think, because the social form also carries with it a standard of courtesy. This makes report writing and verbal presentation a challenge to ingenuity: how

[2]Haywood Alker, Jr., "Logic, Dialectics, Politics: Some Recent Controversies," in *Poznam Studies*, Vol. 7 (Amsterdam: Rodopi, 1982).

to say what is permissible without lying but within the constraints presented by the medium and the audience.

To avoid making this argument abstract and removed from the common experience of the reader and writer of this paper, I want to provide a concrete example to help us think about how we think about policy questions. I use the term "we" in this example to call attention to this shared experience that we all have when we think about questions of policy. I will take as an example the way in which we think about poverty. We all agree that poverty is a real phenomenon and that to be poor means to lack resources. But we can define "lack" in absolute or relative terms. We can think about "resources" narrowly, as meaning money income, or somewhat more broadly, as the cash value of in-kind benefits and services. We can also think of resources as qualities (like power and skill) that are needed to acquire economic resources, or we may regard them even more encompassingly as the components of the level of living, which concretely comprise our health, our involvement in political life, the quality of our life at work, in the family, and at play, and so on.[3] Thus, though we know that poverty is a real phenomenon, the size of the problem, its character, and the course of action that policy should accept in combating it will depend largely on how we define and conceptualize poverty. In other words, the facts we attend to depend upon the construction we impose on reality. We construe reality; it is our only way of understanding it.

The construal of reality, in turn, depends upon our purposes. We cannot have an inquiry or a discourse without appreciating how our conceptualization of what is at issue depends upon our purpose. While some may believe that

---

[3]The level-of-living approach to the study of the distribution of well-being is exemplified in the Swedish study of the level of living.

purposes are an outgrowth of values, I believe that values are the generalization of our situationally specific purposes.

The position I develop here is perhaps controversial, since the line of causality is at issue. Do I first value something (like material objects) and then, based on this value, act acquisitively? In this view, the collection of objects is an expression of my prior value position. In the position I want to develop, I assume that the line of causality runs the other way: I begin by action. My activities can be described by myself and others as those of a collector of material goods. In my everyday life, I see myself as executing such purposes as buying a tablecloth suitable for a projected dinner party, or studying new cars in a showroom with a view to acquiring a vehicle more up to the neighborhood standard. Values are abstractions that summarize my activity and assign it a general meaning: valuing material objects. This assignment of meaning then reinforces the activities and permits them to be generalized beyond the immediate situation.[4]

Purpose takes a concrete meaning when grounded in an institutional locus to which interests are attached. What could be described at one level as the valuing of material objects appears in daily life as a response to my interest in being a good housekeeper; this, in turn, can be generalized as values of family and community solidarity.

Consider a more policy-relevant example. If my purpose in studying poverty is the elimination of misery and extreme hardship, then I will seek to reduce suffering. I pursue this purpose because I see myself as a charitable person, although some might prefer to think of me as a bleeding heart. But if

---

[4]Other scholars have also been dissatisfied with the term "values." Vickers uses the term "appreciative system" instead. An appreciative system has two dimensions: normative and reality judgments. Concrete purpose arises from weighing the desirable against the predictable. See Sir Geoffrey Vickers, *The Art of Judgment*, (London: Chapman & Hall, Ltd., 1965).

I feel that social inequality is shameful because it reveals the loss of a sense of community and a shared common purpose, then I am likely to think about poverty not only in terms of the lack of material resources in some absolute way but also as a lack of power and/or as a lack of integration within a community. What I see as the relevant facts in the situation depends upon which of these purposes I pursue—the restoration of community or the relief of suffering. The facts I study in policy analysis depend on my purpose. A discussion of values that is not linked to purposes and to our interests tends to become abstract and forced from the context of interpretation and action. The theory–fact–value dilemma takes on its most vivid meaning in the context of purposes.

John Dewey's transactional theory gives an explanation of this relationship. Dewey postulates that *"knowings* are always and everywhere inseparable from the *knowns*—that the two are twin aspects of common fact."[5] A generative relationship exists where each forms the other. The knower, through the process of knowing, forms the known, and the known is active in relation to the knower.

The Value Aspects of Facts

We can certainly study the facts of poverty, but our assessment of these facts will depend upon our purposes and values. The facts therefore derive their meaning from the values and purposes that inspire them. If we accept this interpretation, then the tital of Wolfgang Kohler's famous book *The Place of Value in a World of Fact* appears to be curiously misspecified. Rather, we want to inquire into the place of fact in a world where values and purposes dominate and shape the facts we attend to and care about. In brief, then, there

[5]John Dewey and Arthur F. Bentley, *Knowing and the Known* (Boston: Beacon Press, 1949), p. 52.

are no facts independent of the theory that organizes them, and theory cannot be separated from human purposes and hence from values.

Even if, as Hillary Putnam has pointed out, I take as my purpose the search for truth,

> the idea that truth is a passive copy of what is "really" (mind-independently, discourse-independently) "there" has collapsed under the critiques of Kant, Wittgenstein, and other philosophers, even if it continues to have a deep hold on our thinking.. . .Someone's telling us that they want us to know the truth tells us really *nothing* as long as we have no idea what standards of rational acceptability the person adheres to: what they consider a rational way to pursue an inquiry, what their standards of objectivity are, when they consider it rational to terminate an inquiry, what grounds they will regard as providing a good reason for accepting one verdict or another on whatever sort of question they may be interested in. Applied to the case of science, I would say that to tell us that "science seeks to discover the truth" is really a purely formal statement . . . *truth is not the bottom line*: truth itself gets its life from our criteria of rational acceptability, and these are what we must look at if we wish to discover the values which are really implicit in science.[6]

Purpose and values are therefore absolutely essential to any inquiry into facts. While there is clearly a reality and while truthfulness consists in trying to behave so as not to deceive oneself or others, we cannot grasp reality independent of the categories of understanding we impose, and these categories depend upon our purposes and values. Values, in brief, give us the questions to ask. Without values, we would have no questions. For any given fact that you present to me, I will want to know not only if it's true but why you are presenting

[6]Putnam, pp. 145–46.

it. "Know why" is inextricably linked to "know what." In other words, I need to know why the problem is set in a particular way such that these become the relevant facts for my inquiry. An analysis into the value aspects of facts drives us into a concern for problem setting. Where do our questions come from and how do the questions we ask of reality influence the facts we inquire into? I am not satisfied with the factual answer because I can probe further and inquire why anyone would want to know these facts. Behind every answer lies a question. And in order to understand why we are interested in that question rather than some other question, we must recognize that we always integrate facts and values. This is not only unavoidable but also inevitable as well as desirable. Values give us our energy to think. They inspire our curiosity because they offer attachment, concern, and commitment. The more we try, as an ideal, to root values from our inquiry, the more uninteresting and pointless the inquiry becomes.

The Factual Aspects of Value

We cannot leave the matter here. We need also to inquire into the factual aspects of our values. Recall that values, as we use the term, follow activity and purposes. We keep the terminology of value but use it to denote the abstract phase of the concrete expression of action. The facticity of the world cannot altogether be repudiated. As we pursue our purposes and values, we do confront facts, and these facts force us to come to terms with the nature of our intent. We cannot, however, presuppose how our values will take the facts of the situation into account.

To explore the factual aspects of values, let us consider the case of the impact of an income guarantee on family stability. As suggested earlier, it is a value condition that leads to the construal of poverty as a lack of money. Economists working in the Office of Economic Opportunity in the mid-

1960s formulated this conception of poverty as a reaction against the sociological view of poverty—as a lack of power or skill—that inspired the thinking behind the Community Action Program. One of the policy implications of viewing poverty as a lack of money was to design the program so that it did not conflict with other values we equally cherish, such as the incentive to work and the maintenance of family solidarity. The negative income tax experiment was an attempt to show that we can safely redistribute income in such a way that it would not conflict with these other values. However, the facts of our inquiry turned against the ideals of the reform that inspired them. The evidence seemed to suggest that an income guarantee breaks up family life. Here we face the question of the factual aspects of our values. We can't simply live with values alone if they merely reflect wishful thinking and illusory ideals. How then do we respond to the facts as presented in our inquiry?

What happens in the confrontation between values and facts? It seems that we can identify at least three different reactions. First, we can accept the facts as given but begin to question the value position. Essentially, we can argue that the facts do not matter because we are committed to individual welfare. If the pursuit of individual welfare has the unintended effect of breaking up families, it is not important. Indeed, it might be desirable to dissolve families that are not really working well. For example, if the guaranteed income makes it possible for a wife to leave an unfaithful and irresponsible husband, then the fact of family breakup may be desirable. On the other hand, if it is the responsible husband who, now recognizing that government largesse will support his wife, leaves the family in good conscience, we might then take a different view of the matter. But, our empirical evidence tells us only that there is a family breakup and not the social circumstances that brought it about. Thus we can either reaffirm our abstract values while accepting the facts as they are presented or dig into our normative position and suggest that the facts are incomplete.

An alternative reaction is to challenge the facts. It is not difficult in the particular example that I am citing to find anomalies. Why, for example, is it that the lower income guaranteed to the family, the more likely that family will be to break up? Why do families tend to break up in the second and third quarters but not in the later quarters of the experiment? Why doesn't the income guarantee affect blacks, Puerto Ricans, and whites in the same way?[7] One could go on elaborating the point, but it is rather obvious that every study has its limits and that it is reasonable and rational to challenge the facts, especially if they assault our cherished purposes and values. Social science inquiry is seldom so decisive as to settle the matter unequivocally. Facts typically can be challenged because they are not decisive and, moreover, are open to different interpretations. Hence we can challenge the facts and remain agnostic about our values. That is to say, we could argue that we might change our values, but not on the basis of these facts as presented.

A third reaction is to alter our value position. More precisely, in this case we might be prepared to make a somewhat different tradeoff when our purposes are in conflict. If my purpose is to maintain family solidarity while at the same time relieving economic hardship and I discover that these values conflict, then I do not simply repudiate my purposes but find some way of reconciling the newly discovered tensions that exist between them. I might, however, conclude that providing unrestricted cash grants is not the way to relieve hardship, and hence I might be forced to find some way

---

[7]Lee Rainwater, "Observations on Marital Instability in Seattle and Denver Income Maintenance Experiment," Harvard University, n.d. (Mimeographed.)

other than the redistribution of money income to achieve my goals.

There are, of course, other ways of dealing with the value aspects of facts. For example, sophisticated policy analysts have learned from experience that if a study is designed to convince opposition rather than to convert oneself, it is important to avoid asking the kinds of questions that can undermine the value position they hold. Systematic inquiry may not prove a political ally. For example, if I am trying to make the case for the redistribution of resources, it will probably be unhelpful to do a study of subjective attitudes toward deprivation. Most studies that make use of subjective indicators of well-being show that people manage to adjust to the world in which they live and, in the effort to make peace with their lives, are not deeply discontented. Their objective economic and social position might seem distressing to an independent observer, but the individuals involved manage to feel more cheerful than their circumstances might indicate. This example is not altogether hypothetical. Swedish policy analysts insistently refuse to use subjective indicators in their study of the distribution of well-being. They insist on restricting their analyses only to objective indicators because they understand that a study of subjective well-being would force a confrontation between values and facts.

The Policy Problem

I now want to summarize and restate the position I have tried to develop about the interdependence of theory, fact, and value. Not only are there no facts independent of the theories that organize them but there are no facts independent of the methods we use to describe or account for the theory we advance. Both the theory and the methods we use depend on our purposes, from which we can infer our values. The nature of reality is such that every attempt to grasp it requires that we impose some constructs for simplification. Reality then consists in multiple descriptions: the bit, the event, the phenomenon—the experience we are trying to describe is itself many things. Hence, no single summary is ever adequate. The questions we ask of reality depend upon the perspective we take in approaching the phenomenon, and it is this perspective that shapes the categories we use to impose order and give meaning to reality. In this sense, then, we construe reality by the categories of understanding we impose, the questions we ask, and the perspectives and purposes with which we approach our inquiry. However, this does not mean that we reject the facticity of the world and its underlying reality, even though facts are seldom so compelling that they repudiate and decisively refute our previously held interpretation of how the world is and ought to be put together. Hence, the factual aspects of our values and theories are seldom conclusive. We know that nothing we say about reality is definitive, authoritative, and fully settled. There is always some different way to see reality or to describe it. There are very few interpretations of reality which are not contentious and could not be questioned by someone who had a different line of thought (theory), or was trying to get somewhere else (purposes), or made use of a different method of understanding, which proceeded by different starting assumptions about what is important to understand in the world (*a priori* assumptions and analytic methods).

I am leaving aside our ideals about what the nature of social science knowledge might be at some future time and am describing in this summary the present state of disciplinary knowledge in the social sciences. We know that policy problems do not lend themselves to the strict methodological and theoretical strictures of each social science discipline. However, we appear to be a long way from a unified social science. We continue to yearn not for a theory of politics or economics or sociology but for a theory of political economy that takes account of the historical and social contexts. In the absence of such a unifying theory, we are faced with multiple perspectives as a description of the world we inhabit at present. We can speculate about the future. Some believe that, in time, knowledge will be cumulative and, as a greater consensus within social science is reached, we will reduce the variety of conflicting perspectives we now encounter. I doubt that social science knowledge is cumulative and convergent. Rather, it appears to me that the more sophisticated we become, the less knowledge tends to be reductive in character—that is, reducible to a few principles. Rather than producing more consensus, increased knowledge only deepens the disagreements and exacerbates the problem of multiple perspectives. Perhaps we can elevate the disagreement to a higher level of understanding, where we can appreciate why the disagreements we hold are important.

These problems become exacerbated in the field of policy analysis, where the action implications of theories and facts provide the central rationale for undertaking the analysis. In the field of policy, the questions of purpose and values are central. They call attention not only to the factual questions of where I am at the moment but also to where I want to go. Hence, questions of purpose are central in any policy undertaking.

But where does this argument lead us? I think that it suggests two directions. First is the need for a new concept broad enough to encompass the issues we have reviewed. Of particular importance is the development of an analytic concept that addresses the question of purpose and the action implications embedded in our theory. Second, after developing briefly the concept of frames, I want to explore the implications of the theory of frames for policy analysis and policy discourse.

THE IDEA OF FRAMES

A frame is a way to understand the things we say and see and act on in the world. It consists of a structure of thought, of evidence, of action, and hence of interests and of values. In brief, a frame integrates theory, facts, interests, and action.

What is especially distinctive about this concept of frame is my insistence on the need for an analytic construction that rejects the conventional approach implying that questions of theory and questions of practice must be ruthlessly separated because, if we integrate facts and values, we are beset with the demons of bias. If we accept my position of where we stand in the interrelationship between theory, fact, and value, then I believe we are driven to repudiate the separation of thought and action. Hence, we need a way of thinking about our thought processes that includes our commitment to act on our puzzlement about the world.

Before explicating the concept of frame further, I want to comment on the use of the term *frame* and refer to some of our earlier intellectual tradition in which it is grounded.

Erving Goffman used the concept of frame to describe his efforts to stop or freeze action so that it could be inspected.[8] The image he was drawing on was that of a movie film, where the action is portrayed as continuous. But when the film is stopped, one is examining a given frame of the film. I am not using the term *frame* in the same way that Goffman does. A recent article by Tversky and Kahneman comes closer to the way in which I want to use the term. They explain that

> We use the term "decision frame" to refer to the decision maker's conception of the acts, outcomes, and contingencies associated with a particular choice. The frame

[8]Erving Goffman, *Frame Analysis: An Essay on the Organization of Experience* (Cambridge, Mass.: Harvard University Press, 1974).

> that a decision maker adopts is controlled partly by the
> formulation of the problem and partly by the norms,
> habits, and personal characteristics of the decision maker.[9]

In this approach, the concept of a frame draws upon the metaphor of perspective. Taking different perspectives redefines the actions as well as the outcomes and contingencies confronting a decision maker. It is the metaphor of perspectivity that captures my use of the term *frame*.

The concept of a frame draws philosophically on Dewey and Bentley's work *Knowing and the Known*, in particular their insistence on the importance of introducing action as an essential part of the knowing, naming, and thinking process.[10]

A frame, then, deals with the perspective by which we see reality and act on it. A frame provides us with a vision in a world of doubt and permits us to see where we are getting with our ideas. Moreover, it grounds our interests and permits us to integrate facts and values. A frame provides us with a whole structure by integrating interests, values, actions, theory, and facts. A frame is broader than a theory because it contains the normative action implications of the theory and the interests served by it. A frame provides a "research program" in the sense in which Lakatos[11] used the term and is thus much broader than a single, specific research project or undertaking whose meaning can only be grasped

---

[9]Amos Tversky and Daniel Kahneman, "The Framing of Decisions and the Psychology of Choice," *Science*, 211 (Jan. 30, 1981), pp. 453, 458.

[10]Dewey and Bentley.

[11]A research program contains an irrefutable core of metaphysical assumptions that are not subject to confirmation or refutation, a protective belt of auxiliary assumption more amenable to review, and finally testable theories—a restricted domain in which empirical observation is accepted for disconfirmation. I. Lakatos, "The History of Science and Its Rational Reconstruction," in *Boston Studies in the Philosophy of Science*, ed. by R. S. Cohen and C. R. Buck, VIII., (Dordrecht, Holland: D. Riedel, 1971).

by seeing where the project fits in the broader research program.

By its very nature, the focus on framing makes problematic the way in which our understanding of a problem is formulated. Thus problem setting becomes a critical element of the frame because it calls attention to some things and neglects the importance of others, because it names certain events, and because of the normative implications of viewing the world in this particular way.

It is useful to provide a concrete example of the difference between a theory and a frame. Dollard's famous formulation of the relationship between frustration and aggression provides a useful example. Dollard was attempting to develop a theory about the causes of frustration.[12] However, it is only when the normative implications of the theory are explicated that we begin to understand the frame. Moynihan's recent obituary on Dollard makes the point brilliantly clear.[13] If frustration leads to aggression, then we must find ways of avoiding frustration. Hence, when ghettos riot, we must cool them out by allaying the frustration that underlies the aggressive act. Moynihan rejects this thesis and is searching for an alternate action for ghettos. He argues that aggression may be rewarded by incentive rather than by frustration. We act aggressively as a way of getting what we want. If this is the case, then the kind of action required is a change in the incentive structure. Thus the worst thing one can do is to provide resources to individuals who have rioted. They will simply interpret it not as a way of allaying frustration but as an incentive for acting aggressively.

---

[12]John Dollard et al., *Frustration and Aggression* (Ann Arbor, Mich.: Ann Arbor Institute of Human Relations, 1939).
[13]Daniel Patrick Moynihan, "Remembering John Dollard," *New York Times Book Review*, Nov. 9, 1980, p. 35.

We move from theory to frame when the action implications are explicated. However, the task is more complicated because the same theoretical perspective may, in fact, lead to quite different action implications. There is only a very loose joining between interests, actions, and theories because there is no explicit rule for explicating action that is inherent in the theory itself. We discover a frame once its action implications are made explicit. There is therefore an important asymmetry in the conception of a frame. It is not so much that a frame provides an individual with a prescription for action but rather that once we have a prescription for action, we can discover the implicit frame organizing the action and integrating theory, activities, interests, purposes, facts, and values. Hence, the action implications are the critical component of the frame concept. Moynihan's frame centers on a concern for social control and the prevention of riots. Dollard's frame has to do with the experience of those who suffer frustration and who may manifest that suffering through rioting. There is a difference between the concern for order in society and the concern for human experience.

In brief then, a frame is not reducible to interests or action, although interests and actions are understandable in terms of frames. This arises largely because a given frame can serve many interests. Because frames, interests, and actions are only loosely coupled, the question of the nature of the frame becomes an empirical issue and not simply a logical argument that can be derived from the axioms of the frame structure.

A frame, then, is not merely an explicit value position but also a view of the world. A frame provides an individual with a way of inquiring, of making sense as well as masking sense of the world in which we live. A frame offers a way of grounding values in a descriptive picture of reality that can be praised for its action implications. The productivity and adequacy of a frame is accounted for by its ability not only to describe the facts and to predict events but also to lead us to a place we want to go, to a destination we regard as desirable. Both, of course—the final destination as well as the road we travel to reach it—are important in judging the productivity of a frame. We want a frame that provides us with a scenic route to the better place we hope to arrive at. The scenic route gives us many things to see and provides us with a richer experience of the journey.

Implications

A theory of frames provides a way of dealing explicitly with the way in which theory, fact, value, and action are internally related, that is, mutually constitutive of each other's identity. What are the concrete implications of this way of thinking about thought? Most of the field of policy analysis takes as its main task working within a given frame and treating that frame as established and nonproblematic. There is much useful work to be done within a frame. I do not propose to eliminate such studies, but I do think it is important to identify a different kind of inquiry, one that starts with frame awareness as its central puzzle.

I want briefly to consider two implications. The first concerns the kinds of policy studies that explicitly take frames into account. I call this kind of frame-sensitive policy inquiry "value-critical policy analysis." Both inquiry and discourse take as their central concern a reflection on frames. This reflection takes as its primary task the question of problem setting—that is, thinking about the way we think about the formulation of problems in public policy.[14] We reflect by dis-

---

[14]For a discussion, see Martin Rein and Don Schon, "Problem Setting in Poverty Research," in *Using Social Research in Public Policy Making*, ed. by Carol H. Weiss (Lexington, Mass.: D. C. Heath and Company, 1977).

tancing ourselves from our frame in order to get perspective on our own frames, on those held by others, and on the broader question of multiple frames. When we do this, we have to resist drifting into "hopeless pluralism" while at the same time recognizing that *ad hoc* assumptions can rescue any frame from the empirical difficulty it encounters. Hence, we live in a world described by John Watkins as a "haunted house," that is, a world that is partially confirmable, nonfalsifiable, and methodologically influential.[15]

Reflection on frames forces us to brush against the problem of "hopeless pluralism" and the phenomenon of the "haunted house," where refutation is rare. To assert that refutation is impossible to achieve moves us to hopeless relativism, but to assert that it is rare still leaves the question open.

VALUE-CRITICAL POLICY INQUIRY

A value-critical policy inquiry takes frames as the object of its analysis. A frame is a way of describing how people think about reality and linking this description to human purposes. A value-critical analysis probes the categories of people's thoughts, examining where these thoughts come from, where they lead, and what ambiguities and inconsistencies they contain. (Obviously one needs a frame to criticize a frame because we never start *de novo*; all knowledge is linked somehow to purpose.)

There are, of course, many different ways of carrying out a value-critical policy analysis. At its best, a good value-critical analysis tends to be both analytic and synthetic. It includes an empirical search for regularities, an interpretation of these

---

[15]J. W. N. Watkins, "Confirmable and Influential Metaphysics," *Mind*, 66 (July, 1958), pp. 354–65.

realities, and, finally, a critique of that reality that has a practical interest in realizing alternative courses of action. As Bernstein points out in a discussion of Habermas's work, the spirit that animates critique is not to treat these aspects of observation, interpretation, and criticism as distinct but as three internal moments of theorizing about social and political life.[16]

Habermas has a thoughtful discussion of the critical approach in his book on *Theory and Practice*. He distinguishes three functions of the critical task: first, the formation and extension of critical theorems; second, the process of enlightenment where the theorems are applied and tested by a process of reflection that takes place within the groups toward which the processes are directed; and third, the selection of appropriate strategies for action—which includes decisions about tactical questions on the conduct of political struggles. Critique, in this formulation, includes a concern about true statements, authentic insights, and prudent decisions.[17]

Especially interesting in Habermas's formulation is the emphasis on participation with the groups who are affected by the critical interpretation. Theory, standing by itself, can never justify political action. Habermas's work is thus an attempt to integrate the knowing and the acting person. The primary task of critical analysis is not only to interpret the situation, critically gaining insight "into the casualties of the past," but also to initiate among the actors a process of self-reflection that contributes to the political consensus. In the concluding discussion on discourse, I will return to this theme sketchily. Neither Habermas nor I have a very clear way of doing this. However, we both recognize its central importance for value-critical inquiry.

[16]Richard J. Bernstein, *The Restructuring of Social and Political Theory* (Philadelphia: University of Pennsylvania Press, 1978), p. 216.
[17]Jürgen Habermas, *Theory and Practice* (Boston: Beacon Press, 1976), p. 32.

I want to discuss briefly three types of value-critical analysis that take frames as their starting point: the criticism of frames, the building of frames, and the redefinition and integration of frames.

The Criticism of Frames

Frame criticism is perhaps the most common. It is a kind of inquiry that seeks to bring into focus the taken-for-granted assumptions of established policies and the context nourishing these tacit assumptions. Because it is so common, it does not require elaboration. A recent example of criticism is Gilbert Steiner's book on family policy.[18] The study involves a detailed exploration of the movement in the United States to press for a family policy. Steiner argues that the idea is compelling in the abstract and impossible in its details. To argue his case, he examines abortion and family planning, day care, employment, and neglect and abuse to show the practical impossibilities of pursuing a family policy because it leads to conflicting and ambiguous goals.

The Building of Frames

The concern for frame creation arises out of discontent with a framework of action because of its failure to deliver on its implicit moral promise. When established conventional frames lead people into a moral position they do not accept, they may search for an alternate way to think about the issues so it will be more congruent with their normative position. Frame creation usually arises from a variety of social processes designed to enable the participants to reframe their experience. For example, there are encounter groups, demonstrations, consciousness-raising groups, and so on. The research

[18]Gilbert Y. Steiner, *The Futility of Family Policy* (Washington, D. C.: The Brookings Institution, 1981).

analogy to these collective engagements with personal experience is field research, either participant observation or interviewing. This mode of inquiry permits the analyst to come into contact vicariously with the on-line experience of others. It provides the researcher with an opportunity to encounter the experience and stories of the people who are actively engaged in action. Their experience provides the grounded information that stimulates the researcher to invent a new frame.

The work of Michael Piore illustrates this kind of value-critical analysis. Piore thinks that the maximizing assumptions underlying the behavioral model of economic theory are wrong and have failed to deliver the promise of economics as a moral science—that is, offering policy solutions that are morally acceptable to him. The methods and theory of conventional economics lead him to a place where he does not want to be. Briefly, macroeconomic theory in economics is concerned with the model of economic humanity purposively maximizing utility in a field of constraints. The econometric methodology starts with a formal behavioral model assuming that every quantified variable in the model has a distribution divisible into a random element and a systematic element; the task is to assign the nonrandom variation to the several different variables that are believed to explain the behavior.[19] To remedy his disaffection with the theory and method, Piore makes use of institutional economics. The institutional frame offers a way of developing not only a different theory about what economic activity is about but also a different method of interpretation—namely, qualitative case analysis. The critique of theory implies a critique of method as well. Piore's research is designed to tell a different story about economics. Qualitative inter-

---

[19]Michael Piore, "Qualitative Research Techniques in Economics," *Administrative Science Quarterly*, 24 (December, 1979), p. 564.

viewing is a way of being stimulated by the experience of economic actors as an aid to developing this new story; this method of uncovering a story cannot also be used to verify a story. Piore's account of his quest for an alternate frame and his criticism of the present modes of economic theory and method illustrate how value-critical policy analysis tries to build frames.

The Redefinition and Integration of Frames

Redefinition is an attempt to take different frames and make them compatible. There are, of course, many reconciliation strategies. The work of Kenneth Boulding provides one example.[20] I believe that Boulding is attempting to reconcile the Quaker frame of action with the economist's frame of economic growth. The two aspects of Quaker doctrine that are central to this effort are the concept of "right livelihood" and "responsible stewardship." In the former, work is regarded as a moral endeavor. It is important to earn one's living in a way that is morally and socially meaningful. In respect to the latter, people who control economic resources have a moral responsibility to do so on behalf of society and not merely for the sake of self-interest. By contrast, economics tends to define work as being concerned with the production of material values and places its faith in the invisible hand of markets rather than depending on "responsible stewardship" to produce desired social outcomes.

Boulding rejects what he calls "cowboy economics"—that is, using resources up recklessly. He believes that we are entering a new era of "spaceship economics" characterized by a steady state rather than by economic growth. Steady-

[20]Kenneth Boulding, "The Economics of Spaceship Earth," in *Collected Papers*, 11 (Boulder: University of Colorado Press, 1971).

state economics can address the twin questions of meaningful work and stewardship.

Problems in Carrying Out Value-Critical Policy Analysis

There are basically two difficulties that warrant special concern: the problem of method and the problem of audience. If frames arise from purpose and interests, then the identification of whose purpose and whose interests are served by the value-critical analysis becomes a central concern.

By and large, value-critical policy inquiry is done in the university by scholars who, from this position of privilege, can remove themselves from the political fray. Scholars who carry out value-critical analyses present their analyses in such a way that their own interests remain invisible. But this is an illusion. The university is, after all, organized along interdisciplinary lines with each discipline providing an intellectual framework for inquiry. Policy analysis is no exception. The dominant school of thought in policy analysis arises from an attempt to apply microeconomic thinking to the policy arena. Those who carry out value-critical analysis reject the disciplinary roots of policy analysis. Value-critical analysis is a way of addressing the interest of policy analysts who are politically "homeless," in the sense that they do not take the disciplinary home as the base for their policy analysis. But the university environment and culture support scholarly rather than critical inquiry. This has the tendency of driving value-critical inquiry into a metalevel where the philosophical assumptions of the whole process of inquiry and thinking can be examined. When such a tendency becomes entrenched, the analysis drifts away from the political realities it attempts to understand and runs the risk of deepening the separation between thought and action.

The experience of the Frankfort school is relevant here. Although it was deeply committed to critical thought, it took as its practical purpose the radical critique of capitalism as a way of transforming society. Nevertheless, it had for its audience other scholars and nonactivists and it never resolved the disjunction between theory and practice. The writings became increasingly abstract, philosophical, and "meta" in their modes of inquiry. To avoid the experience of the Frankfort school, what is needed is a form of value-critical inquiry that is politically engaged in arguments about the past yet remains relevant to the future. But the university is not the best setting for this form of political engagement, which requires a commitment to a strategy of what is to be done. Such a strategy must address the question of who is the audience and who are the agents of change, transformation, or revolution because it is the purposes of these active agents, and not of the scholars, that must inform inquiry.

The task, then, is to create a process that is not university-based and driven by the privileged position of university actors and their interests. A politically engaged process must be set in motion—one that is critical in its nature and capable of producing new frames in a grounded way. University scholars can participate in this process but should not dominate it. These concerns about the limits of value-critical inquiry lead to a discussion of discourse.

Cross-Frame "Discourse"

Because of the intimate connection between the ideas we have and the kind of life we lead, we are not emotionally neutral about frames.[21] It is precisely because socially relevant ideas have such a deep bearing on the conduct of our social life that we also have an interest in effective cross-frame discourse, an interest not merely in debate but in reaching agree-

---

[21]For an interesting explication of this argument, see Brian Fay, *Social Theory and Political Practice* (New York: Holmes and Meier Publishers, 1976), p. 11.

ment. The most interesting and probably the most important policy questions involve politically engaged cross-frame discourse, but the very factors making such discourse urgent also make it difficult to carry out.[22]

Rather than starting with ideal discourse, I believe we need to begin with a much deeper understanding about how discourse in the lived world takes place. I do not therefore propose a method for improving discourse but only some preliminary ideas for inquiring into it. And, I restrict my observations to discourse about the kinds of policy inquiries discussed in this essay.

Effective discourse across frames in many respects is a prototype of a transactional process. I gain a deeper understanding of my own interests and purposes as I see someone else's interpretation of what I am about. My intent is reflected in your construction. If I, in turn, respond by modifying my original content, I have participated in a mutually determined transformation of my position. Frame reflection is itself a form of discourse, because the discourse always also implies less overt discourse between myself and others. The process I want to describe is not adequately characterized as successive mutual approximation or consensus building. That is what political debate is about. A politically engaged debate where conflicting interests are at stake is about compromise and consensus. Discourse is about engagement and transformation.

Three areas of frame discourse seem to be important: awareness, level, and arena.

Awareness of Frames. Groups and individuals have different degrees of awareness of their frames. We can identify at least four different types of awareness.

---

[22]For analysis, see Jane J. Mansbridge, *Beyond Adversary Democracy* (New York: Basic Books, 1980).

1. There are those who have little awareness of the frame in which they operate. Among academics who do policy research, we find those who accept their disciplinary frame and work within it. Seldom questioning the assumptions on which their practice rests, they organize their lifetime academic careers within the terms of this frame. How extensive such frame insensitivity is among policy analysts is an interesting question to pursue. One might speculate that the very experience of carrying out policy-relevant, action-oriented research would force one to a high degree of frame awareness. Alternatively, the doubts and uncertainties arising from frame awareness might very well produce a protective response against doubt, leading to a very low degree of awareness.

2. There are those who are searching for a frame. Students typically fall into this category. They are learning their way around the world, trying to find something they can believe in and work within, which will give "meaning" to their activities.

3. There are those who enjoy criticizing other people's reality but never their own. Here the analyst is at work criticizing someone else's frame but not seriously questioning the limits of his or her own.

4. There are those who criticize their own frames. They have doubts about themselves because they cannot find a way to make sense of the reality they experience. They deal with doubt and dissent by trying to understand their frames. They are very sensitive to frames because the frames they have do not work for them.

Levels of Frames. Most policy discourse takes place at the level of what I call policy dichotomies. A listing of some of these dichotomies suggests the kinds of issues that are the subjects of many policy studies: centralized versus decentralized, cash versus in-kind, loans versus grants, sensitivity versus specificity, universal versus selective, and so on. The specific dichotomies that comprise the center of the policy debate depend on the concrete policy areas under review. Many of these dichotomies take the form of dilemma. Economists prefer the term "tradeoff." This difference in the name given to the dichotomies is important but cannot be developed here. When these dichotomies are nested together, they form a broader social ideology. When a choice is made within a dichotomy, the analyst moves from broader ideology to the detailed questions of program design: for whom is the program designed, what benefits should recipients receive, how should the program be financed and administered, and so on. In brief, then, there are at least three different levels of discourse: midrange policy dichotomies, broader-purpose ideology, and specific choices about the details of design.

Frame Arena. There are several different arenas within which discourse can take place. There is the solitary discourse that an individual carries on alone. There is the discourse that scholars have within the community of inquirers to which they belong. And there is a public discourse in which the media plays a central role. Of course, the three levels of discourse are closely related to each other. Any solo discourse also involves, at least implicitly, a discourse with others. A debate within oneself is a debate that takes account of other people as a reference point. And similarly, the public debate takes into account both the community of inquirers and ourselves as actors. The nature of the discourse with oneself, within one's community, and within the broader public takes a somewhat different form.

I believe that, if we are to understand discourse, a useful starting point is to take account of the degree of frame awareness of the actors, of the level within which the discourse takes place, and of the arena of discourse. This can be done by examining how discourse takes place in the politically engaged world. Perhaps the most typical discourse is at the level of dichotomies or design, within the community of inquirers, among those who have low degrees of awareness of their frames. But obviously discourse takes place at other degrees of awareness, at other levels, and in other arenas.

The intellectual challenge that discourse poses is how to gain a better understanding of the nature of the kind of reflective inquiry into action that we bring to cross-frame conflicts and, within this inquiry, to examine the kinds of resolutions that are possible and the grounds for them. It is the understanding of the resolution and management of conflicting frames that is most problematic. While we can speculate about how we reach agreement when frames conflict, very little is known about the resolution of frame conflicts in practice. An empirical inquiry into action is needed as a first step in trying to improve frame discourse.

Reflection about discourse will not enable us to make a decisive choice among conflicting frames or to decide which frames provide us with a more productive set of questions for inquiry and action. It is based on the more limited assumption that if we think about our own thought (where thought is conceived of as dealing not only with puzzlement but also with action), the quality of our thinking will be improved and the actions we take within our frames will be more effective.

6

EMANCIPATORY SOCIAL SCIENCE AND SOCIAL CRITIQUE

KAI NIELSEN

Developing as a systematic alternative to positivistically oriented social science, critical theory emerged from the work of the Frankfurt school in the between-wars period and was continued by them during the Second World War, principally in the United States. Under some of its original leadership, the Frankfurt school was reinstated in Frankfurt in the postwar years and continued the development of critical theory there. This work, in turn, has been continued and indeed radically transformed by Jürgen Habermas. Utilizing and synthesizing a considerable array of contemporary developments in social science and philosophy, we have in Habermas's work a subtle and developed, as well as developing, concept of an emancipatory social science. I shall elucidate it, critique it, build on it, and show some of its implications for policymaking.

I begin by noting a series of difficulties that beset a social

KAI NIELSEN □ Professor of Philosophy, University of Calgary, Calgary, Alberta, Canada.

science that attempts to be both scientific and emancipatory. In section II, I then set out the general lines of Habermas's response to these difficulties, including his response to what he takes to be scientistic and ideological assumptions in some of the very ways these difficulties are posed. I also make clear how he conceives his nonscientistic alternative: emancipatory social science. In sections III and IV, I turn to a critique of Habermas's account. I argue that his "universal speech ethic" and his theory of communicative rationality do not provide him with the Archimedean point he requires to give him secure criteria for social evolution or for a universal ethic in accordance with which he could critique social practices and whole social formations. In section V, moving from nay saying to yea saying, I give both a reading of historical materialism and a critique of Habermas's reworking of it. The rationale for this discussion is to indicate how it can give us a basis, without constructing an ethical theory or articulating cross-culturally valid criteria for moral development, for making judgments about social evoltuion that would enable us to transcend a historicist or relativist perspective. In the final section I consider the implications for policymaking of such an emancipatory social theory.

I

If we want both a social science with a human face and a social science having something approximating a tolerable rigor and a responsibility to empirical constraints, we will quickly be led to reflect (1) on how the relationships between social research and policymaking should be conceived, (2) on the moral responsibilities of social scientists to society as a whole, and (3) on the kind of overall rationale there could be for the development of social policies by the social sciences.

Social scientists have not infrequently overestimated the

intellectual power and the predictive reliability of social science research.[1] But be that as it may, it is also true that, rightly or wrongly, our societies are becoming increasingly dependent on social science research. However, we should not forget how problematical much social science research is. Neither social science's claims to knowledge nor its methodologies are secure. Even the very idea of what, if much of anything, a social science could come to is deeply contested. Indeed, it may in reality be something—like true art or genuine democracy—that is *essentially* contested. The concept of objectivity is itself multiply ambiguous and the status of objectivity claims in the social sciences is unclear—as is, even more obviously, the extent of objectivity in the social sciences. We do not have agreement about the nature of social science, or indeed science generally, or about its relationship to society.

A picture emerges here that is very natural and which, in some important respects, critical theorists such as Habermas want very much to resist.[2] Social science, this picture has it, where it is genuinely and rigorously scientific, must be normatively neutral. To be objective, it must be based on value-free research and remain utterly nonpartisan and neutral on policy issues. Such an account must be free of ideological bias and underlying ideological assumptions, though there is little stress, in such accounts, that one of its crucial functions is to engage in a critique of ideology. Such a neutralist account of society, it is claimed, will give us a genuinely scientific account of society, one that will be superior to any single participant's knowledge or understanding of society.

[1]Derek Allen, *Abandoning Method* (San Francisco: Jossey-Bass, Inc., Publishers, 1973); and Charles Lindblom and David K. Cohen, *Usable Knowledge* (New Haven, Conn.: Yale University Press, 1979).
[2]Jürgen Habermas, *Erkenntnis und Interesse* (Frankfurt: Suhrkamp, 1968). Jürgen Habermas, *Knowledge and Human Interests*, trans. by Jeremy S. Shapiro (Boston: Beacon Press, 1971).

With such a conception of social science—a conception Habermas would surely consider thoroughly scientistic—it is natural to adopt what, until recently, has been the standard model of scientific methodology for social research. We should quantify wherever possible and develop sophisticated statistical approaches. We need ideologically decontaminated, testable knowledge with a high degree of predictive reliability. The goal of social science research should be the discovery and the systematic display of regularities (probabilistic laws) that show, where societies are viewed both synchronically and diachronically, the structure of society and its underlying mechanisms. From lawlike statements of these regularities, together with statements of initial conditions, we need, for social science to progress, to be able to derive predictions or retrodictions concerning tolerably specific bits of social behavior and social action. But most fundamentally we need to be able to discover, and not just ideologically invent, these underlying regularities. Most fundamentally we want to know who we are, how we got to be that way, and who we are likely to become.

Faced with such a conception of the nature of social science and the goals of scientific research, we confront a whole series of problems concerning the relationship between "ethics and public policy." The relationship between social research and policy formation becomes very problematical indeed. Some of these difficulties, when they are thought through, raise serious problems for that tolerably mainline conception of social science.

Probably the most obvious one turns on the place of values in such an account and, given that placement, on what advocacy would legitimately come to. If the above account is on the right track, there could be nothing comparable to an "immanent morality of law" for social science. Rightness and wrongness, goodness and badness are rigidly excluded from social science domains. *Qua* social scientists we can, of course, study what people *believe* to be right or wrong, desirable and undesirable, and there can be various explanatory accounts, as distinct from justificatory accounts, of why people have the moral beliefs they have and of what role these play in their lives. But by way of justification, defense, or systematic elaboration with an eye to rational reconstruction or use in advocacy, there can be in social science, on this rather standard understanding, no taking account of values or norms. That is taken to mean that, within the domain of a genuine social science, there can be no establishing or disestablishing of the claims to truth or validity of any categorical norms or judgments of intrinsic value.

But there is, as we all know, applied research, and social scientists are not infrequently engaged in the articulation of social policy or at least of scenarios for what is put forth as desirable or rational social policy. Does this mean that the tough-minded scientific view of the matter is that what we have here are social scientists for hire? That we should, where they leave pure theory, view social scientists simply as the *technicians of the social life?* This conjures up the picture of social scientists quite legitimately, as far as their science is concerned, working away at pacification programs for the Americans in Vietnam, stabilizing programs for Saudi Arabia, destabilizing programs for Angola, and constructing plans for the rational regulation of concentration camps. The picture is this: take whatever goals you wish as given, we social scientists can show you the best way to achieve them. But it is not and cannot be our business as social scientists to pass judgment on the goals themselves. Whatever value frameworks social scientists may happen to have, they are not and cannot be part of their scientific framework. Important as they are, they are external to that framework.

This picture, even when it is modified in various ways,

presents a series of problems for anyone other than the purest of the pure social theoreticians. It surely raises issues for those social scientists who see themselves as also having some normative function vis-à-vis policymaking or as providing social critique. Social scientists, if they are not social anthropologists studying distant primitive societies, are usually participants in the society they study; they partake of its aspirations and fears and, in one way or another, suffer its alienations and oppressions. And they, like almost everyone else, have a certain picture of a good society. It sometimes, perhaps typically, is a rather blurred one, as it is for many others as well, but all the same it is a picture they have. And it is natural to be concerned about the relation of that picture of a good society to what they as social scientists know about society. Whatever we want to say about the "is" and the "ought," it is natural to believe that somehow their conception of a good society ought to be more adequate than the plain person's, if they really have a reasonable grasp—a grasp not everyone has—of the way society works.[3] If there is, in any considerable dimension, something like social science expertise, that ought to provide a crucial input into the social scientist's conception of a good society. It ought to help make it the case that social scientists, to the degree that they really have a reasonable mastery of social dynamics, will, *ceteris paribus*, if they are also morally reflective, have a more adequate conception of the good life than someone similarly morally reflective but without such an understanding.

Perhaps an example would clarify what I have in mind here. It is common knowledge (with some it is knowledge by description and with many it is knowledge by acquaintance as well) that much work in industrial societies is deeply al-

[3]Kai Nielsen, "On Deriving an Ought from an Is," *Review of Metaphysics*, 32 (March, 1979), pp. 488–515.

ienating. A reaction of dismay and an overwhelming feeling of the horror of it is not uncommon when the nature of the work done by many people is faced and reflected on concretely. But many will, all the same, also take it, like a fact of nature, as something that is inescapable. However, a social scientist who has worked extensively in these domains should have a conception of what causes and sustains such work relations, what possible alternatives there are to them, how realistic these alternatives are and what their costs are. Such a social scientist should, as well, have some understanding of what, more generally, the alternative ways of organizing society would look like if they were translated into the concrete, and how these alternatives might plausibly impede or aid human flourishing. This would shed light on what is the case, what can be the case, and what is desirable. Examples of actual works that exhibit this are Samuel Bowles's and Herbert Gintis's *Schooling in Capitalist America* and Harry Bravermann's *Labour and Monopoly Capitalism*. The discussions of work in America in *The Capitalist System*, edited by Richard C. Edwards and associates, also vividly illustrate what I am talking about.

Such considerations, among others, have led some social scientists to practice and defend social critique as one of the legitimate functions of social inquiry. But, in a way that Frankfurt school theorists have attacked, social scientists with the conception of their discipline that is dominant in their society will have fears that social critique will conflict both with the objectivity of social science and with the canons of what they take to be scientific rationality. The social scientist, it is feared, cannot be both an analyst and a critic. The standards for what is true or false, plausible or implausible, important or unimportant are partially internal to the discipline itself and partially determined by the way the world is, that is, by the empirical facts. They cannot legitimately be determined by what goals one thinks are desirable or what ends one takes to be emancipatory or as answering to human needs and interests. Such considerations are external to the discipline and are irrelevant to its claims to truth or validity. Whether we are engaged in discipline research, policy research, or advocacy research, the standards of truth and adequacy remain the same and remain (1) internal to the subject and (2) determined by the empirical facts in a way that is not dependent on our conceptions of moral rightness or human appropriateness.

II

Frankfurt school theorists generally, and Habermas in particular—whose work is a continuation, though in a more rigorous manner, of the critical theory distinctive of the Frankfurt school—would regard many of the problems sketched above as pseudo-problems generated by a scientistic understanding of social science.[4] Indeed, the very conception of social science sketched above is a scientistic one, a conception which, far from being nonideological and *wertfrei*, expresses the dominant ideology of our time, an ideology which disguises itself as a scientific and perfectly nonnormative view of the world. (I am not, of course, suggesting that this is something which is done self-consciously by the social agents involved.) When, Habermas would have us understand, we are free from the domination of that ideology, many of these problems will dissolve, along with many of the other problems about the alleged conflicts between the roles of a social scientist as an academic, a discipline researcher and a policy researcher.

To understand Habermas's attack on the ideology of

[4]Martin Jay, *The Dialectical Imagination* (Boston: Little, Brown and Company, 1973).

scientism and what he would take to be a specious scientistic conception of objectivity, where objectivity gets identified with neutrality and freedom from normative commitments, it is essential to understand some of the core elements in Habermas's account.[5]

Habermas's alternative conception of social science and his rejection of scientism is closely linked with his critique of what he calls positivism, a term which he uses, as do Frankfurt school theorists generally, in a very wide but still, I believe, nonarbitrary way.[6] On this account, not only the philosophers usually classified by philosophers in the Anglo–American tradition as positivists are called positivists but, from the vantage point of analytical philosophy, such archcritics of positivism as Popper, Quine, and Armstrong would be classified as positivists.

In spelling out what is involved here it is well to note initially that Habermas believes that there are three irreducible types of knowledge related to three distinct types of interest, none of which are taken to have cognitive superiority over the others and all three of which have essential roles in human life and human understanding.[7] Positivism, on his account,

[5]Noam Chomsky in several of his political writings has shown an acute understanding of the relation between neutrality and objectivity, as has Robert Paul Wolff in his *Ideal of the University* (Boston: Beacon Press, 1969). See, as well, Alan Montefiore, ed., *Neutrality and Impartiality* (London: Cambridge University Press, 1975).

[6]The special use of "positivism" plus the reasonableness of it came out rather clearly in his exchange with Popper and Albert in Theodore W. Adorno, ed., *The Positivist Dispute in German Sociology* (New York: Harper & Row, Publishers, Incorporated, 1976).

[7]Jürgen Habermas, *Knowledge and Human Interests*. Thomas McCarthy's discussion of this is extensive and enlightening. See his *Critical Theory of Jürgen Habermas* (Cambridge, Mass.: MIT Press, 1978), chaps. 1 and 2. I have tried to say something about this issue in an extremely simple way in my "Some Theses in Search of an Argument: Reflections on Habermas," *National Forum*, 59 (Winter, 1979), pp. 27–32.

acknowledges as legitimate just one of these types of knowledge related to one of the types of interest. But, in effect, by such a cricumscription, positivism takes an imperialistic approach to knowledge in regarding natural scientific knowledge and knowledge based on this model as the sole legitimate form of knowledge.

Positivism is centrally concerned with the control of nature and is officiailly normatively neutral. As such it is widely regarded as the very model for objectivity and rationality. Values or norms, on such an account, are nonscientific and nonobjective. They are choices or preferences, perhaps always universalizable choices or preferences; they are not knowledge claims, something capable of being either true or false, but prescriptions about how to act. As such they are nonrational, rationality itself being construed as instrumental reason—that is, a reason concerned with consistency and with the taking of the most efficient means to achieve whatever ends one happens to have, but the ends themselves are not something which can properly be said to be either rational or irrational. Values or norms are construed as choices, decisions, preferences, or commitments and, as such, must be (1) excluded from scientific domains and (2) regarded as neither rational nor carriers of knowledge or warranted belief.

Positivism is a scientism because it remains imperialistic about knowledge, collapsing all human knowledge into one of its legitimate types, namely natural scientific knowledge, and utterly failing to recognize that there are three different types of human knowledge rooted in three fundamental human interests: (1) our interest in controlling our natural environment (including, of course, our human environment); (2) our interest in communication, that is, understanding each other and acting together in the context of common social traditions; and finally (3) our interest in emancipation, that is, our interest in being free of ideological mystification and irrational, unjust social constraints. The three types of knowledge, corresponding to these three types of interest, are natural scientific knowledge, social scientific knowledge (a knowledge rooted in our need to understand each other and our social institutions and traditions), and the knowledge of critical reflection.

So-called mainline social science, making what in effect are positivist and scientistic assumptions, identifies knowledge with natural scientific knowledge and the instrumental control of nature; it regards social science where it is nonideological as the instrumental control of human nature and social institutions. Where there is genuine social science knowledge it is of the same type as natural scientific knowledge, for that, according to positivism, is the only genuine type of knowledge. Such knowledge must be normatively neutral and must, in its methodology, be continuous with the methods of the natural sciences. There cannot be, as Winch and Evans-Pritchard believe, a nonscientific but not antiscientific type of knowledge on which most of our social scientific knowledge is finally dependent.[8] We must recognize that what science—construed as knowledge of the natural scientific type—cannot tell us humanity cannot know. There can be no knowledge or understanding between human beings that is not of this type and there can be no knowledge of norms or knowledge of a rational foundation of norms. They are matters of subscription and commitment, not of knowledge. But this, Habermas claims, is to define, illegitimately but persuasively, "knowledge" as "scientific knowledge" and to deny conceptual space to other forms of knowledge rooted in other interests by what in effect is a convertionalist's sulk.

[8]Peter Winch, *The Idea of a Social Science* (New York: Humanities Press, 1958); and E. E. Evans-Pritchard, *Essays in Social Anthropology* (London: Faber & Faber, Ltd., 1962), chaps. 1 and 3.

If we appeal only to our interests in controlling nature, then, of course, there can be no other forms of knowledge; but to do this is to engage in arbitrary stipulation in the interests of a scientistic ideology. Once we recognize that there can be other types of knowledge that are equally legitimate, there is no need to insist that such social science knowledge as we can obtain must always be normatively neutral and free from an emancipatory intent. Social science—or, if you will, social studies or social inquiry—is not a subspecies of natural sicence with the same methodological commitments. But it need not be any of the worse for all of that.

We need to recognize that, in social science, judgments concerning the rationality of social practices and human actions are unavoidable.[9] In trying to understand some stretch of behavior or the function of some social institution or social practice, we have to make for ourselves, as social theorists, judgments of rationality even to classify what we are trying to understand let alone to explain it. Societies, to take an obvious example, have religious belief systems. If we understand them as Freud or Leach does, on the one hand, or as Evans-Pritchard or Robin Horton does, on the other, we will make rather different judgments about their rationality and their role in social life. Here our own understanding about what it is *reasonable* to believe must enter into our own social analysis, and not as an external factor that can be expunged from our analysis and separately appraised. Social science, where it says much of anything that is significant about social life, Habermas argues, cannot be normatively neutral. A *wertfrei* social science is both an unnecessary and an incoherent scientific ideal. Indeed, to make it appear that social science to be genuine science must be *wertfrei* is one of the important

[9]Alasdair MacIntyre, *Against the Self-Images of the Age* (London: Gerald Duckworth & Co., Ltd., 1971), pp. 244–59.

ideological mystifications of scientism.[10] This very posture of moral neutrality is a valuable ideological tool in protecting the *status quo* with its class domination, for, by methodological strictures, social science is prevented from critiquing the goals of a society or the underlying rationale of its social institutions. This Habermas regards as arbitrary and debilitating.

The Frankfurt school, along with Lukacs and Korsch, stresses the need for social theory to develop an overall critical theory which would be sufficiently encompassing to provide an Archimedean point for cultural criticism of whole social orders. Habermas very much shares this viewpoint and has tried to lay the foundations for such a theory. He differs from the Frankfurt school, and from Adorno and Marcuse most particularly, in his belief that such a theory must, eschewing impressionism, be systematic and must take into account work in structuralism, transformational grammar, speech act theory, and developments in contemporary analytical philosophy. At the foundation of Habermas's social theory is a theory of universal pragmatics, communication theory, and a theory of distorted communication which he regards as essential for understanding the diverse forms that ideology can take. He also takes his theory of communicative competence and of socialization as essential for his reworking and reconstruction of historical materialism.[11]

It is Habermas's belief that scientism (crudely, the belief that what science cannot tell us humanity cannot know) is the dominant ideology of our time. With it goes the phenomenon of technocratic consciousness, which so deeply affects

---

[10]Jürgen Habermas, *Technik und Wissenschaft als "Ideologie"* (Frankfurt: Suhrkamp, 1968). See particularly his discussion of Weber and Marcuse. [The last essay in the translated volume *Toward a Rational Society*, trans. by Jeremy Shapiro (Boston: Beacon Press, 1971), is particularly relevant.]

[11]Jürgen Habermas, *Communication and the Evolution of Society*, trans. by Thomas McCarthy (Boston: Beacon Press, 1979).

a large portion of contemporary intelligentsia that they can barely conceive of the possibility of rational argumentation over the ends of life or any fundamental critique of the social institutions actually in place. Such critiquing is viewed by scientistic ideology as the irrational ideological posturing of irresponsible and utopian value-oriented intellectuals. Responsible policy-oriented intellectuals—the Brzezinskis and Kissingers of the world but not the Russells or the Chomskys—will not engage in such ideological posturing.[12]

Habermas attempts to establish that this scientistic attitude results from a confused epistemology which conflates all knowledge with natural scientific knowledge and conflates rationality with instrumental rationality.[13] To be rational, on such an account (as we have remarked), is to be consistent and to take the most efficient means to whatever ends you happen to have; to have knowledge is to know how to control nature, including, of course, human nature. What gets simply ruled out from the beginning, by implicit persuasive definition, is self-reflective knowledge and the very possibility of either the rationality or irrationality of our ends. This ideology, Habermas contends, makes impossible the rational criticism of institutions. There can be no room for it, according to such an ideology, in either philosophy or social science, and it renders invisible the existence of our practical interest in mutual understanding and our emancipatory interest in understanding and facing the forces that dominate us. Previous ideologies have expressed in a distorted form a vision of the good life and a conception of how a rational human being is to live. Scientism is a unique ideology in that it denies the very rationality of any such vision.

---

[12]Noam Chomsky powerfully and ironically criticizes this way of dividing things up.

[13]Jürgen Habermas, *Theorie und Praxis* (Frankfurt: Suhrkamp, 1971), and the last essay of *Technik und Wissenschaft als "Ideologie."*

However, when scientism is recognized for what it is, social science will no longer be robbed by it. To recognize, firmly and nonevasively, something as an ideology is to free ourselves from its domination. Acknowledging that we have *practical interests* in making collective social activity and dialogue possible, *emancipatory interests* in attaining self-knowledge, and *technical interests* in gaining control over nature, we will come to recognize that an understanding of society goes not just with the type of knowledge generated by technical interests but with other interests as well. *Science* and *scientific,* as Max Black once stressed, are honorific terms with contestable criteria: there is no more reason to give scientism its persuasive definition of *science* than to give it its persuasive definition of *knowledge.*[14] Once this is recognized, advocacy and critique, as well as analysis and hypothesis construction, can be a part of social science, and normative knowledge need not be a Holmesless Watson. Self-reflective inquiry, like technical inquiry, can be a part of social science. Indeed, Habermas contends, just this mode of inquiry is reflected in the practice of psychoanalysis and in the very practice of critical theory itself. Just as there is knowledge of the control of nature, so is there knowledge of human emancipation, of what would constitute an escape from the control of powers both institutional and libidinal that undermine our autonomy and cause suffering, deprivation, and alienation.[15] Inquiry into this is not *wertfrei,* and it carries with it a form of *advocacy* and a conception of the good life and of the sort of institutions and life policies that could make this more than a reified ideal. An inquiry into this is surely neither neutral nor detached, but it can be objective and nonideological for all of that; it is not something, Habermas argues, which is external to social

[14]Max Black, *Problems of Analysis* (Ithaca, New York: Cornell University Press, 1954), pp. 3–23.
[15]Habermas, *Knowledge and Human Interests,* chap. 10.

science but is internal to its proper practice and gives it its rationale. It is a principal task of critical theory, and thus of philosophy and social science (two disciplines which should be more closely linked than they typically are), to show how society can and should be altered.

There is, of course, little point in talking about the "should" unless we have an understanding of the "can." Hence the importance of historical materialism and of a critical analysis and, if necessary, a reconstruction of its foundations—for, it is not unreasonable to claim, it alone provides us with a comprehensive theoretical account of the dynamics of social change. However, we need to know not only what kind of changes are possible and likely and what the instruments of those changes are but also which of the historically possible changes are genuinely emancipatory. This requires some nonideological understanding of what a good life and a truly human society would look like.

We live in a time of a very pervasive cynicism about the very possibility of anything like that. If Habermas is correct, this reflects the dominant ideology of our time. But be that as it may, critical theorists have powerfully and plausibly argued that human beings, with their distinctive capacities and interests, can become self-conscious agents capable of self-reflective knowledge; they can become genuinely self-formative beings who affect the formative processes of self and society. Men, as Marx has reminded us, make their own history, but they do not make it just as they will under conditions of their own choosing. But as makers of their own history, as self-formative beings, they must be capable of reflective self-knowledge. Indeed, the self-reflective knowledge of human beings should be one of the principal ends of social inquiry. In that way it should be an emancipatory science. With their distinctive abilities and with this emancipatory knowledge, human beings can attain a historically conditioned autonomy. It is a principal aim of a critical sociology to aid in this human emancipation.

III

The above remarks merely touch the surface of a few facts of Habermas's complex and systematically ramified social theory.[16] In a more developed account of his views there is a range of additional elements which would surely be important to bring into focus. The most important of these is his theory of communication. I have tried to focus on the most central elements relevant to reflections on the functions of social science and on its relations to questions of critique and policymaking. And perhaps here we do have enough in view to help us face from an altered perspective some fundamental issues about the rationale of social theory and some of its implications for policy analysis and human emancipation. We have, that is, enough of Habermas's account before us to see why he would hold that the relationship of theory to policy, in what is sometimes called mainline sociology, is fundamentally misconceived. It is not so much that we must deny, though skepticism here is not without point, that there can be results of social science research which in some circles, and relative to certain ends, are useful. If you want less trouble from the workers in the auto industry, there may very well be some social scientists who can tell you what to do, and if you want to pacify blacks or Indians or disoriented radicals, there are perhaps some social scientists who can tell you what to do. If that is so, these "mainline social scientists" should indeed congratulate themselves on the fact that the social sciences can be highly useful to the policymaker. Critical theorists are not at all concerned to deny that that is an empirical possibility. But critical theorists generally do not see that kind of practical activity as the proper activity of critical social theory, for critical social theory seeks to be an emancipatory social theory. Definitions here will not settle anything, and people can continue to conceive of the goals of social science differ-

[16]McCarthy, pp. 61–125.

ently. But if one has an interest in human liberation, one will take the critical theory model very seriously indeed.

But then there is its execution, and here my ambivalence runs very deep. First off, I should remark that I am utterly in sympathy with what Habermas is trying to do, though I am deeply skeptical about whether it can be pulled off in anything like its present form, and I am only moderately and intermittently hopeful that, in some radically reconstituted way, a critical social theory with an emancipatory rationale can be developed—a theory which would, in important ways, replace or supplant what is now in the mainline view taken to be what philosophy and sociology properly are. In my penultimate section, I shall give, with some misgivings, some reasons for not being so skeptical.[17]

What I shall say first will, however, be negative and skeptical. I will argue that, left over from Habermas's probing twin critique of what he calls positivism and historicism, there are recalcitrant issues concerning social evolution and moral knowledge that put seriously in question the capacity of his critical sociology to delineate the direction of social emancipation or detect the mechanisms by which it can be achieved. It is a core claim of Habermas's social theory and of his account of knowledge that (1) the very ideal of a presuppositionless knowing is an illusion and (2) that fundamental human interests shape the situations of inquiry in which data are collected for these forms of knowledge. The link between knowledge and interests is so tight that knowledge without interests is impossible. Our various criteria for what is to count as knowing are determined by our interests. Yet Habermas also believes that we have objective criteria for the individual moral development of persons and parallel objective criteria, some of them irreducibly moral, for social evolution. He also believes that there is objective transcultural knowledge of right

[17]But the critical theory I shall defend is closer to Marx than it is to Habermas.

and wrong and of the foundations of morality, and that an understanding of what this is is crucial for an understanding of the criteria for social evolution. It is here, I believe, where Habermas's argument is the thinnest and where a form of skepticism has its strongest day. It isn't that we can return to a *wertfrei* sociology but that the objectivity of our moral conceptions and principles is very much more in doubt than Habermas realizes.[18] (Though what this comes to requires a careful reading.) More positively, I shall argue that there are plausible readings of historical materialism, readings which do not require Habermas's reconstruction of it, which give us an important methodological key to how social science can be both emancipatory and, without falling into the ideology of scientism, scientific and (if that is not pleonastic) objective in a reasonable sense of that multiply ambiguous conception. Habermas, as several critics have noted, importantly misreads Marx here, making him more scientistic than he actually is.[19] Both Marx and Habermas have a conception, which they embed in their complex theories, of increasingly maturer forms of corporate social life. Habermas believes that to establish this it is not sufficient to have an account of the development of the productive forces but that we must also have a properly validated theory of the autonomous development of norms. I am not convinced that this is necessary for the articulation

[18]J. L. Mackie, *Ethics: Inventing Right and Wrong* (Baltimore: Penguin Books, Inc., 1977) and Gilbert Harman, *The Nature of Morality* (New York: Oxford University Press, 1977). I have tried to convey some sense of the complexity of the issues here in my "Reason and Sentiment: Skeptical Remarks about Reason and the Foundations of Morality," in *Rationality Today*, ed. by Theodore F. Geraets (Ottawa, Ontario, Canada: University of Ottawa Press, 1970), pp. 248–79. See there also my remarks about Habermas, pp. 205–6, and about Apel, pp. 340–46.

[19]Julius Sensat, Jr., *Habermas and Marxism* (Beverly Hills, Calif: Sage Publications, 1979), chap. 6, and his review of *The Critical Theory of Jürgen Habermas, The Philosophical Review*, 89 (January, 1980), pp. 121–4; Roger S. Gottlieb, "The Contemporary Critical Theory of Jürgen Habermas," *Ethics*, 91 (January, 1981), pp. 280–95.

and defense of the emancipatory program of critical sociology. Recent work of a rigorously analytical sort on the conceptual foundations of historical materialism is beginning to give us a picture of it which is nonscientistic and yet gives us a non-ideological picture of social evolution to maturer forms of social life. This is all done without the elaboration of "the ethical foundations of Marxism" or articulating, by some transcendental arguments, the objective ground of moral norms. There may or may not be such objective grounds. Weber may be right concerning ultimate standards of the moral life. We may just have a rationally irreconcilable conflict of the "warring gods." It is not evident to me that we even have any very clear understanding of what is at issue here. But I shall argue that we do not need such an account to develop an account of social evolution that would give us a conceptual underpinning for a critical sociology with an emancipatory thrust.

I shall turn first to my negative second-saying. Habermas, like anyone deeply influenced by Hegel and Marx, stresses the importance of a consciousness of history and of situating theories in their historical contexts. However, Habermas believes, in addition, that there is progress not only "in objectivating knowledge" but also "in moral-practical insight."[20] For understandable reasons, or at least understandable causes, there is, in our societies, a not inconsiderable cynicism about this. But Habermas does claim, against scientism, that certain fundamental moral values—the moral values of freedom and justice preeminently—have an objective justification. He regards his account of universal pragmatics as so crucial partly because he believes that there is presupposed at the very basis of communication the unavoidable binding force of such

---

[20]Habermas, *Communication and the Evolution of Society,* p. 177.

norms.[21] They are built into our communicative competence and must be presupposed in any ideal speech situation. As Habermas puts it himself,

> In adopting a theoretical attitude, in engaging in discourse—or for that matter in any communicative action whatsoever—we have always (already) made, at least implicitly, certain presuppositions, under which alone consensus is possible: the presupposition, for instance, that true propositions are preferable to false ones, and that right (i.e., justifiable) norms are preferable to wrong ones. For a living being that maintains itself in the structures of ordinary language communication, the validity basis of speech has the binding force of universal and unavoidable—in this sense—transcendental—presuppositions.[22]

We are not free, he goes on to tell us, "to reject the validity claims bound up with the cognitive potential of the human species."[23] It is, he tells us, senseless to reject such ground norms. There are principles of the rightness of actions—principles of justice and freedom—which are logically linked to the very idea of what it is to be reasonable or to act in accordance with reason. And it is senseless, he tells us, "to want to 'decide' for or against reason, for or against the expansion of the potential of reasoned action."[24] A proper understanding of the conditions for undistorted communication also gives us an understanding of how it is that moral claims can be true or false; a proper understanding of universal pragmatics provides us with an objective basis for the moral judgments which result from critical reflection. If we reflect carefully on the presuppositions of human communication, we

[21]Ibid.
[22]Ibid.
[23]Ibid.
[24]Ibid.

will come to recognize that we are committed to norms of justice and freedom. Against positivists, Habermas argues that norms have "an immanent relation to truth."[25] Norms are not just choices, even universalizable choices, but they are guides to action that can be justified. They are defended, along procedural lines, as something which would be adopted in an ideal speech situation. A norm is rational or true if it is what would be adopted in a constraint-free consensus. Ideology, by contrast, is a form of "systematically distorted communication" in which people are kept from understanding their situation and from gaining an understanding of what a rational or valid norm would come to and the conditions for the validity of norms. Indeed, in contemporary scientistic ideologies, ethics is suppressed as a category of life, and people are either kept from recognizing their needs or led to believe that there is no way in which they can be fulfilled given the exigencies of life. All value judgments are thought, by those in the grip of such an ideology, to be merely people's particular biases. People bamboozled by this ideology frequently refer to their considered moral convictions as their biases or prejudices. (This is a common enough cultural occurrence even in academic circles.)

However, Habermas has not shown that intelligent, well-informed, conceptually sophisticated people must adopt such norms of justice and freedom. He has not shown that they, no matter how they are placed, on pain of intellectual mistake or false consciousness, must adopt the norms that would be consensually agreed on in an ideal speech situation—a situation of constraint-free consensus. Intelligent members of the ruling class elites know that, as a matter of fact, they are not in such a situation. Indeed, they are not in anything which even approximates such a situation. They could come to un-

---

[25]Jürgen Habermas, *Legitimation Crisis*, trans. by Thomas McCarthy (Boston: Beacon Press, 1975), p. 95.

derstand reasonably well the difference between their condition of life now and what their condition of life would be if a constraint-free consensus actually obtained. They might, without any failure of intellect or intellectual mistake, not accept the norms Habermas says are true and rationally required and ask, not without point, what intellectual fault they could be tagged with for not accepting them. It is not evident that they must have made any or that Habermas can show that any failure of intellect or failure of understanding would have to be involved.

Habermas appears at least not to have shown that these norms are rationally required and have been rationally justified. He may have shown that they are *consistent* with reason, but he appears at least not to have shown that they are *required* by reason. Accepting them could very well not be in the interest of this ruling class or dominant elite. It might very well be in their rational interest to develop manipulatively a moral ideology to enforce "irrational" social norms that could not survive in a situation of undistorted communication (for example, Wilson asking Britons to keep the social contract). In class societies there are class interests. Why should it be *irrational* for members of that ruling class to prefer a stable situation of distorted communication that protected their interests? If it is replied that they *ought* not to *want* it, how can this be shown to have anything other than a moralistic force? If they do not, after all, want it, how can they be shown to be, in the very nature of the case, less rational than the person who does? And even *if* we employ a substantive normatively nonneutral conception of rationality in which this cannot be said to be rational, essentially the same question can be put by asking whether such members of the ruling class must make any cognitive mistake in not opting for a situation of undistorted communication. It does not appear, at least, to be the case that they must in all situations be making such a mistake. If this is so, it would appear, at least, that commitment may play a larger role in morality than Habermas allows.

It will not do for Habermas to reply that to argue in such a way betrays an unwitting acceptance of the ideology of scientism, for in the above argument no appeal was made to a noncognitivist metaethic or to any metaethic at all, and no claim was made that self-reflective knowledge was impossible and only scientific knowledge was justified. Neither appeal was made nor assumed and the burden would surely be on Habermas to show that it was somehow presupposed. Rather, I developed an immanent critique and simply pressed Habermas on grounds that it would be natural for him to acknowledge—namely, on an appeal to the fact that we live in class-divided societies with class interests and to an argument which returned, as his did, to human interests and to what rational people would choose. Rational elites could very well have a standing interest in the perpetuation of ideologies, that is, conditions of distorted communication. Indeed, as Roger Gottlieb rightly stresses, one of the clear implications of Habermas's analysis of society is that capitalist societies, such as our own, have, in holding themselves together *as capitalist societies*, benefited—more accurately their ruling classes have benefited—from systematically distorted communication.[26] Undistorted communication with its "universal validity claims (truth, rightness, truthfulness), which participants at least implicitly raise and reciprocally recognize" is dysfunctional for such a society.[27]

IV

Habermas's account here is both complex and none too clear. Perhaps I have missed something in his account or at least in his intent which could lead to a reconstructable interpretation and would take us around such difficulties. One

[26]Gottlieb, "The Contemporary Critical Theory of Jürgen Habermas."
[27]Habermas, *Communication and the Evolution of Society*, p. 118.

sympathetic interpreter (Seyla Ben Habib), in the context of examining McCarthy's systematic and informed account of Habermas, interestingly remarks: "nothing would be more erroneous than to assume that the 'ideal speech situation' alone is to be the ground norm of critical theory."[28] Only theoretical discourse, on Habermas's account, is so guided; "practical discourse, by contrast, is governed by the equally counterfactual norm of 'consensually articulable common needs'" and, in determining what would count as a morally legitimate social order, we need, as well, to add a conception of *generalizable interests*.[29] The norms of the ideal speech situations are the procedural norms that people in something like the original position would use and are norms which could be defended nonideologically and impartially where appeal could not be made to class interests.[30] Such norms, in any event, "cannot provide a *material* specification for the ideals of freedom, justice and equality."[31] In this context, it is important to note McCarthy's explication of what a norm is for Habermas. Norms are "intersubjectively binding reciprocal expectations of behavior which regulate legitimate chances for the satisfaction of needs."[32] They provide, as Ben Habib puts it, "socially sanctioned modes of need satisfaction."[33] These socially sanctioned modes of need satisfaction always carry an implicit *claim* to legitimacy. With such additions, as McCarthy points out, Habermas maintains his distance from a Kantian formalism in ethics.[34] Like Marx, Habermas sees

---

[28]Seyla Ben Habib, "Critical Notice of Thomas McCarthy's *The Critical Theory of Jürgen Habermas*," *Telos* (Summer 1979), p. 179.
[29]Ibid.
[30]Ibid., p. 180; and Thomas McCarthy, pp. 303–10.
[31]Ben Habib, p. 180.
[32]Thomas McCarthy, pp. 311–25.
[33]Ben Habib, p. 180.
[34]But he still appeals to a rather special reading of "universalizability" and it is not evident that he has overcome formalistic difficulties. Thomas McCarthy, pp. 310–33.

needs as changing and expanding. Indeed they are not rooted in a fixed human nature, but what our needs are is, in part, dependent on what, in a given historical situation, is possible and what can be attained as well as on a particular culture's historically conditioned conception of what is good.[35] The stress here is on the claim that the "guiding norm for practical discourse is the ideal of 'consensual need articulation.'"[36] This too is procedural and it understandably avoids following Marx and many Marxists (Fromm and Marcuse, for example) in trying to develop an account of true and false needs.

If this is the way we should understand Habermas, it does not enable us to escape my previous criticism. Suppose the members of an established ruling class in a secure class society acknowledged that there is this tight link between legitimate norms and consensual needs. Still, why do such people fly in the face of reason or make any cognitive mistake if they do not acknowledge that their class should act in accordance with that ideal of need articulation? Why should they want a system of need regulation based on undistorted communication? Indeed, it could be argued (as I did) that they as a class have a need for a system of distorted communication—a moral ideology—answering to their class interests. To the response that that is bourgeois ideology becoming cynical and indeed using people manipulatively, the reply could be: "And what is *irrational* about being cynical and so using people?" At times in our history it has paid off very handsomely indeed for the dominant class.

Moreover, to speak of norms as being intersubjectively binding reciprocal expectations of behavior which regulate legitimate chances for the satisfaction of needs does not get us very far until we have some criteria for "legitimate chances."

[35]Ben Habib, p. 180.
[36]Ibid.

And the remark in descriptive ethics that norms are "socially sanctioned modes of need satisfaction" or that they are "intersubjectively binding" cuts no normative ice unless you have already accepted a given moral system in a given society. But the observer can perfectly appropriately ask: Why accept that system? And a person or group of persons can perfectly well ask: Why accept that socially sanctioned mode of need satisfaction with its distinctive scheduling of needs? Members of a ruling class in a stable class society would, of course, at least accept them as useful ideological devices for mass control, but they need not, on pain of irrationality, accept them as binding norms on which they are themselves committed to act. Moreover, it is a textbook truism, which all the same is true, that the mere fact that a system of rules is socially sanctioned does not make these rules right or something that should be accepted.

I do claim that it is in the class interests of ruling-class holdouts (if that is the right word for them) to maintain distorted communication. Indeed, without it their very existence as *a class* would be in grave doubt. But I do not equate their acting rationally as individuals with their acting in accordance with their individual interests. I no more equate "rationality" with "instrumental rationality" than does Habermas, and to do so would simply beg the question with him. Members of the capitalist class, like everyone else, have emancipatory interests. (I am here, of course, speaking of them as individuals.) But I do question whether their so protecting their class interests can be shown always or perhaps even generally to be in conflict with their emancipatory interests, and I do contend that they need not make any intellectual mistake (any deductive or inductive error) if they continue to opt for propagating a moral ideology (recognized by them to be ideology) which protects their class interests. I believe that many of their human needs, including things like at least some of

Rawls's primary social goods, could for them still be met, as they are situated now, under conditions of capitalist class hegemony. What might be argued, and I remain skeptically hopeful that such an argument might turn out to be sound, is that they could not, where they also saw their situation with considerable clarity, maintain their self-respect while sanctioning such a use of moral ideology to maintain their class interests. But Habermas has done nothing to show that this is so.

Something more can be said, giving some sense to the notion of an objective basis for moral norms, if we drop the Kantian and Hobbesian task of trying to get morality out of rationality and instead try to say something about what taking the moral point of view requires. In elucidating the mode of social critique that would result from an acceptance of Habermas's theory of communicative competence, McCarthy makes it clear that Habermas has shown that a discourse of domination—ideological discourse not meeting the conditions of an ideal speech situation—would make impossible the public articulation of the need interpretations of the dominated class. The norms of such a discourse of domination preclude that, but if, as Baier and Rawls have argued, a formal requirement of the moral point of view is that anything which can even count as a moral norm must be publicly defensible, then the norms of such a discourse of domination could not be moral norms.[37] A class society utilizing such a discourse of domination could have a moral ideology but not a genuine morality. Its norms are incompatible with what it is to take the moral point of view. This approach, though not one taken by Habermas, is perhaps a promising one. The formal con-

[37]Kurt Baier, *The Moral Point of View* (Ithaca, New York: Cornell University Press, 1958), pp. 191–200; and John Rawls, *A Theory of Justice* (Cambridge, Mass.: Harvard University Press, 1971), pp. 55, 133, and 167–92.

straint Baier and Rawls put on moral norms is a plausible one; if such a position were adopted and could withstand criticism, it perhaps would provide a way around the difficulties I have pressed against Habermas's account. It would, of course, still be necessary to spell out what it is to take the moral point of view in such a way that moral ideologies and "class moralities" would be excluded, and it would be necessary to provide some answer to the challenge to morality (any morality at all): Why be moral?[38] But here we are on reasonably familiar ground and the task is perhaps not insuperable.

The publicity requirement, if adopted and so utilized, might also help provide us with grounds for making the distinction, one that Habermas is very concerned to make, between a merely *de facto consensus* and a *rational legitimate consensus*. The publicity requirement, as a defining characteristic of the moral point of view, would also be a defining characteristic of a rational consensus. We could not—logically could not—have a *rational* consensus where moral ideologies were in force and some people remained ideologically bamboozled. (To say this is to make what Wittgenstein would call a grammatical remark.) Ben Habib makes a solid point about ideologies in this context when she remarks: "Ideologies are precisely such discourses which pre-empt, reinterpret and misarticulate the needs of dominated groups. The aim of critique is to demystify these frameworks of legitimacy which socialize individuals by providing them with value systems and norms through which to articulate needs."[39] Habermas, with his norms of the ideal speech situation and his understanding of needs, may have gone some of the way toward providing us with a rational underpinning for such a critique

---

[38]Kai Nielsen, "Rationality and the Moral Sentiments: Some Animadversions on a Theme in *A Theory of Justice*," *Philosophica*, 22 (1978), pp. 167–92.
[39]Ben Habib, p. 181.

so that it can become clear to us that we do not need to be in a situation where we pit ideologies against ideologies—where, that is, we are in Weber's situation of the "warring gods."

However, as Rawls remarks, publicity is a very weak constraint. Even with Habermas's procedural norms of the ideal speech situation, we still may not get, even when they are linked with the above account of needs, a material specification of the ideals of freedom and justice and a conception of a humane social order sufficient to give us objective guides to action or moral criteria for social evolution. The critical reception of Rawls's magisterial account of social justice gives us reasons for not being sanguine. It has been about a decade now since its appearance and—given the extensive, varied, and often careful critical assessment of it—we are by now in a position to draw some important object lessons from it. Almost everyone who has studied Rawls's work regards it as a masterpiece, a contemporary work that belongs with the classical works in moral and social philosophy. It has a powerful but controlled moral vision; it is systematic, careful, and detailed; and, like Sidgwick's work, it shows an acute and sensitive appreciation of both its predecessors and contemporary alternatives. Yet, unlike Sidgwick, it also seeks to establish a distinctive moral methodology, to establish the correctness of certain principles of justice and a conception of a well-ordered society which in large measure is based on them. It seeks to refute its main rivals, utilitarianism, pluralism, and a purely rights-based ethic. The upshot of all the varied critical reception of that book is the recognition that it has succeeded in none of these tasks. Disputes about moral methodology remain as deep as ever and all the major nonskeptical alternatives remain in the field: theories of utilitarianism, pluralism, perfectionism, and even natural rights.

Perhaps the renewed moral skepticism defended by J. L.

Mackie and G. Harman could be faulted by Habermas for sharing in many ways the scientistic assumptions of earlier noncognitive theories, but the alternatives mentioned above, none of which has been excluded by Rawls's account, do not always make scientistic assumptions. Neither those nonskeptical normative ethical accounts nor Rawls's rest on such scientistic or, broadly speaking, positivist assumptions. There may be positivistic residues in the thought of some of the philosophers articulating those moral theories, perhaps even in Rawls's, but they are—or so it seems at least—readily excisable from their theories.

If there is such a stalemate in ethics, there is reason to be skeptical that Habermas's account will succeed where these accounts have been failures. In these domains, Habermas's work is much less developed and sophisticated than the work of Rawls and many of his critics and some of the alternative normative ethical theories that have been constructed. (I have in mind here particularly the work of Kurt Baier and Thomas Nagel.) Habermas might respond that even here it is the implicit metaethics of positivism—taking the term in his wide sense—and its underlying scientistic assumptions that is getting in the way. I think that so to respond is mistaken. The stalemate I spoke of is not the one that bothered people such as Blanshard and Frankena in the decade after World War II, when all three of the then dominant metaethical theories had generally acknowledged weaknesses and yet no alternatives were in sight which overcame those difficulties or reasonably clearly pointed the way to the overall superiority of one theory over the other.[40] Rather the situation now is that: it isn't that we can never know or reasonably believe that certain things

---

[40]Brand Blanshard, *The Impasse in Ethics—and a Way Out* (Berkeley, Calif.: University of California Press, 1955); and W. K. Frankena, "Moral Philosophy at Mid-Century," *Philosophical Review*, 60 (January, 1951), pp. 44–5.

are right and wrong. There are moral truisms (commonplaces) that are generally acknowledged. The rival nonskeptical moral theories all agree that it is wrong to torture the innocent just for the fun of it, or to break faith with your friends on a whim, or not to regard the keeping of a promise or the telling of the truth as something one, *ceteris paribus,* must do. They also all believe that pleasure is good and pain is awful, though they certainly do not all believe that pleasure is the sole intrinsic good. Moreover, to take a Moorean turn, it is more reasonable to accept these moral truisms than to accept a skeptical theory which would deny them. But the acceptance of these truisms does not get us very far in constructing a normative ethic on which to ground (partially ground) a theory of social evolution. All the major, and often deeply conflicting, nonskeptical moral theories (normative ethical theories) accept these truisms, though they differ profoundly on the weight they give to them and on the place they have in their theories. For a hedonistic utilitarian the importance of the judgments of intrinsic value that pleasure is good and pain is bad will be more important, in his or her scheme of things, than the deontological judgments that promises must be kept and the truth told or that people must be treated as ends and never as means only. The opposite will, of course, be true for the Kantian. Their disagreement is not over whether these various things are good or bad but over their placement and weight.

What is crucial for us to see is that we have no rational consensus as to which of the alternative normative ethical theories are, everything considered, the more adequate or even the least inadequate. We perhaps know some moral truisms to be true, but we do not have a *systematic* knowledge of right and wrong.[41] Habermas either does not realize this

[41]Nielsen, "Reason and Sentiment," pp. 248–79, and "On Needing a Moral Theory," *Metaphilosophy,* (1982).

or does not face it. Minimally, he does nothing to challenge it or to show that a claim like the one I have made above is even overstated. But how, then, can he reasonably claim that we have made progress in "moral-practical insight," a progress giving us an understanding of social evolution to maturer forms of social integration? How can he rightly claim that, independently of the development of the productive forces, we have moral or normative criteria for social evolution?

It is fair enough to remind us that "Habermas remains faithful to the Hegelian ideal of not providing 'blueprints' for social and political reality in the form of *a priori* normative models," but still, how does he provide us with normative criteria for social evolution?[42] These, it would seem, would have to be tolerably abstract and independent of context.[43] Again it is important to remark, as Habermas does, that "every general theory of justice remains peculiarly abstract in relation to historical forms of legitimation" and then go on to ask whether there is "an alternative to this historical injustice of general theories, on the one hand, and the standardlessness of mere historical understanding on the other."[44] But where is his alternative and how does it—or does it—provide criteria for social evolution?

Social theory for Habermas is importantly social critique. He wishes, as Ben Habib has it, to radicalize the method of immanent critique.[45] But Habermas, unlike Rawls or Baier, does not believe that critique can supply universal norms in the form of ethical imperatives, for, as he puts it, "the melodies of ethical socialism have been played through." He can do no more here than can Popper or Weber. His critique is

[42]Ben Habib, p. 181.
[43]Ibid.
[44]Habermas, *Communication and Human Evolution,* p. 205.
[45]Ben Habib, pp. 182–84.

in no position to reveal the universal content of moral norms while critiquing in late capitalism or bureaucratic socialism their distorted, system-serving, particular realization. Habermas himself claims that such a critique requires a philosophical ethics and that a "philosophical ethics . . . is possible today only if we can reconstruct general presuppositions of communication and procedures for justifying norms and values."[46] But whatever may be true about his account of the presuppositions of communication, he has not succeeded in providing us with convincing procedures for justifying moral norms. It may be, as Ben Habib remarks at the end of her penetrating discussion of Habermas, that "it would be an error to interpret Habermas's later work as reviving the melodies of ethical socialism, or to conflate it with the grandiose self-deceptions of theories of justice that claim to speak from 'the standpoint of eternity.' "[47] But Habermas does claim to have given us a (partially) normative theory of social evolution and a procedure for justifying moral norms, yet it remains both unclear what those procedures are or how they can do their justifying work or that we have been given criteria for social evolution.[48]

V

I want to set forth, as an alternative candidate for providing criteria for social evolution, a reading of historical materialism. I believe that Marx's account requires less reconstructing than Habermas believes is required. I want also to put it forth as a method which might provide us with the

[46]Habermas, *Communication and Human Evolution*, pp. 96–7; and Ben Habib, p. 185.
[47]Ben Habib, p. 185; and McCarthy, pp. 310–33.
[48]Ben Habib, p. 187.

foundations for a critical theory of society: a sociological theory which will both advocate and analyze and, if you will, provide an underlying rationale for policymaking.

Habermas believes that scientistic assumptions are embedded in Marx's statement of historical materialism. In thinking about the crucial causal role of the forces of production in producing social change, and indeed in a progressively liberating social change, Marx, Habermas gives us to understand, saw the organization of social life too much as a technical problem, like the technical control over objects and natural processes, and, with these assumptions in place, Marx came mistakenly to believe that to overcome exploitation and oppression is simply a matter of making social production more efficient. The key to this was in the development of the productive forces. But we must distinguish, Habermas believes, between instrumentally rational production and emancipatory social interaction, and we must realize that social production has, as an essential element, a mutual understanding of people and not just a technical control over objects and natural processes. Social evolution has two logically independent elements, Habermas claims—technical rationalization and practical rationalization. They are, in turn, rooted in two fundamental interests. Technical rationalization has to do with society's control over natural processes; practical rationalization has to do, as we have seen, with the justifiability of norms governing human interaction. Marx, Habermas believes, in developing historical materialism, came to characterize the process of social reproduction as production, incorrectly reducing practical rationalization to technical rationalization. By confusing technical rationalization and practical rationalization—rational production and social interaction—Marx, as well as many later Marxists (Lenin and Kautsky), came to have an inadequate understanding of the dynamics of capitalism. They did not understand, and their theoretical preconceptions inhibited their understanding, how state capitalism can prevent crippling economic crises or how social revolution could not be stage-managed by "experts" from above. But this, as Sensat and Gottlieb have argued, is a misreading of Marx and a misunderstanding of his historical materialism.[49] For him, social production is much more than simply controlling the natural environment. For Marx, practical rationalization is not reduced to technical rationalization, but neither are they, as Habermas believes, logically distinct, with quite different criteria for their development. Rather, on Marx's view, they are two developmental patterns which are inextricably intertwined. They are interdependent aspects of the mode of production. It is crucial in gaining an understanding of historical materialism and social evolution to come to understand how the forces of production can be both fettered and promoted, though not at one and the same time, by the relations of production, and how the fettering impoverishes social life and how promoting it can enhance it.

Marxists, including Marx, believe that the fundamental determinates of social change are in the development of the productive forces and in their clash, as they develop, with the relations of production, relations which first suit them and then, as they further develop, come to fetter them. We human beings are tolerably rational creatures with some understanding of our interests. These interests and our normal, and perhaps rather minimal, rationality lead us to develop our productive capacities. Our productive capacities develop and with that our productive forces develop, until at some point our productive forces will come to clash with the previously well-matched relations of production.

There are two crucial theses involved here, theses which

---

[49]See the references to Sensat and Gottlieb in footnote 19.

G. A. Cohen calls *the development thesis* and *the primacy thesis.* It is important, in thinking about historical materialism, to consider both of these theses, for the latter requires the truth of the former as a necessary condition for its truth. The *development thesis* is the thesis that the productive forces tend to develop throughout history. The *primacy thesis* is the thesis that the nature of the production relations of a society is explained by the level of development of its productive forces, though to assert this is not to deny, as it might seem at first sight, that production relations themselves develop and bring about changes in productive forces.[50] Causal relations go both ways, but the claim of the primacy thesis is that the dominant causal determination is from the forces of production to the relations of production. The claim is that when there are extensive changes in the productive forces, changes in the production relations will occur. As Cohen puts it, "for any set of production relations, there is an extent of further development of productive forces they embrace which suffices for a change in relations.. . ."[51] This will continue throughout history, because it just is the case that the productive forces tend to develop. But to assert this is just to assume the *developmental thesis.*

It is difficult to know how the *development thesis* could be proved, but it certainly appears, at least for Western societies, to be an unassailable historical datum that the "productive forces tend to develop and, indeed do develop."[52] If in reflecting on societies other than Western ones we are forced to be skeptical about the development of productive forces

[50]G. A. Cohen, *Karl Marx's Theory of History, A Defense* (Oxford, England: Clarendon Press, 1978).
[51]Ibid., p. 138.
[52]Ibid.

throughout history, this would indeed surely weaken that claim and make us consider whether there are things special about Western societies that trigger this development. We would also, and more importantly, be less certain that such developments must continue indefinitely in the future. However, it surely seems at least to be an empirical truth that societies rarely replace a given set of productive forces by inferior productive forces. Indeed, it did happen for a time after the decline of the Roman Empire, but massively and generally it tends to be the case, perhaps because we are (to a degree) rational and have a sense of our own interests, that we will not replace the productive forces we have in place with inferior ones and that it is because of this that the productive forces tend to develop throughout history. Perhaps we do not know *why* this is so, but *that* this is so seems at least evident enough in Western societies.

The degree of development of the productive forces is, in turn, the measure of a society's capacity to produce. Productive forces are, of course, what is used in production, and production relations are either the relations of ownership of the productive forces or persons or relations presupposing such relations of ownership. *Ownership* here means "effective control." The economic structure of a society is just the entire set of production relations of a society and the modes of production of a society are the distinctive ways a society has of producing. (It is by virtue of these modes that Marxists periodize history.) The superstructure of a society, as distinct from the base (another name for the "economic structure of society"), is the noneconomic institutions of society: its legal system, its morality, its religion, its rituals, its kinship system, and the like. Just as the base (the economic structure of society) has the general character it has because of the character of the productive forces, so the superstructure has the general character it has because of the character of the base.

What we have here is a claim to the primacy, in speaking of social change, of the productive forces. They are the fundamental determinates of the whole historical process. The productive forces tend to develop throughout history and the level of development of these productive forces explains why it is that we have the productive relations we have during a given era. The productive forces determine the general direction in which the production relations will change, and the production relations, in turn, explain the general character of the noneconomic institutions of society and the general direction of their change.[53] The key to understanding social development is to understand the changes, and the likely direction of future changes, in the development of the modes of production.

It is important to see that the character of the forces of production functionally explains the character of the relations of production. In times of stability, the production relations are of the type they are because they are the sort of relations which are suitable to the use and development of the productive forces at that time. Where we are in an epoch of revolutionary conflict and the relations of production for a time persist in spite of the conflict, the explanation is as follows: the production relations are of the kind they are because they once were suitable to the use and development of the productive forces at an earlier time. In both cases we use functional explanations. (We have here functional explanations without functionalism.[54]) When new relations of pro-

[53]Ibid., p. 136.
[54]Ibid., pp. 158–60.

duction come into being, they do so because they are the sorts
of relations which will promote the development of productive forces. The *primacy thesis* requires such an appeal to functional explanations. Relations of production will stably obtain
over time only if, and because, they suit the development of
the productive forces. The relations are as they are because
they suit the development of the forces of production. (Note
how teleological all that is, but it is not, for all of that, unem-
pirical.[55])

There need be nothing scientistic about this claim. In
trying to understand the wheel of history, it indeed gives
considerable weight to technological considerations, to the
way labor power and the means of production develop. But
even here, at the level of the forces of production, we are also
talking about human knowledge and human inventiveness.
Moreover, social production—the whole mode of production—involves much more than technical control over objects;
it involves a fundamental understanding of how humans are
to relate together and the forms that that social cooperation
can take.

Such a view does not impugn our rationality or render
morality or moral development impossible. Even if we say
that a certain human development is inevitable—and I do not
suggest that we should talk that way—the "inevitabilities"
do not exist *despite* what human beings do but, because of
what they, being rational, are bound predictably to do.[56] This
gives us an understanding of how people, even in a deterministic world, if such it be, make their own history. We can

[55]Charles Taylor, "Marxism and Empiricism," *British Analytical Philosophy,*
    ed. by Bernard Williams and Alan Montefiore (London: Routledge & Kegan
    Paul, Ltd., 1966), pp. 227–46.
[56]Cohen, p. 147.

see on this account how human actions count. On such an account of historical materialism, an account I believe was Marx's account, we can see how there is an extensive coincidence between the development of the productive forces and the growth of human faculties.[57] With an ever greater control of nature, as the productive forces develop, there is an ever greater amassing of social wealth, an enhancement of human rationality, and more and more leisure for more and more people within the societies where that wealth obtains, with a consequent development of the capacities for reflection and esthetic appreciation and an expansion, for more and more people, to an ever greater degree, of their capacities to act autonomously. Imperialism puts temporary wrinkles on this, but over the long haul there is this enhancement of human powers. With the development of the forces of production, our mastery over nature and, potentially, over our own lives is enormously expanded. We are in a very different position than the Athapascan Indians. If the core notion of human liberty is conscious self-direction and the opening of ever wider possibilities for choice; the development of the productive forces enhances that. It increases, at least poten-

---

[57]In addition to the masterful general statement of historical materialism in Cohen's book, important related accounts occur in William H. Shaw, *Marx's Theory of History* (Stanford, Calif.: Stanford University Press, 1978); John G. Gurley, *Challengers to Capitalism: Marx, Lenin and Mao* (San Francisco, Calif.: San Francisco Book Company, 1976); and John McMurtry, *The Structure of Marx's World-View* (Princeton, N.J.: Princeton University Press, 1978). Cohen's and Shaw's account has been powerfully but sympathetically criticized by Henry Laycock, *Canadian Journal of Philosophy*, 10 (June, 1980), pp. 335–56. Even if Laycock's acute criticisms are sustainable, they will not, I think provide a ground for altering the use I made in my text of Cohen's arguments. Similar things should be said for Richard Miller's powerful probing of Cohen's theses in his "Productive Forces and the Forces of Change," *The Philosophical Review*, 90 (January, 1981), pp. 91–117.

tially, our control over our own lives and adds to the richness and potential for variation in our lives. As the productive forces develop—and it is not unreasonable to believe that over history they do—we are less and less yoked to the realm of necessity.[58] There is there a firmly materialist but not reductionist or morally insensitive conception of freedom from human bondage. With this, we by degree achieve greater and greater moral autonomy and make, again by degrees, more tangible the realization, for more and more people, of the good of self-respect.

This relatively unreconstructed historical materialism thus provides the basis for an emancipatory social theory and a social science which can, in good conscience, advocate and make policy as well as analyze and critique. Even without Habermas's complicated picture of moral development and his transcendental grounding of norms, we have, on a perfectly materialistic basis, sufficient key to moral progress and human emancipation reasonably to ground a critical social theory with an emancipatory thrust.

VI

If a policymaker in a Western capitalist society were to accept such an account of emancipatory social theory so buttressed by historical materialism, how, if at all, would it affect her or his approach to policymaking? One response—a response I mean entirely seriously—is that he or she might very well give up all efforts at policymaking in such societies and in some way or another go over to the extraparliamentary opposition, as many intellectuals have done in the past. (The ways in which this can be done are varied.) The rationale

[58]When we consider only Western history, it is plain that these productive forces do so develop.

would be this: only after such societies have been radically transformed in a far more humane direction is there much point in worrying about policymaking. The question is the gaining of state power and not that of trying to tinker with the system within the existing parameters of power. (This is not, of course, to say that policymaking would not be a worthwhile activity in a different kind of society.)

This response is a natural response, but it is perhaps not utterly inescapable. We do not have to be committed to piecemeal social engineering to recognize that there are evils to be overcome, including injustices to be rectified or at least ameliorated. Something (though often not very much) can be done about some of these ills in almost any society, and one way of doing something about them is by institutional action or (more rarely) inaction. There plainly is work here for policymakers. Their scope may often be modest and their room for maneuver slight. But if they have a tolerably clear conception of what they are to aim at and some reasonable grasp of the empirical facts, it is seldom the case that nothing can be done.

It is also well to have a sense of the relevance of context when questions are raised about the poliymaker's role. (Remember we are asking what this role would be assuming the work were informed by critical theory.) In what Western capitalist society is the policymaker seeking to work? Sweden and Iceland are not the United States and South Africa. Moreover, it very much depends on what his or her own role in the society is. But suppose he or she is middle aged, a social scientist, and has been a policymaker for some years; suppose further he or she becomes convinced that some such form of critical social theory as I have outlined is roughly correct. What then is this person to do? Again it depends on how close he is to power, the possibilities for change within the existing state apparatus, and the like. To be reasonably placed in the central planning office of Zimbabwe is a challenge; Chile is something else again. And the United States is not Sweden.

However, suppose we pose the question, in terms of their position in the state apparatus, of statistically standard policymakers in the United States in 1982. If they go on in that role at all (and it seems to me they should seriously question whether they should), they should, I think, approach their work with considerable wariness and cynicism. (Given the elected and appointed officials they are responsible to, how could they do anything progressive without engaging in some form of trickery?) Most fundamentally, for a critical theorist turned policymaker or a policymaker convinced by critical theory, there would be a difference in attitude from that of a conservative or welfare-state liberal in the approach to policymaking. He or she would not view the future to be achieved as merely some improved, possibly a little more efficient and a little less inhumane, version of the present or be wedded to structural–functionalist assumptions, nor would he or she expect societies, with the continued development of the productive forces, to change, and in certain epochs fundamentally and radically change, and indeed develop in a generally liberating direction. Our policymaker would not have the cultural pessimism of a Freud. Moreover, he or she would have a conception of the general direction those changes would take and, with a recognition that there is causal interaction between base and superstructure, between the economic and political–legal realm, would seek to develop social policies that would help unfetter the production relations in the society. (A recognition of the primacy of the economic does not commit one to economism.) This would consist most fundamentally in struggling to bring into being policies that would weaken capitalist-class hegemony over the society. Central in such an endeavor would be (1) the articulation of policies that would further movement in the direction of workers' control over their places of work and (2) policies that would move in the direction of achieving democratic rather than business control of the mass media and indeed over the whole consciousness industry. Policymaking, informed by the commitments of critical theory, would also be directed toward achieving free and universally accessible higher education, health care, day-care centers, facilities for the elderly, legal aid, and the like. In fine, policies would be articulated whose probable effect would be to weaken class divisions—and thus undermine the hegemony of the capitalist class—and sexual and racial inequalities. The underlying rationale of policymaking, consonant with the emancipatory ends of critical theory and with devices that would accelerate the development of productive forces instrumental to those ends, would be the articulation of policies which would work to *equalize power within the society* and in this absolutely central way democratize society and make possible the existence of the public sphere that Habermas, like J. S. Mill, takes to be essential for a truly human society.[59]

There should be very deep pessimism about whether policymakers in bureaucratic structures, even if they had such ends, could do much to further them. Liberation is not likely to come from such sources. After all, we must not forget who their masters are. But at least such policies as are formed should not impede such class struggles and further strengthen the repressive, deeply ideologized, elite control of capitalist society.[60] A critical social science informed by historical materialism would sensitize us in this direction and would provide the policymaker with intellectual support for such a cluster of commitments and such attitudes in policymaking.[61]

[59]Jürgen Habermas, *Strukturwandel der Öffentlichkeit* (Neuwied, West Germany: Luchterhand Verlag, 1962). See also Jürgen Habermas, "The Public Sphere," *New German Critique,* 3 (1974), pp. 49–55.
[60]For a window on how it works, see Noam Chomsky, "Resurgent America," *Our Generation,* 14 (Summer, 1981), pp. 11–22.
[61]I should like to thank Bruce Jennings, Elisabeth Nielsen, and Daniel Callahan for comments on early versions of this essay.

II

SOCIAL SCIENCE AND POLITICAL ADVOCACY

7

THE BRITISH TRADITION OF SOCIAL ADMINISTRATION

Moral Concerns at the Expense of Scientific Rigor

MARTIN BULMER

American social science is, tentatively and perhaps belatedly, discovering ethics, particularly in issues surrounding the uses of social science research for policymaking. Although the concern may seem novel to many social scientists, in fact the discipline is rediscovering its roots. In Britain the links between ethics and social science were never so completely severed but were forged in a quite distinctive way, through the creation of the field of social administration. The development of social administration, with its particular strengths and weaknesses, offers a useful basis for comparing the American and British experience.

Less than a century ago the social sciences in Britain and the United States were directly and explicitly concerned with ethics. In their teaching, American sociologists such as Albion Small and E. A. Ross combined scientific analysis and direct

MARTIN BULMER □ Department of Social Science and Administration, London School of Economics and Political Science, Houghton Street, London, WC 2A 2AE, England.

ethical prescription.[1] From 1906, sociology at Harvard University was taught in the Department of Social Ethics. In Britain, leading figures such as the social philosopher L. T. Hobhouse and the early social investigator Seebohm Rowntree combined scientific concerns with specific ethical and political interests. A recent history of British social science between 1870 and 1914 is titled *Ethics and Society in England*.[2] To modern eyes, several of these figures now seem distinctly quaint, if not anachronistic, throwbacks to the origins of social scientists from the ranks of Protestant ministers. The university professor (mis)using his position to preach prescriptive doctrines, a practice that Max Weber so fiercely attacked, is the prototype.[3]

THE NEW SCIENTIFIC SPIRIT

These early tendencies were not sustained, and those who advocated a fusion of social science and ethics were eclipsed by those who favored more scientific approaches to social questions. This new conception of social science first and foremost insisted upon the objective, detached, and *scientific* character of the academic study of society, modeled (to some extent at least) upon the natural sciences. Around the end of the First World War, new and distinct disciplines (such as sociology, political science, and anthropology), each characterized by particular theories *and* methods, took a shape

---

[1]Cf. V. K. Dibble, *The Legacy of Albion Small* (Chicago: University of Chicago Press, 1975); J. Weinberg, *E. A. Ross and the Sociology of Progressivism* (Madison, Wis.: State Historical Society of Wisconsin, 1972).

[2]R. N. Soffer, *Ethics and Society in England: The Revolution in the Social Sciences 1870–1914* (Berkeley, Calif.: University of California Press, 1978).

[3]Max Weber, "Science as a Vocation," in *From Max Weber*, ed. by H. H. Gerth and C. W. Mills (London: Routledge & Kegan Paul, Ltd., 1948), pp. 129–56.

still recognizable in those disciplines today. Their practitioners concerned themselves with scientific and analytic ends in which moral and prescriptive explorations played little or no part. Indeed, moral concerns were regarded as an intrusion more characteristic of muckrakers, do-gooders, and reformers than appropriate to new disciplines striving for professional status.

In the 1920s the University of Chicago, home of famous "schools" of political science, sociology, and economics, was a leading exponent of these trends. In political science, Charles Merriam pointed the subject more in the direction of rigorous and quantitative inquiry and pressed for a more systematic and expanded study of public administration.[4] The scientific purpose of the enterprise crystallized at the national level in the Social Science Research Council, set up by Merriam in 1923.[5] In sociology, Robert Park represented the new scientific spirit, advocating the detached scientific study of social phenomena, untrammeled by political or philosophical ends. One of Park's major interests was race relations, which he effectively established as a field of academic study (though there had been one or two precursors, notably W. E. B. Du Bois).[6] The fierce academic passions that the study of race arouses today—it is enough to mention the Moynihan report on the black family of 1963, the article by Arthur Jensen on race and IQ in the *Harvard Educational Review* of 1969, and the James Coleman–Thomas Pettigrew exchanges over busing[7]—stand in sharp contrast to the dispassionate and scholarly approach

---

[4]B. Karl, *Charles E. Merriam and the Study of Politics* (Chicago: University of Chicago Press, 1974), p. 155.
[5]Karl, *Charles E. Merriam,* chap. 7.
[6]Cf. D. S. Green and E. D. Driver, *W. E. B. DuBois on Sociology and the Black Community* (Chicago: University of Chicago Press, 1978).
[7]Cf. T. F. Pettigrew, "Race Ethics and the Social Scientist," *Hastings Center Report,* 9 (October, 1979), 15–18.

that Park was able to maintain. As Ernest Burgess recalled in a memorial *festschrift*,

> Students attracted to the field of race relations, whether white or negro, generally held strong sentiments against racial discrimination and for negro rights. They were predisposed to fight valiantly for them. Park told them flatly that the world was full of crusaders. Their role instead was to be that of the calm, detached scientist who investigates race relations with the same objectivity and detachment with which the zoologist dissects the potato bug.[8]

Despite its academic base, social science was regarded as relevant for policy formulation and the guidance of government. Merriam had been actively involved in city politics for twenty years, nearly being elected mayor in 1911. Park had been secretary to Booker T. Washington and was the first president of the Chicago Urban League.[9] Both encouraged academic studies of a markedly applied kind, relating to policy problems. However, these studies were to be carried out scientifically, within the framework of an academic discipline (whether sociology or political science) with its own body of general ideas and its own developing scientific methods of investigation. William F. Ogburn carried on this tradition when he joined the Chicago department and undertook (together with Wesley Mitchell and Merriam) the work for Herbert Hoover's Commission on recent social trends.[10] Here was explicit

[8]E. W. Burgess, "Social Planning and Race Relations," in *Race Relations, Problems and Theories*, ed. by J. Masuoka and P. Valien (Chapel Hill, N.C.: University of North Carolina Press, 1961), p. 17.

[9]F. H. Matthews, *Quest for an American Sociology: Robert E. Park and the Chicago School* (Montreal: McGill-Queens University Press, 1977).

[10]President's Research Committee on Social Trends, *Report of the President's Research Committee on Social Trends* (New York: McGraw-Hill Book Company, 1933).

policy research (a forerunner of the modern social indicators movement, which attempts to measure social change statistically), conceived within a rigorous scientific framework of detachment and objectivity, from which ethical concerns were entirely excluded.

The tendencies begun in the 1920s have been strongly maintained in American social science to the present. The exclusion of value concerns is reflected in methodological principles such as "value freedom" in sociology, a definition of economics ("positive economics") as the study of means to given ends, and the use of rigorous experimental designs in psychology. It is also revealed in empirical studies of society. In sociology, for example, the scientific social survey has become the dominant methodology and the most widely used technique in policy research, although other types of research design also exist.

Why were philosophical elements so rigorously excluded? The main reasons lie in the conception of social science as science and the drive to professional respectability. Scientists generally believed that moral and ethical judgments introduced a weakness and flabbiness into scholarly work. Western social thought in the twentieth century widely reflected the philosophical distinction between "is" and "ought," fact and value, the positive and the normative. Social scientists, it was argued, should not permit their own judgments about the good society to permeate their work any more than historians, linguists, or classical scholars allowed moral and ethical values to color *their* work. The institution of slavery, for example, might be evil and pernicious; nevertheless, the task of the social scientist was to understand it as an economic and social system and to explain why it persisted for so long, not to pass judgment on those who originated and perpetuated it. As a recent survey by Donald Warwick, a social psychologist, has shown, ethics acquired distinctly pejorative overtones in the teaching of some social sciences.[11]

Accompanying the rise in scientific objectivity was the salience of social science in America and its integration into the policymaking processes of the government. Although the enterprise may not seem so vast to American social scientists, the volume of funding, the size of particular projects, and the number of social scientists involved take a Britisher's breath away. The status of social science policy research in the United States is grounded in its *scientific* rigor. Such respectability as it has—which certainly should not be exaggerated—rests on methodological competence and sophistication and the ability to produce representative and reliable evidence bearing on relevant policy problems.

FUNDAMENTAL QUESTIONS

Recently, however, some social scientists have argued that the claims to scientific rigor have been oversold, that the discipline cannot deliver the goods that it promises to produce.[12] It is certainly not clear that more social science data have led to greater clarity about policy objectives. One thinks, for example, of David Cohen's account of the effects of educational

---

[11]Donald P. Warwick, *The Teaching of Ethics in the Social Sciences* (Hastings-on-Hudson, N.Y.: Institute of Society, Ethics and the Life Sciences, 1980).

[12]For critical discussions, see, for example, Martin Rein, *Social Science & Public Policy* (Baltimore: Penguin Books, Inc., 1978); C. H. Weiss, "Improving the Linkage Between Social Research and Public Policy," in *Knowledge and Policy: The Uncertain Connection,* ed. by L. E. Lynn, Jr. (Washington, D.C.: National Academy of Sciences, 1978), pp. 23–81; and C. E. Lindblom and D. J. Cohen, *Usable Knowledge: Social Science and Social Problem-Solving* (New Haven, Conn.: Yale University Press, 1979).

research on policy in the twenty-five years since the *Brown v. Board of Education* desegregation decision.[13]

True, critical voices have been raised before. Throughout the last half-century, some have asked whether academic social scientists were as disinterested as they claimed to be. Writers such as Thorstein Veblen, Karl Mannheim, Robert S. Lynd, Gunnar Myrdal, and C. Wright Mills pointed to the various ways in which social background, material interests, political beliefs, and moral concerns entered into the background assumptions, analytical frameworks, and conclusions of mainstream social science. But their critiques failed to have a major impact until the late 1960s and early 1970s. At this point a variety of developments coalesced.

Social ferment, particularly in universities in the industrial world, led to critical questioning of received theories of social science such as "structural functionalism" and marginalist economics. Attacks by thinkers as diverse as Charles Taylor, Herbert Marcuse, Barrington Moore, Jr., Alvin Gouldner, and Richard Bernstein evoked support that had formerly been lacking. Greater openness to philosophy began to characterize several social science disciplines. Major ethical and political discussions focused on particular pieces of empirical social science research, from the secret tape recording of the Wichita juries in the 1950s, through the Moynihan report, the U.S. Army-sponsored research in Chile (called Project Camelot) in the 1960s, to the covert observations of homosexual encounters described in Laud Humphrey's book *Tearoom Trade*, and the Coleman–Pettigrew debate over busing in the 1970s.

In the last fifteen years federal support for social science

[13]D. K. Cohen and M. S. Garet, "Reforming Educational Policy with Applied Social Research," *Harvard Educational Review*, 45 (1975), 17–43.

has increased dramatically, following the enormous increase in federal expenditure on social welfare. New styles of policy research, such as social experimentation and evaluation research, have tended toward the hard, more scientific end of the spectrum of social science methodologies. But the growth of such research has also led to penetrating questions about the ends that were being pursued and the alternatives that might be chosen. Even apparently "scientific" enterprises such as the large-scale negative income tax experiment led to queries about whether the experimenters were not circumscribing the policy options in order to make their work more acceptable to legislators. The applications of social science to public policy raised philosophical questions more fundamental and more problematic than had hitherto been suspected.

ETHICS IN THE WELFARE STATE

Ethical issues underlying social science policy are now firmly on the agenda for public discussion. British experience seems likely to be relevant here, particularly in its tradition of social administration. Why has one particular academic area of study—that of social policy and administration—evolved a markedly different relationship among the social sciences, policy analysis, and the policymaking process, in which ethical concerns figure as central? This discussion is *not* an account of British social science as a whole, or of British sociology or British political science. It focuses on *one* particular field of study in order to examine the relationships between academic social science and public policy.

Social administration has no precise academic parallel in America. Its nearest equivalent in the United States would be a hypothetical department that embraced applied economists, applied sociologists, political scientists interested in policy analysis, social historians of the state provision of welfare, and social philosophers with interests in citizenship and social justice. To my knowledge, no such department exists. Social administration's most remarkable feature is its ability to blend analysis with moral concern to produce a subject of practical import.

Social administration exists in British universities in separate departments of that title, distinct from departments of sociology, political science, and economics. Nor is it to be confused with the teaching of social workers, which is a distinct and separate function. It is interdisciplinary, bringing knowledge from different fields to bear on understanding how welfare policies have developed in fields like housing, education, social services, income maintenance, health, race relations, and social deviance. The contributory disciplines include sociology, psychology, political science, economics, philosophy, history and—in a different relationship—statistics.[14] It is an academic, not a professional, subject, though some undergraduates go on to professional courses in social work later.

Social administration in Britain does not have a monopoly on policy studies. Political scientists study policymaking processes. The field of international relations is, of course, well developed either on its own or as part of political science. On the domestic front, industrial relations is usually taught in separate departments and not covered in social administration teaching. In a few universities there are special departments of criminology and/or race relations, but more usually these

---

[14]For representative texts defining the scope of the subject, see T. H. Marshall, *Social Policy in the Twentieth Century* (New York: Humanities Press, 1975); D. Donnison *et al.*, *Social Policy and Administration Revisited* (London: George Allen & Unwin, Ltd., 1974); and K. Jones *et al.*, *Issues in Social Policy* (London: Routledge & Kegan Paul, Ltd., 1978).

are part of social administration. Though professional social work training is separate, teaching and research on *policy* in the personal social services (that is, the delivery of social work services) *are* part of the field.

There is a close connection between the subject of social administration and the development of the British welfare state. The subject focuses on *identifying social needs* and determining the structure of administration necessary to satisfy them. It studies the nature and distribution of social benefits and social costs, the rights and duties of the citizen both as contributor to and consumer of social services, and the three systems of welfare (social, occupational, and fiscal) that constitute collective intervention to meet selected needs. The administrative structure that meets these needs includes state education, social security, the National Health Service, local authority housing (what Americans call public housing), and other directly administered services and transfer payments. Benefits may be provided—needs may be met—either in cash (for example, social security payments) or in kind (for example, free hospital services), but in all cases government and not the economic market is the allocating agent for rights, duties, and collective consumption. The ideal toward which government is striving is "integrated community services, preventive in outlook and of high quality for all citizens in all areas irrespective of means, social class, occupation or ethnic group."[15]

The academic study of social administration as a distinct subject originated with the growth of the welfare state. The subject developed in British universities in the period after 1945, when large-scale welfare legislation was being passed. In addition to empirical analysis of its actual workings, there

[15]R. M. Titmuss, *Commitment to Welfare* (London: George Allen & Unwin, Ltd., 1968), p. 81.

was direct discussion of philosophical issues. Many of the subject's most distinguished practitioners—Richard Titmuss and Peter Townsend in Britain and Martin Rein in America,[16] to name but three—have emphasized the role that positive value choice has played in the direction of their academic research. Many of its British practitioners have either been active members of the Fabian Society—a small, elite intellectual group of social democrats founded by Beatrice and Sidney Webb and George Bernard Shaw in the 1890s—or have maintained close links with civil servants and politicians in London.[17] Others, coming from a background in economics, have pointed to the operation of market forces in welfare provision and have been less identified with social democratic politics.

At the academic core of the subject is a concept of need, which is philosophical and value-laden in a way that concepts in other subjects (social system in sociology, government and power in political science) are not. It provides a direct link to ethics and an avenue by which ethical criteria may be fed into social science. The importance of this value element has been recognized by leading social scientists such as R. H. Tawney, Gunnar Myrdal, and C. Wright Mills; their writings are widely used in teaching social administration.

"Need" is usually defined with reference to an existing state of affairs and a desired end that is different from the status quo. "To speak of a need is to imply a goal, a measurable deficiency from the goal, and a means of achieving the goal. The goals may be set by some sort of consensus within society, by the person in need 'felt' need) or by experts with a knowledge or specific means for achieving particular

[16]Cf. *inter alia* M. Rein, *Social Policy* (New York: Random House, Inc., 1972); Rein, "Social Science and Public Policy," in *Dilemmas of Social Reform*, ed. by P. Marris and M. Rein, II (London: Routledge & Kegan Paul, Ltd., 1972).
[17]See D. Donnison, "Research for Policy," in *Social Policy Research*, ed. by Martin Bulmer (New York: Humanities Press, 1978) esp. pp. 54–9.

aims."[18] In specifying need several different approaches have been followed, including the postulation of ideal norms ("good health"), minimum standards ("freedom from want"), comparative definitions (cross-national comparisons of low-income groups), or "felt" needs (relative deprivation).

Writers in the British tradition have been readier to employ the concept of need than to analyze it deeply. Recently, they have come under attack from fellow practitioners with backgrounds in economics for indulging in "needology"[19] and for making heavily value-laden statements of the need for more and better public services, whether in the health, housing education, social security, or personal social science fields. Economists such as Alan Williams and A. A. Nevitt urge an approach based on demand rather than need or a redefinition of social needs as "demands which have been defined by society as sufficiently important to qualify for social recognition as goods or services which should be met by government interventions."[20] According to this view, if a social need has not been recognized and converted into a public demand, it behooves those who have identified it to change public taste and show that other goods and services should be deferred in order to meet the new demand that this need creates.

This controversy continues, but both sides recognize that the allocation of resources between competing ends in the social field involves choices that are partly a matter of value judgment. Whether needs or demands are postulated, ethical

---

[18]A. Forder, *Concepts in Social Administration* (London: Routledge & Kegen Paul, Ltd., 1974), p. 39. On need, see also D. Miller, *Social Justice* (New York: Oxford University Press, 1978), parts 4 and 8; and A. J. Culyer, "Economics, Social Policy and Social Administration: The Interplay Between Topic and Discipline," *Journal of Social Policy*, 10 (July, 1981), pp. 311–29.

[19]A. Williams, "'Need' as a Demand Concept," in *Economic Policies and Social Goals*, ed. by A. J. Culyer (London: Martin Robertson, 1974).

[20]A. A. Nevitt, "Demand and Need," in *Foundations of Social Administration*, ed. by H. Heisler (London: Macmillan & Co., Ltd., 1978), p. 115.

criteria are relevant in determining how social priorities should be ranked in allocating resources.

SOCIAL CHOICES IN ALLOCATING RESOURCES

An excellent example of this approach is provided by the last book of Richard Titmuss, the founder of social administration in Britain and undoubtedly its greatest figure. Titmuss was professor of social administration in the Department of Social Science & Administration at the London School of Economics, the leading department in the subject in Britain. He held that post from 1950 until his death at the age of sixty-five in 1973. Titmuss was a most unusual man, not least because he was appointed to the senior chair in the subject without ever having held a university post. Like Robert Park, who came to sociology late by way of journalism, Titmuss was then over forty. Unlike Park, who had a Harvard M.A. and a German Ph.D., Titmuss had no university degree at all and never obtained one (other than honorary degrees). Yet by the time Titmuss died, "he had created a new discipline and was one of the few truly original social scientists of his generation."[21]

The Gift Relationship, published in 1970,[22] is a study of the provision, in different societies, of human blood for transfusion. Medical services require a regular and predictable supply of blood; modern medicine requires blood in even larger quantities. How is that need to be met? To show that different societies meet the need in different ways, Titmuss developed

---

[21]Margaret Gowing, "Richard Morris Titmuss, 1907–1973," *Proceedings of the British Academy,* 61 (1975), 401–28, at p. 401.

[22]Richard M. Titmuss, *The Gift Relationship: From Human Blood to Social Policy* (London: George Allen & Unwin, Ltd., and New York: Random House, Inc., 1970).

an eightfold typology along a continuum from the paid donor at one extreme to the voluntary community donor at the other. The paid donor is motivated solely by the promise of cash compensation; the voluntary community donor strictly by the altruistic desire to give to strangers regardless of what he or she gets in return. In between are various arrangements with different degrees of compensation to the donor in cash or kind or the granting of rights and privileges for the receipt of blood to individuals or groups in return for individual donations. Titmuss concluded that the differences among, say, Britain, the United States, and Russia could not be attributed simply to administrative and organizational structures of blood supply systems and patterns of medical care services. "Different social and political structures and value systems," he argued, "strongly determine" which type of donation is characteristic of a particular society. "Explanations—and admittedly explanations can never be more than partial—have to be sought in the history, the values and the political ideas of each society."[23]

This statement exemplifies a more general principle. Social policy presupposes social choices, which presuppose social values. These values must evolve from widely held attitudes rather than being imposed from above by a power elite. Societies, like individuals, must make choices, and in a democracy these choices must be made collectively. Titmuss says, "Social policy models . . . with all their apparent remoteness from reality, can serve a purpose in providing us with an ideological framework which may stimulate us to ask the significant questions and to expose the significant choices."[24]

The Gift Relationship considered in detail the ease with

[23]Ibid., p. 196.
[24]Richard M. Titmuss, *Social Policy* (London: George Allen & Unwin, Ltd., 1974), p. 136.

which blood is obtained under different systems, its purity, its cost per unit, its perishability (human blood has a "shelf life" of not more than three weeks), and hence its wastage. It also examined who the donors were, and why they sold, lent, or gave their blood. This led to a study of the social relationships involved in blood donation, the "quality of life" implied on the one hand by response to the market and on the other by giving for the general good. In addition to exploring the connection between different systems of blood provision, the book examined the objectives of social policy, altruism in society, and gift relationships—hence the title. Nor was Titmuss wary of prescription. He demonstrated that the national–collectivist blood transfusion system in Britain was far more efficient than the market systems in other societies (such as the United States) on almost any criterion—availability, cheapness, purity of blood, economy in its use. (The blood debate goes on, however, with some critics charging that the American market system is not nearly so disastrous or the British voluntary system so rosy as Titmuss claimed.[25]) Because British donors gave blood entirely on a voluntary basis, with only a cup of tea as their reward, Titmuss linked this finding to a broader philosophical principle, the role of altruism in modern society. Altruism, he argued, is present in many different types of social relationships, including those for social provision. Analytic social changes—such as economics—that fail to identify such social relations have omitted a main motive power in human existence.

A different field of empirical research, the study of poverty, also exemplifies the fusion of moral and philosophical concerns with empirical inquiry. A long British tradition of

[25]Harvey M. Sapolsky and Stan N. Finkelstein, "Blood Policy Revisited—A New Look at *The Gift Relationship*," *The Public Interest*, 46 (Winter, 1977), 15–27.

poverty studies goes back to Henry Mayhew, Charles Booth, and Seebohm Rowntree. In the recent past, several notable inquiries have demonstrated the extent of poverty in contemporary Britain and argued for state action to meet the needs of those living on low incomes. The most notable studies are Brian Abel-Smith and Peter Townsend's *The Poor and the Poorest*[26] and Townsend's *Poverty in the United Kingdom*.[27] The latter makes a considerable theoretical contribution, as do W. G. Runciman's *Relative Deprivation and Social Justice*[28] (which incorporates an explicit discussion of John Rawls) and Dorothy Wedderburn's symposium *Poverty, Inequality, and Class Structure*.[29] These studies will give the American reader the flavor of British social administration. But for those who wish to peruse the wide range of empirical studies in the different specialist fields mentioned earlier, a useful bibliographical guide is available.[30]

DISTINGUISHING TRAITS

What follows is an attempt to roughly summarize the more distinctive features of academic social administration. Because Titmuss was so central in the development of the subject, his work figures prominently. First, social administration is a continuation of a strain in academic social science

[26]Brian Abel-Smith and Peter Townsend, *The Poor and the Poorest* (London: G. Bell, 1962).
[27]Peter Townsend, *Poverty in the United Kingdom* (Berkeley, Calif.: University of California Press, 1979).
[28]W. G. Runciman, *Relative Deprivation and Social Justice* (London: Routledge & Kegan Paul, Ltd., 1966).
[29]D. Wedderburn, ed., *Poverty, Inequality and Class Structure* (Cambridge, England: Cambridge University Press, 1974).
[30]T. Blackstone, ed., *Social Policy and Administration in Britain: A Bibliography* (London: Frances Pinter, 1975).

that sees moral criticism as the legitimate concern of the scholar. Distinguished figures such as Thorstein Veblen, R. H. Tawney, Gunnar Myrdal, John Kenneth Galbraith, and C. Wright Mills, though differing in discipline and orientation, all show a marked philosophical bent in their writing. Similarly, in social administration fundamental debate about society's pruposes and ways of meeting various conditions and circumstances is recognized as a proper part of academic study. In many areas of social policy, radical choices have to be made between competing social values. The realization that ultimately these decisions are made by the executive arm of government and by politicians does not rule out their academic study. Two notable examples of this type of analysis are Rawls's work on justice and Tawney's classic *The Acquisitive Society*. Though more sardonic in tone, some of Veblen's writing might fall into the same class. In the last analysis, Titmuss wrote, human welfare is an ethical concept.

Second, in social administration one of the most important dimensions of choice is the manner in which certain social needs (health care, for example) are to be met: by the individual or by the government? Through individualism or collectivism? Titmuss was originally a Liberal politically, and his belief in collectivism was not a doctrinaire position but arose out of observation of the "enterprise, efficiency and compassion" with which the British central government after Dunkirk and through the blitz met the need for national mobilization.[31] He came to believe strongly in services that were provided universally rather than selectively, services free of social discrimination, services that involved the pooling of risks and the sharing of national resources. The English National Health Service, for all its imperfections, exemplified many of these features.

[31]Gowing, p. 410.

It is important to emphasize that this belief in collectivism was no mere whim or value choice but an integral part of an intellectual enterprise, closely linked to an analysis of the social consequences of industrialism and urbanism for a complex and highly differentiated society. This theme is not unique; Harold L. Wilensky, C. L. Lebaux,[32] and Gaston V. Rimlinger,[33] for example, have developed similar ideas. Such a position contrasts sharply with the individualist tenets of certain other social scientists. A leading economist at the University of Chicago and his wife have recenlty been extolling in the media the virtues of individualism and of the market as mechanisms for resource allocation. Whether he expresses these views in popularizations or in his more scholarly work, Milton Friedman is one among many who builds value premises into the propositions from which his theory is constructed. Within social administration there is lively debate between collectivists and individualists, proponents of the state and of the market, of legislative or voluntary solutions to social welfare provision. Titmuss was a staunch collectivist, but the subject as a whole is no longer collectivist in outlook.

Third, social administration takes as a central theme a concern with citizenship, developing further the seminal ideas of T. H. Marshall.[34] Two important questions to ask of modern industrial societies are: (1) Who is a member of the society?

---

[32]H. L. Wilensky and C. L. Lebaux, *Industrial Society and Social Welfare: The Impact of Industrialization on the Supply and Organization of Social Welfare Service in the United States* (New York: The Free Press, 1965).

[33]C. V. Rimlinger, *Welfare Policy and Industrialization in Europe, America and Russia* (New York: John Wiley & Sons, Inc., 1971).

[34]T. H. Marshall, *Class, Citizenship and Social Development* (Chicago: University of Chicago Press, 1977), esp. chap. 4, "Citizenship and Social Class." See also T. H. Marshall, *The Right to Welfare* (London: William Heinemann, Ltd., 1981).

and (2) What rights do members have? Foreign migrant labor, which now constitutes 12 percent of West Germany's work force and between 2 and 5 percent of the American work force, poses this sort of issue very sharply.[35] Thirty years ago the questions related much more to the position of the working class in Britain and to that of blacks in the United States. An important element in Titmuss's belief in collectivism held that common access to social services was a badge of citizenship, the only way of distributing social rights without discrimination and stigma. Hence this tendency to favor universalism, with positive discrimination to divert resources to the poor, handicapped, and minority groups.[36]

Fourth, a further characteristic of social administration is its social empirical base. Titmuss's early work focused on population and public health in the British tradition of "political arithmetic" (the compilation of statistical data about a society, particularly demographic and sociomedical data). His later work retained this meticulous factual documentation meshed with a broad philosophical perspective.

AN AMERICAN COMPARISON

This very brief and compressed characterization highlights the distinctiveness of the social administraion approach, which should be of interest to American social scientists and policymakers. A comparison of American developments with

[35]Cf. R. C. Rist, *Guestworkers in Germany* (New York: Frederick A. Praeger, Inc., 1978); and M. J. Piore, *Birds of Passage: Migrant Labour and Industrial Societies* (Cambridge, England: Cambridge University Press, 1979).

[36]For a critical discussion of this and many other aspects of Titmuss's work, see the useful essay by David A. Reisman, *Richard Titmuss: Welfare and Society* (London: William Heinemann, Ltd., 1977).

those taking place elsewhere can throw fresh light on the choices open to American social science policy studies at the present time, particularly given the doubts that are being expressed about their general objectives. What can be learned from a comparison with this British tradition?

In the immediate postwar period, America was still markedly individualistic in its approach to welfare provision, with widespread political hostility to extension of government welfare.[37] But since 1965 the proportions of the gross national product spent on social welfare have narrowed between the United States and Britain, with the American share rising. An English academic commenting on America has to beware of presenting a caricature of America as it was fifteen or twenty years ago, though in the health policy field the differences are still extremely marked. One explanation for the development of American policy studies, evaluation research, and social experimentation is surely this enormous increase, particularly in federal government expenditure on social welfare. The consequent academic growth in America has been in "hard" or "harder" social sciences of this type. In Britain this has not been the case.

It is a truism to say that "government" does not mean the same thing in Britain and in America. Not only do the political systems of the two countries differ markedly, but (more relevant here) they differ in the respect accorded to academic experts in each society, in the position of the social sciences, and in institutional support for social sciences. The wide public hearing that social science expertise commands in the United States contrasts with greater skepticism within

---

[37]For a recent comparative discussion, see R. A. Pinker, *The Idea of Welfare* (London: William Heinemann, Ltd., 1979).

the smaller, close-knit world of the British political elite. The relative position has been summed up by Oxford political scientist L. J. Sharpe, who compares the British social scientist visiting America to the English chef visiting Paris.[38]

The connections between social administration and Fabian activism are particularly revealing of the close relationship between the academic and political worlds in England. The Fabian Society embraces Labour politicians, academics, and some civil servants. It is allied loosely to the Labour party but distinct from it. Titmuss was a committed Fabian, as are his contemporary successors such as Abel-Smith and Townsend. (To a British observer it is puzzling that Daniel Patrick Moynihan may move from advising Richard Nixon to become a Democratic senator. In Britain such a change of sides would likely be political suicide.) An illuminating recent study be Keith Banting has shown how close the political and academic links can be and what a marked impact British academic intellectuals had on social policies in relation to poverty, housing, and education during the 1960s.[39] Whether such close links with policymakers and "political administrators" are good for the health of the social sciences is another matter.

The role of theory in the social sciences also differs sharply

[38]L. J. Sharpe, "The Social Scientist and Policy-Making in Britain and America: A Comparison," in *Social Policy Research*, ed. by Martin Bulmer (Atlantic Highlands, N.J.: Humanities Press, 1978), pp. 302–380.

[39]K. Banting, *Poverty, Politics and Policy* (London: Macmillan & Co., Ltd. 1979). The role of social research in the work of British Royal Commissions may play a similar role. See H. Acland, "Research as Stage Management: The Case of the Plowden Committee," in *Social Research and Royal Commissions*, ed. by Martin Bulmer (London: George Allen & Unwin, Ltd., 1980) pp. 34–57. For a more general comparison, see M. Bulmer, "Applied Social Research: The Use and Non-Use of Empirical Social Inquiry by British and American Governmental Commissions," *Journal of Public Policy*, 1 (Autumn, 1981) 353–380.

between the two countries. It may be only a slight exagger-
ation to say that strong theoretical interests and strong applied
interests seem antithetical in the British social sciences. British
sociology is strong on theory, moderate on empirical research,
and notably weak on policy applications. By contrast, social
administration (which historically and departmentally usually
branched off from sociology) is strong on application, moderate on empirical research, and extremely weak on theory.
The absence of scientific rigor in social administration can be
seen as much in the realm of theory as in methodology. Many
of its practitioners conceive of it less as a science than as
humanistic *social* science with strong links to history, philosophy, and ethics. It is not distinguished by a coherent body
of theory, though it does make use of a set of distinctive
concepts that include need, welfare, and citizenship.

As one critic has pointed out, the peculiar blend of empirical data and philosophy thrives at the expense of theory—
"too much is prescribed, too little is explained." Robert Pinker
suggests that "in British social policy and administration we
begin with fact-finding and end in moral rhetoric, still lacking
those explanatory theories that might show the process as a
whole and reveal the relations of the separate problems to
one another."[40] Here British social administration diverges
most markedly from American social science and policy studies. People of the caliber of Merriam and Park gave American
social science its cutting edge by insisting first and foremost
that social science was *science*—not philosophy, not social reform, not history. Whether this goal has been achieved is

[40]R. A. Pinker, *Social Theory and Social Policy* (London: William Heinemann,
Ltd.; and New York: Crane Russak, 1971), esp. chap. 3, "Ideology, Rhetoric
and Evidence." See also M. Bulmer, *The Uses of Social Research: Social Investigation in Public Policy-Making* (London: George Allen & Unwin, Ltd.,
1982), chaps. 1 and 2.

highly debatable, but several generations of social scientists have acted to a considerable extent as if it had succeeded.

Britain and America differ significantly, too, in the place of empirical data and the role of research methodology in social science. Although British social policy research (both academic and governmental) is highly empirical, the use made of empirical data is still largely "empiricist" in the correct (and pejorative) sense of that term; that is, it is based on the view that the facts speak for themselves. Such a view verges on the prescientific in the sense that a data-collecting activity like the census, though providing materials for social science, would not in itself be regarded as social science. Here the differences between Britain and America seem to be greatest. This poses a fascinating question: To what extent is there a tradeoff between scientific rigor and ethical commitment? Does one tend to drive out the other? To what extent can philosophical and ethical premises be introduced explicitly into general frameworks in social science without fundamentally changing the nature of those frameworks? The undoubted strengths of British social administration are its blend of philosophical concerns, historical sense and specificity, and policy focus. But these strengths are achieved at the expense of formal theory and rigorous methodology as those are usually understood, particularly in the United States. Does the former set of characteristics tend to preclude the latter?

Is it possible to integrate formal theory and rigorous methodology with historical and ethical sensitivity? If some American "policy science" reads like arid scholasticism, which does little to illuminate the real world, some British work on social policy reads like moral rhetoric, resisting systematization and methodologically weak. Excessively scientific policy research is equally unattractive, preoccupied with formalization and methodological rigor and without attention to the moral ends of policy or the historical circumstances in which policy is enacted.

Some middle way is surely possible. The overblown claims of "policy science" need to be firmly resisted, and the belief that the social sciences constitute a new "social engineering" must be exposed for the self-serving cant that it is. The social sciences should provide a general framework within which social processes can be examined—the "enlightenment" model.[41] They need not provide definite predictions about the direction of social change or offer technocratic solutions to discrete problems. But the framework must necessarily take account of the ends of social action and deal with the moral dimension of human affairs.

On the other hand, American social science has demonstrated over the last sixty years that methodological standards matter and that empirical inquiry needs to be both rigorous and systematic while also being located within a proper theoretical framework. In these respects, British social administration is singularly inadequate and could greatly strengthen its theoretical and methodological backbone. If the goal of social science is understanding and explanation, much more attention needs to be paid to the structure of the explanations that are being offered. It is possible, for example, for critics to dismiss *The Gift Relationship* as a flawed and polemical moral tract, and there is a slight element of truth in the charge, despite the illustrative empirical material included in it and the overall conviction of the comparative analysis.

Moral concerns do have a place in social policy research,

[41]Cf. the various writings of Morris Janowitz, including his *Sociological Models and Social Policy* (New York: General Learning Systems, 1971); and C. H. Weiss, ed., *Using Social Research in Public Policy* (Boston: D. C. Heath and Company, 1977), chap. 1. The point made here is elaborated in M. Bulmer, "'Engineering' and 'Enlightenment' Models of Applied Social Research," *Knowledge: Creation, Diffusion, Utilisation*, 3 (1981): 187–209.

but this place is not preeminent, as Park and Merriam clearly recognized long ago. If moral concerns are preeminent, as in certain British social policy writing, then the persuasiveness and influence of the writer is significantly weakened, since his or her work can be dismissed as mere emotional rhetoric. The answer is not to discard a moral dimension altogether but to combine it with an adequate theoretical and methodological structure. In this respect, Gunnar Myrdal's magisterial survey of American race relations more than a generation ago, *An American Dilemma*,[42] remains a model of the fusion between ethics and science that is both compelling and methodologically adequate.

---

[42]Gunnar Myrdal, *An American Dilemma: The Negro Problem and Modern Democracy* (New York: Harper & Brothers, 1944).

8

SOCIAL RESEARCH AND POLITICAL ADVOCACY

New Stages and Old Problems in Integrating Science and Values

JEANNE GUILLEMIN AND
IRVING LOUIS HOROWITZ

The study of the relationship between social research and political partisanship is scarcely a novelty. This linkage has characterized investigations in sociology and anthropology for the last fifty years. The work of the prototypical and part-mythical post-World War I Chicago School of W. I. Thomas, R. E. Park, Louis Wirth, and E. C. Hughes, to mention but a few figures, is characterized by a keen sense of accurate reporting, a perspective on the raw materials that raised issues of stratification and societal values, and—in the cases of Park

---

JEANNE GUILLEMIN □ Associate Professor of Sociology, Boston College, Chestnut Hill, Massachusetts 02167.   IRVING LOUIS HOROWITZ □ Hannah Arendt Distinguished Professor of Sociology and Political Science, Livingston Campus, Rutgers—The State University, New Jersey 08903.

and Wirth —strong political recommendations.[1] What distinguishes this earlier phase of social ethnography from later development thus becomes a problem to be discussed, not simply a history to be described.

What sets the past apart from the present is certainly not a matter of sophistication. It would be entirely debatable whether earlier or later forms of ethnography were more intellectually advanced. True enough, new elements arose: more refined methods of research based on survey sampling rather than cartographic sampling, a sense of the national rather than the community context in which ethnography takes place, and an emphasis on different types of populations omitted from reckoning by earlier field studies. These points stated and registered, the heart of the matter has not yet been established. For these are essentially peripheral distinctions, tending to indicate the strength rather than the weakness of linkages between past and present.

An alternative explanation of the differences, one that underscores the basis for this effort, is the meliorative context of the old ethnography and the radical context of the ethnography that followed. Whatever differences there were in the Chicago school types, whatever designation may be assigned to them, they certainly were not revolutionary or manifestly ideological in their political orientation. These researchers believed in the social system—in the ability of the democratic potential of that larger system to correct problems within the subsystems—whether they were problems of deviance, minorities, or urbal blight. Not so the latter post-World War II ethnographers. For their part, they tended to be less concerned with policy inputs than their forebears because they were less convinced that the system contained solutions. In-

[1]Edward Shils, "The Confluence of Sociological Traditions," in *The Calling of Sociology and Other Essays in Pursuit of Learning* (Chicago: University of Chicago Press, 1980), pp. 134–64.

deed, they were often convinced that the system was the problem.[2] The new partisans assumed that the power alliance of the social scientist was with marginal groups whose conditions were direct evidence of trouble at the core of the social system. The new field researchers were armed not simply with ethnographic description but with materials for a weakly formulated but generally leftist political critique. It was during this period, from the mid-1960s to the early 1970s, that advocacy research came to represent a watershed in the history of social scientific domestic policy formulation, presaging the pervasiveness of the language of social science as well as of social scientists themselves in government. For some, belief in political redress was commensurate with a profound distrust of the very government programs from which they were deriving largesse. Identification with the underdog was a means of countering oppression and avoiding personal and political compromise; there could be no policymaking until global revolution arrived. But at this point, a critical problem arose: the revolution never came. Prophecies of doom remained unfulfilled; worse, the new utopia posed by the "other side," usually in the form of socialist bloc countries, failed to indicate anything better. Quite the contrary, as information filtered back, culminating in Aleksandr Solzhenitsyn's *Gulag Archipelago*—a smashing piece of ethnography—it became evident that both revolutionary posturing and meliorative faiths were naive and unconvincing, offering little sustenance to the very groups under the research knife. At the same time, the politicization of outsiders and their incorporation within interest groups obliterated the need for volunteer paraintellectuals. Presented with such a cul-de-sac, the new sociological par-

[2]Kathleen Gough, "Anthropologie et impérialisme," *Les Temps Modernes,* 293–94 (December–January 1970–71) and 299–300 (July–August. 1971). Reprinted in *Anthropologie et imperialisme,* ed. by Jean Copans (Paris: François Maspero, 1975), p. 70.

tisans lost heart and there was a consequent falloff of research in this area. To trace the empirical and normative characteristics of this natural history in the rise and fall of a particular social scientific style of work with a political cutting edge itself becomes a significant aspect in the history of social research.

RESEARCH AND POLICY

In the general context of relevance seeking that has characterized academic life in the postfunctionalist stage and which achieved its maximum impact in the mid-1960s, a small but significant number of sociologists and anthropologists produced accounts of deviant and marginal groups which, as published works, successfully combined tough-minded reporting with tenderhearted indictments of social inequalities. In retrospect, the synthesis of social science and ideology achieved by Goffman,[3] Liebow,[4] Becker,[5] Lewis,[6] Lofland,[7] Humphreys,[8] and other classic ethnographic ventures gave their authors and audience a new potential for social advocacy. The small-scale empirical study of two decades ago opened doors to political action in the name of the group which was described in ways in that earlier, qualitative research had failed to achieve. Crossing the threshold from academic work to practical involvement in the mobilization of deviant and marginal groups proved a direct though not irreversible change of role from scientific observer to social actor.

[3]Erving Goffman, *Asylums: Essays on the Social Situation of Mental Patients and other Inmates* (Chicago: Aldine Publishing Company, 1962).
[4]Elliot Liebow, *Talley's Corner* (Boston: Little, Brown and Company, 1967).
[5]Howard S. Becker, *Outsiders: Studies in the Sociology of Deviance* (New York: The Free Press, 1973).
[6]Oscar Lewis, *La Vida* (New York: Random House, Inc., 1968).
[7]John Lofland, *Doomsday Cult: A Study of Conversion, Proselytization and Maintenance of Faith* (New York: Halsted/Wiley, 1977.
[8]Laud Humphreys, *Tearoom Trade: Impersonal Sex in Public Places* (Chicago: Aldine Publishing Company, 1970).

The current sharp decrease in this type of ethnography in the 1980s, and the corresponding decline of partisan roles it so well facilitates, raises abundant questions about the complex relationship between social science methods, ideological commitment, and political advocacy. Paramount is the contextual question: Under what circumstances does a particular kind of ideological persuasion appear fully to inform all phases of social science work—from posing the research question to proposing policy? The effect of partisanship on the quality of academic performance is one central issue, insofar as the partisan role demands zealous adherence to a cause even at the expense of the quality of research performed.[9] Advocacy as a commitment expressed in specific acts of counsel, intercession, and public defense raises parallel questions of professional integrity in empirical research and in the use of knowledge to legitimize one or another interest.

The atmosphere in the 1980s is one of divided opinion about the uses of social science information by growing numbers of practitioners—economists, psychologists, sociologists, political scientists—actively engaged in policy-related research and analysis. Like the proverbial "gentleman" unconsciously speaking in prose, social scientists often advocate policy without knowing it. From one perspective, the definition and resolution of social policy problems are best left to the government, with the social scientist offering nonpartisan information.[10] From another perspective, social scientists preserve their critical expertise by maintaining university affiliations while independently addressing policy issues.

Since social scientists have served in a variety of advocacy

[9]Howard S. Becker and Irving Louis Horowitz, "Radical Politics and Sociological Research: Observations on Methodology and Ideology," *American Journal of Sociology*, 76 (July, 1972), 48–66.
[10]Daniel P. Moynihan, *Maximum Feasible Misunderstanding* (New York: The Macmillan Company, 1969); and Harold Orlans, *Contracting for Knowledge* (San Francisco: Jossey-Bass, Inc., Publishers, 1973).

roles, responding first to the government market in programs for the needy and then to drift toward cost-benefit assessment, this distinction between the polity and the academy becomes somewhat strained. To chart the huge penetration by social psychologists and sociologists of the federal bureaucracy in the 1960s is to understand how these particular personnel came to represent a constituency and even to create an articulate interest group demanding still wider access to government. In the late 1970s and continuing into the present, the larger role of institutions like Brookings, American Enterprise Institute, or the presidential Council on Economic Affairs indicates a shift of emphasis not simply toward economists and away from sociologists but toward a belief in a savings and work policy and away from a spending and welfare policy. There are lags and inconsistencies in these patterns. But as a general rule, it is fair to say that the period between 1960 and 1972 witnessed a large-scale sociological penetration of government, and the period from 1973 to the present saw a corresponding rise of the economic penetration of government.[11] Of course, social scientists from the various fields can and do accommodate changing fiscal policies, but the selective emphasis contributes to the articulation of those policies.[12]

According to one set of critics,[13] the ascendance of economic theories and methods has produced conflict over policy alternatives. Constructive policy decisions are undermined by the multiple dissection of issues as if only data—of which

[11]Irving Louis Horowitz and James Everett Katz, *Social Science and Public Policy in the United States* (New York: Frederick A. Praeger, Inc., 1975), pp. 159–78.

[12]Irving Louis Horowitz, ed., *Constructing Policy: Dialogues with Social Scientists in the Modern Political Arena* (New York and London: Praeger Publishers/ Holt, Rinehart and Winston/CBS, Inc., 1979).

[13]Steven E. Rhoads, *Valuing Life: Public Policy of Dilemmas* (Boulder, Colo.: Westview Press, 1980); and Paul F. Lazarsfeld and Jeffrey G. Reitz, *An Introduction to Applied Sociology* (New York: Elsevier Publishing Co., Inc., 1975).

there is never enough to justify action—mattered. This tendency to precise but partial analysis based on statistics alone blocks the open expression or admission of ideology while feeding the national mood to delay innovations by introducing new and costly health and welfare programs.[14] The constraints of a savings policy have undoubtedly curtailed long-range planning and forced the transformation of ideology into interpretations of statistical tables. This has not prevented thousands of social scientists from implementing, evaluating, and regulating existing programs as well as participating in occasional dismantlings and innovations; presumably they act according to identifiable sets of social values, overt or covert. The difference in the present decade, under the Reagan administration, as opposed to ten or fifteen years ago is the difficulty of predicting the responses of any group of social scientists or intellectuals to a controversial issue or of placing them professionally in one or another political camp. Just as American liberalism has been eclipsed by the new mood of conservatism, the easy association of past and future academics with a presumed liberal Democratic party has vanished, leaving behind a more extensive and complex network of social science and government connections than ever dreamed of in the Kennedy–Johnson years. Both the character of government largesse and the sentiments of its recipients have changed. Federal funds are sought in the 1980s much more vigorously and with far fewer qualms than in the late 1960s.

FROM PRAGMATISM TO RADICAL IMPERATIVES

As an empirical method, field research is sorely out of fashion except in those few select areas that involve community-impact studies. The length of time it takes to do fieldwork—a two-year immersion according to classical anthro-

---

[14]Henry J. Aaron, *Politics and the Professors: The Great Society in Perspective* (Washington, D.C.: The Brookings Institution, 1978), pp. 16–64.

pological tenets—the high yield of qualitative information, and problems with scientific reproducibility are deficits in an information market seeking quick statistical returns and even quicker fixes. Not only the investment of protracted time but the development of international ties and a sense of identification with the community and group members distinguishes the ethnographer from the social scientist who works at a greater informational remove from the people whose behavior he or she studies. While methods scarcely predict ideology, the association of ethnography with liberal pluralism did emerge in recent past history, not in its politically quiescent form as nostalgia for the traditional community but as part of a ground swell of social criticism and interest-group support.

The first half of this century witnessed the development of a Chicago school of sociology; a tradition of investigatory field research coupled with a populist view of the social order. In the two decades following World War II the polarization of sociology into the Columbia–Harvard camp, stressing universalistic value in the profession of sociology, and the softening orientation of the Chicago school also represented a methodological drawing of lines between the former's qualitatively geared positivism and the latter's attempts to develop a pragmatic package that contained not only hard data but also ethnographic observations and value orientations.[15]

The Chicago school of ethnography was postulated as a unique, even laudatory definition of the nature of human groups, which profoundly dictated the researcher's relationship to such groups. At Michigan, Charles Horton Cooley's early articulation of the humanizing function of society af-

[15]Irving Louis Horowitz, "Social Science and Public Policy: Implications of Modern Research," in *The Rise and Fall of Project Camelot: Studies in the Relationship Between Social Science and Practical Politics* (Cambridge, Mass.: The M.I.T. Press, 1967), pp. 339–76.

firmed the moral value of the small, semirural community, placing ultimate worth on prolonged social interaction among primary groups over substantive judgments of a group's wider activities as either illegal or deviant. Mills's perception of the conservatism inherent in Cooley's community definition of "moral order" remains quite relevant: "The notion of disorganization is quite often merely the absence of the *type* of organization associated with the stuff of primary-group communities having Christian and Jeffersonian legitimations."[16] The bias favoring a notion of community order notwithstanding, detailed reporting of social cohesiveness among such unlikely populations as slum dwellers, criminals, immigrants, and racial and ethnic minorities became a widely adopted characteristic of social research in the Midwest. Sociology as a Christian calling served to validate a general notion of moral order even among deviant populations.

The research investigations of faculty and graduate students alike were underwritten by a belief in the responsibility of social scientists to make a contribution to the populist revision of the notion of social order. The pragmatism of men like Louis Wirth, Robert E. Park, Walter Reckless, and Everett C. Hughes rested on a new populist undercurrent. They wrote not only about urbanization as a source of criminal behavior but also about how crime can be minimized and channelized, not only about Negro–white relations but also about how, through mutual support, such relations can be humanized. Their sociological commitment was strongly influenced by their belief in political and moral reform.

It took a major confluence of historical circumstances in the 1960s to give ethnographic information the power of gen-

---

[16]C. Wright Mills, "The Professional Ideology of Social Pathologists" (1943), in *Power, Politics and People: The Collected Essays of C. Wright Mills*, ed. by Irving Louis Horowitz (New York: Oxford University Press, 1963), pp. 525–52.

eralization and to increase opportunities for the researcher to assume an activist role. Herbert Kalman concisely summarized what he experienced as the three major changes in postwar conditions in the United States that touched every area of academic work.[17] First, there was the weakening of barriers against speaking out as McCarthyist forces became discredited and a new generation of uncautious students forged by the civil rights movement added impetus to activism. Second, the interplay of knowledge and values became redefined as the central business of the university, with students demanding greater relevance and also with faculty taking their own political assumptions more seriously. Third, there developed a sense of urgency about social science participation in political change which complemented the heightened feelings of social responsibility. The war in Vietnam, East–West nuclear confrontations, and international race and class struggles involving the Third World fueled the volatile atmosphere of the time.

The need for information about who had been bearing the burden of political and economic inequities was filled in great measure by reform-minded figures who were relatively marginal to academic life and certainly not viewed as central to the historic evolution of sociology and ethnography. Set to wage a domestic war on poverty, the War on Poverty proceeded with practically no aggregate data identifying who the poor were, why they were poor, or what might best be done about it. In this statistical vacuum, the broad general statements of John Kenneth Galbraith,[18] Michael Harrington,[19]

---

[17]Herbert C. Kelman, *A Time to Speak: On Human Values and Social Research* (San Francisco: Jossey-Bass, Inc., Publishers, 1967), pp. 300–305.

[18]John Kenneth Galbraith, *The Affluent Society* (2nd rev. ed.; Boston: Houghton Mifflin Co., 1969).

[19]Michael Harrington, *The Other America* (New York: The Macmillan Company, 1952).

Dwight Macdonald,[20] and, somewhat earlier, Gunnar Myrdal[21] and Herbert Gans[22] were supported by sympathetic ethnographic accounts of disadvantaged groups.

The only serious challenge to this poverty model of any policy consequence in the 1960s concerned the "culture of poverty" hypothesis versus environmental influences. This was based on the formulations of anthropologist Oscar Lewis. Detailed descriptions of the daily lives of blacks, Mexicans, Puerto Ricans, lower-class groups, and deviant people provided evidence corroborating social inequities which were not only statistically undocumented but experientially beyond the ken of most Americans. The works of Lewis in particular persuaded powerful elements of the cultivated new class that the poor lived and that they might live better and more freely with their help. These beliefs became a matter of social convention which went considerably beyond either professionally defined commitments or scientifically gathered evidence.

For those ethnographers who took up the mantle of partisanship, the means for further weakening barriers against speech and activism were cast in terms of ideological ultimates. Laud Humphreys, in mandating the liberal position on activism, wrote: "If those he studies cry out for liberation [the researcher] . . . must help with that liberation—and on their terms."[23] Actual confrontation with sources of actual authority—police, prison systems, information agencies, and foreign government officials—matched in drama the new rhetoric of radical moral imperatives for field workers. Yet

---

[20]Dwight Macdonald, *Discriminations: Essays and Afterthoughts* (New York: Grossman Publishers, 1974).

[21]Gunnar Myrdal *et al.*, *An American Dilemma: The Negro Problem and Modern Democracy* (New York: Harper & Brothers, 1944).

[22]Herbert Gans, *Urban Villagers: Group and Class in the Life of Italian Americans* (New York: The Free Press, 1962).

[23]Myron Glazer, *The Research Adventure* (New York: Random House, Inc., 1976), p. 160.

when the pertinent social scientific question of specific goals for social change was asked, the unmasking function of ethnographic reportage appeared to have less to do either with revolution or reform than with the capitulation of dedicated amateurs and paraprofessionals to civil servants in the business of social reform.[24]

THE DECLINING VALUE OF SOCIAL SCIENCE AS INFORMATION

The most surprising phenomenon of the times was the rapidity with which the revelatory characteristics of social research and analysis, that aspect which Peter Berger called "the first wisdom of sociology,"[25] would fail as negotiable policy currency. The golden age of social research as partisanship in the 1960s and early 1970s was not coincident only with the liberalism of the War on Poverty but, more important, also with the actual expansion of social services predicated on the local community as the focus of programs engineered at the federal level. By the early 1970s several truths had emerged. For one, it was patently obvious that once marginal groups could generate their own framework for organization on which to base entitlement, they could make a strong bid for government recognition, representation, and support quite without sociological advocates. The initial mobilization of ethnic groups, drug users, homosexuals, prisoners, women, and the aged may have required the legitimizing participation of social scientists; but the broadening of channels of appeal appeared to eliminate the necessity for scholarly validation. Social science was thereby reduced from

[24]Alvin W. Gouldner, "The Sociologist as Partisan: Sociology and the Welfare State," *The American Sociologist*, 3 (1968) 103–16.
[25]Peter L. Berger, *Invitation to Sociology: A Humanistic Persepctive* (Garden City, N.Y.: Anchor Books, Doubleday & Company, Inc., 1962).

advocacy to testimony[26] or sometimes testimony as advocacy.[27]

From the standpoint of American communities and organizations, political invisibility ceased to be a problem, since government categories for program recipients had proliferated. The central point of tension became competition with other groups of similar outlook wishing to allocate resources, a competition that disallowed impartial, potentially critical long-term research by social scientists and lent to marginal groups the same defensive restrictions—what Everett Hughes described as "protecting the secrets of the temple" associated with bureaucratic organizations. In this changing scenario, the partisan role of the field researcher has been sharply revealed as action in the interest of others rather than in the interests of a profession or for a larger cause or vision of society. The gentle academic phrasing of social research as an opportunity to break down the hierarchy of credibility that slights the perspectives of the disadvantaged[28] succumbed to reconstruct social science morally and politically for the sake of practical service.

Some pressure groups came from within and relied on a moral construction of the class struggle. In the rhetoric of the late 1960s, scholarly investigations within an advocacy framework as such were denounced as "ripoffs"—aiding and abetting the repression of the poor. In one of the more extreme posturings along this line, Nicklaus wrote: "Sociology has risen on the blood and bones of the poor and oppressed. It owes its prestige in this society to its putative ability to give

[26]Lawrence Rosen, "The Anthropologist as Expert Witness," *American Anthropologist*, 79 (1977), 555–78.

[27]Howard S. Becker, "Whose Side Are We On?" *Social Problems*, 14 (1967), 240–41.

[28]Marvin Wolfgang, "The Social Scientist in Court," *Journal of Criminal Law and Criminology*, 65 (1974), 239–47.

information and advice to the ruling class of this society about ways and means to keep the people down."[29] Short of a total retreat from empirical research, social ethnographers have had little choice but to let the definition of the fieldwork contract rest exclusively with informants as they saw the potential use of social science. For social anthropologists with ties to native American tribal organizations, there were obligatory responses to personal calls to do research on topics defined by the group, whatever the merits of the claims.[30]

In overseas analysis, political upheavals were invariably attended by severe indictments of the complicity of social scientists with colonial regimes. The demands of the natives took on a frightening cast: "The pacific or pacified objects of our investigation, primitives and peasants alike, are even more prone to define our field situation gun in hand."[31] At home and abroad, social scientists became identified with the translation of public service priorities to the community level, an *ipso facto* redemption via national government contracts or employment by local groups. The intellectual and professional price for continued ethnographic access has been high. Major comparative work which would relieve community and small-group studies of their unstinting resistance to generalization has not been forthcoming, nor has the successful integration of qualitative and quantitative methods or an historical appreciation of national development emerged from the numerous efforts in applied research.

Post-Vietnam War ethnography of America was hard hit by waning faith in local-level administration of programs for

[29]Martin Nicklaus, "Remarks at the American Sociological Association Convention," *The American Sociologist*, 4 (1968), 154–6.

[30]June Helm, "Long-Term Research Among the Dogrib and Other Dene," in *Long Term Field Research in Social Anthropology*, ed. by George M. Foster (New York: Academic Press, 1979), pp. 145–63.

[31]Eric R. Wolf, "American Anthropologists and American Society," in *Reinventing Anthropology*, ed. by Dell Hymes (New York: Random House, Inc., 1969), pp. 257–8.

the poor and by the expansion of PPBS (planning, programming, and budgeting system) as a predominantly cost-benefit
evaluation effort of the Office of Economic Opportunity and
the Department of Health, Education, and Welfare. Support
for community autonomy emerged only fleetingly in President
Nixon's 1972 campaign, and then with disatrous consequences, by the decentralization of the Bureau of Indian Affairs.[32] The pullback from the local community was based in
part on the locus of reform moving upward from the local to
the national level. More accurately, the notion of federally
generated reform was abandoned even as the size of the social
service administration continued to grow and federal funds
continued to flow into state and local agencies.

Justification for cutbacks in certain parts of poverty programs was sought and found in the program planning methodology, the cost-effectiveness effort instituted simultaneously with the War on Poverty. The outcome for expenditures
on community-level and neighborhood programs consistently
failed to meet cost–benefit criteria.[33] Evaluators cast doubt on
the entire relationship between policy and social change. Results meant not only that the poor were getting the same
quality of educational and health services as the nonpoor but
that these services were meeting some new tests of effectiveness that had never before been applied. In this exercise, the
poor served as pawns in the contest to reform all government
policies—in which the best became the enemy of the good.
Appraisals of the budget against poverty became entangled
with discoveries that the links between educational spending
and learning and between medical care outlays and health
are not clear.[34]

[32]Jeanne Guillemin, "Federal Policies and Indian Politics," *Society*, 17 (May
    1980), 29–34.
[33]Rita D. Berkson, "Community Health Centers After Fifteen Yea ., ' *Health/
    PAC Bulletin*, 12, (June 1980), 6–14.
[34]Robert J. Lampman, "What Does it Do for the Poor? A New Test for National
    Policy," *Public Interest*, 34 (1974), 74–75.

The command that government agency and department heads exert over research has permitted contract houses to do the bulk of policy work, if only because the intellectual fit is far better between the federal bureaucracy and Abt, Rand, Bendix, or Systems Development Corporation than between the same bureaucracy and a university environment where time frames are looser and the preemptive claims to generate extraneous, apparently nontarget knowledge are protected. The net effect of the increasing bureaucratization of channels of funding and program evaluation has been even sharper competition among organizations and communities acting as special interests totally resistant to nonpartisan inquiry which exposes them to closer observation. Even if the researcher is sympathetic, qualitative data alone offer more informational chaff than grain and are virtually useless in holding the attention of officials or generating models of change.

POWER AND CLOSURE IN RESEARCH

The double jeopardy of the field researcher is inherent in the methodological problem raised by the researcher being subject to the group's definition of issues and yet preventing the methodological approach from becoming too unwieldy (i.e., dealing with cultural entities rather than social aggregates); the deficit is shared less by those social scientists employing strictly quantitative methods. Nonetheless, the restraints that influence the potential for empirical research in fieldwork have equal repercussions for other academic research ventures. The allocation of power is increasingly defined by the flow and control of information. It is a crucial matter in any inquiry, and its transformations directly affect the empirical base of social scientific thought. The political activation of deviant groups, from homosexuals to drug users to pederasts, has profoundly transformed their image; where they once appeared to be among the helpless, needy, submerged sectors of American society, they are now seen as robust interest groups, competing on an equal footing with other groups, from antiabortionists to antinuclear activists. But this also signifies a deep change in the research posture that social scientists can take toward these presumably marginal groups. It raises new questions about how these groups perceive what social scientists can still do for them. As the price of entrance into future research projects, social scientists are being asked to become increasingly partisan, (e.g., researchers have to declare their homosexuality and not simply describe the homosexual "scene"). Access remains a big issue for social researchers. The social scientists for their part want the taste of victory, a sense that their activities have directly and organizationally been responsible for changes in social attitudes and political dominance. Self-declarations become a simple way to achieve both research and emotional ends.

There is a more subtle aspect to this partisan role: in every interaction the possibility always exists of "going native"—not only in the traditional overseas sense of becoming romantically attached to the Kwakiutl or Trobrianders but in terms of beliefs in the context of advanced societal research. If an Eric Lincoln or John Howard studies the Black Muslims, the belief system of the group may well prevail or modify the structure of social scientific reporting. Higher values may prevail—racial or religious identification in these cases. Ethnography invariably exposes the relativity of power: it turns out that welfare mothers are not as helpless or hapless as early researchers would have had it. Homosexual communities are not huddling in closets or on dark streets. Street gangs, in fact, have a good deal to say about turf ownership in ghettoes. As a result, the researcher comes to a point where he or she must identify not so much with powerlessness as a sympathetic value but with forms of power that have an attraction and a magnetism of their own. The same situation holds true for overseas work. The articulation of local groups with a central government which has its own agenda for development makes scholarly investigation a personal mission on the part of the ethnographer who otherwise should be aiding agricultural development, population control, or labor organization. Advocacy for informants becomes a manifest political act, one of clear partisanship, which must often take place outside the national context in which research has been done— as in pleas for the protection of the Amazon tribes[35] or against the Indonesian government's military attacks on East Timor.[36]

The power of local groups to detach researchers from an impersonal scholarly model and draw them into the political model has parallels in entire range of interest groups. This corresponds to the power of other bureaucratic institutions to impose all-or-nothing conditions of access—to claim allegiance or reject the intrusion of social scientific inquiry. Such regulated institutions as hospitals, prisons, mental instituions, and schools have evolved a defensive attitude toward researchers and, unless otherwise convinced, will restrict access on the basis of claims to protect inmates and clients. A nonpartisan report or survey may involve the release of particularly dangerous information if an institution is already dealing with regulatory review and is heavily dependent on government funding for its survival.

The capacity of social scientists to reveal unknown, unseen, or unexamined aspects of institutional life has been severely reduced by the compromises demands—under threat of exclusion from research sites—for permission to do research, such as an adherence to confidentiality that protects not primarily individual subjects but the institution itself. In-

[35]Shelton H. Davis, *Victims of the Miracle: Development and the Indians of Brazil* (Cambridge, England: Cambridge University Press, 1978).
[36]Shepard Forman, "Human Rights in East Timor," *Society*, 15 (July, 1978), 78–80.

stead of sociological "unmasking," with its academic tone, journalistic exposure and legal advocacy have become the *modus operandi* for informing the public about what transpires behind the doors of nursing homes, schools for the retarded, and intensive care units. As one indication of the current restructuring of access, a most effective way of obtaining research information comes from participation in legal cases and court-ordered investigations.

The climate of institutional organization has been deeply affected by federal review and regulation in a way that ultimately can deny both public interest and social research. In such institutions, managerial problems, failure to deliver services, and changes in the definitions of problems are inadmissible because they jeopardize assessment and funding. The same problems in the private sector have fueled the activities of industrial sociologists for years and continue to do so. The public rendering of accounts takes place in a political context of intense positivism, of a decline in officially sponsored reform, and in a bureaucratic context that frowns on support to such deviant projects. In other words, as social pressures urge increased identification of the investigator with the investigated, the need for fiscal support argues in favor of value neutrality.

In yet other arenas where social scientists might seek written records and information on behavior, either empirical data are inaccessible or the coercive power of the group threatens the autonomy of the individual researcher. Certain religious cults are in this category insofar as they resist inquiry or demand life membership. Government organizations, such as the Department of Defense and the Pentagon, have both the power of secrecy and general coercive power to restrict access and will therefore offer nothing but externalized public stances on which the internal organization of decision making can only be conjectured.

The ideal classical component of social research, "a description of culture in such a way that we feel that we are dealing with real and specific men and women, with real and specific situations, and with real and specific tradition,"[37] is now construed as a threat to social life if not a violation of the right to privacy. Concurrently, the empirical basis of the social sciences has shifted to survey data. The repercussions for members of the different disciplines who confront issues of science and values have been complex. The best times offered us a plurality of consulting roles in government and a profusion of research opportunities not only in governmental service but also in law and industry. Each option for engagement in public interest problems presents a secondary option to assume an advocacy position which will mitigate the struggle between nonpartisan professionalism and ideology.

The range of advocacy roles is great. We have seen and still do see in ethnographic work the singular reality in the investigatory spectrum where the hazards of sacrificing social science to political action on behalf of others become manifest. There are other varities of advocacy that deserve discussion because they illuminate both the universality of the struggle to integrate knowledge and values and the choice of postures that seem to resolve the dilemma; the latter, however, invariably promise more than they deliver.

First, advocacy can mean active partisanship or, more aptly, participation in political parties or causes. In the cases of earlier committed scholars such as V. F. Claverton[38] or Bernhard Stern,[39] there was a strong presumption that ad-

---

[37]Paul Radin, *The Method and Theory of Ethnology* (original ed., 1933; New York: Basic Books, Inc., Publishers, (1965), pp. 22–46.

[38]V. F. Calverton, ed., *The Making of Man: An Outline of Anthropology* (New York: Modern Library, Inc., 1931).

[39]Bernhard J. Stern, *Historical Sociology: The Selected Papers of Bernhard J. Stern* (New York: Citadel Press, 1960).

vocacy, as part of the tide of history, serves to inform social research and create the basis of objective truth. For others, such as Peter Berger and Murray Weidenbaum, membership in the Republican party does not at all guarantee such scientific truths. In this approach, membership is simply isomorphic with the belief system of the scholar.

Second, advocacy in a slightly less obvious sense has to do with social movements that turn political (e.g., deviant movements or welfare mothers' movements). Scholars like Laud Humphreys not only write about homosexual communities but also participate in the propagation of homophile societies. Others like Frances Fox Piven and Richard Cloward[40] likewise participated in the organizational phase of the welfare rights movement.[41] At this level the presumption is that to write about such outside groups is to accept some mandate to participate in rectifying the problems written about.

Third, advocacy in a still weaker form has a positivist gloss—a tacit assumption that to write about outside groups in an empathetic manner invites broad support for such groups. Bitter ethnography in itself makes for higher public receptivity. In this category we find academics like Howard S. Becker[42] on drug users and John Lofland[43] on cult groups. Although there is no explicit presumption mandating the use of drugs or enlistment in cults, there is a hope that their writings will elicit broad public support or eventual legislative relief.

Fourth, there are scholars for whom research and advocacy have absolutely nothing organic to do with each other.

[40]Frances Fox Piven and Richard Cloward, *Regulating the Poor: The Functions of Public Welfare* (New York: Pantheon Books, Inc., 1971).

[41]Guida West, *The National Welfare Rights Movement: The Social Protest of Poor Women* (New York: Praeger/CBS Publishing, 1981), pp. 292–4, 303–4.

[42]Howard S. Becker, *Outsiders: Studies of the Sociology of Deviance* (New York: The Free Press, 1973).

[43]John Lofland, *Doomsday Cult: A Study of Conversion, Proselytization and Maintenance of Faith* (Englewood Cliffs, N.J.: Prentice-Hall, Inc., 1966).

Facts and values are distinct. Yet values or citizenship roles are perfectly acceptable and carry greater weight precisely because of the presumed objectivity of the scientists involved. Hence, social scientists like Robert Bierstadt can function as members of the executive board of the American Civil Liberties Union without forfeiting any claims to objectivity in the research process.

Fifth, there are individuals who become part of the policy apparatus or the political mechanism, such as Daniel Patrick Moynihan[44] and Henry Kissinger.[45] For such people, social research is a sensitizing device and a preliminary training agency for the political life which helps make for better and richer decision making. There is a clear recognition that social science information is important, but that it remains relatively neutral with respect to mandating certain courses of action. However, the main commitment, the way in which such individuals make a living or do work, involves shifting directly from an academic to a political locus, quite unlike members of the previous four categories who remain attached to academic social science research.

The types of advocacy roles a social scientist can play clearly extend in practice beyond these model categories. Therefore, the question of social science's impact on policy becomes more a matter of individual participation in the process of decision making than of a bloc force of intellectuals whose total influence can be characterized in terms of a single ideology. The easy association of academics with liberal causes cannot be taken as a given, as it was ten or fifteen years ago. The entire political base for action—the party system, the or-

---

[44]Daniel P. Moynihan, *Maximum Feasible Misunderstanding* (New York: The Macmillan Company, 1969).

[45]Henry Kissinger, *The White House Years* (Boston: Little, Brown and Company, 1979, and *Years of Upheaval* (Boston: Little, Brown and Company, 1982).

ganization and relations of federal and state governments, and the needs and wants of the polity—have undergone drastic changes from Johnson to Reagan. Party affiliation no longer determines how an elected official votes on public welfare or foreign policy or how citizens judge issues or political performance. New oppositions—between the Sun Belt and the Frost Belt and between old allies and even old enemies on the international front—have evolved in innovative and unanticipated ways. In the meanwhile the education and social service sectors are, at all levels except that of the community, more intellectually problematic than could have been imagined twenty years ago.

The lack of ideological consensus among intellecutals or of intellectual consensus among ideologues is much less worrisome as a phenomenon than observable inroads on the firm empirical foundation of social science research by which informed by policy decisions can be made. Closure in scholarly research opportunities, loss of comparative perspective, and emphasis on a single, quantitative methodology will have the ultimate effect of changing the nature of social science influence in government rather than canceling it out. As Lindblom and Cohen remind us, the continuation of research efforts is the major social science contribution to policy and to social change. The principal impact of policy-oriented studies—say, on inflation, race conflict, deviance, or foreign policy—including those studies specifically designed to advise a specific policymaker at a particular time, is through their contribution to a cumulating set of incentives for a general reconsideration by policymakers of their decision-making framework, their operation political or social philosophy, or their ideology.[46]

The burden of these remarks examining the historical

---

[46]Charles E. Lindblom and David K. Cohen, *Usable Knowledge: Social Science and Social Problem Solving* (New Haven, Conn.: Yale University Press, 1979), pp. 5–6.

antecedents of activism in social research is to show how different types of advocacy are employed to give social science an extra push in the direction of those values deemed beneficial to the future well-being of humankind. But despite the deep weakness in any one form of partisanship, it would be inappropriate to conclude on a note of extreme relativism. To do so would merely serve to cast doubt on social research as a whole and to accept at face value the argument that since scientists have values, all research is *a priori* value-saturated to a point beyond hope. More dangerous yet is to deny the universality of science, to assert instead that the essential difference between the social and physical sciences is that the former are irretrievably connected to subjectivity, relativity, and partisanship, and hence must simply be harnessed to one or another form of ideology, whether that be expressed in terms of the maintenance of divine institutions or of climbing aboard a mythical railroad of history.

The scientific standpoint remains relevant for social research as it delivers messages to the political system. That standpoint is simple enough: whatever be the disputation of any court of enquiry, legal edicts, professional sanctions, political obligations, or religious persuasions, the earth will continue to orbit about the sun in terms of laws observed with respect to the motion of all celestial bodies. While one cannot seriously assert the same universal, lawlike status for findings of social research, it is still possible to come reasonably close. Ideology may remain a stimulus and a prod to good research as well as poor research, but the test of the quality of research remains the experiential context and evidential base of ethnography and inquiry generally.

If social scientists forfeit the right to criticize the political establishment from a posture of autonomy, they risk becoming agents of the political apparatus, whatever the level of policy engagement. The concept of evidence on which research is based is the fundamental guarantee for professional autonomy. In its strength, it stands as a protection against the subversion of social science to a partisan model for promulgating certain kinds of persuasions and beliefs. The appeal to empirics is itself the essential, nay the quintessential, social scientific response to the relativity of beliefs, values, and postures found in social research. If science is the source of so many questions about the advocacy status of findings and events, it also offers the means of resolving ideological disputes and partisan differences.

IDEOLOGY, INTERESTS, AND INFORMATION

The Basis of Policy Positions

CAROL H. WEISS

What used to be called applied social research and is now commonly called policy research is a large, multiform, and complex enterprise. In essence, it is the application of social science concepts and methods to the study of issues on the practical agenda, these days commonly on the agenda of government decision makers. Over the years, it has been the object of grandiose hopes and doleful disappointments.

HISTORICAL VIEWS OF POLICY RESEARCH

Expectations for policy research have always been embedded in an image of how political positions are taken and political decisions made. The social scientists who engage in policy research, their sponsors in government and foundations, and the people on the sidelines cheering them on have all tended to believe that policy research would add a

CAROL H. WEISS □ Harvard Graduate School of Education, Cambridge, Massachusetts 02138.

measure of rationality to the hurly-burly of policymaking. By providing objective evidence, such research would counteract the special pleading and selfish interests that seemed to dominate the political process. Somehow it was expected that however self-seeking politicians might be and however cautious and inert public bureaucracies might be, research would be above the fray. By producing objective, valid, nonpolitical data and conclusions, research would win attention on its merits and help to overcome the excesses of "politics" in its most pejorative sense. Research was a quintessentially rational way to help solve policy problems. Although political actors were often irrational, as these observers saw it, they would somehow *have* to use the evidence that research provided. Why they would use it—in violation of all their accustomed modes of operation—was not clear, but the tacit assumption seemed to be "because it was there."

Since long before the Progressive Era, reformers have taken on faith the adage that knowledge is power. They assumed that adding to the stock of knowledge about social conditions, causes of social problems, and strategies effective for their amelioration would have a beneficent effect on the direction of public policy. In the early years of the century, progressives were intent on compiling data about such issues as the ravages of child labor and the prevalence of industrial accidents in order to make their case for reform. Implicit was the belief that once the society knew, really *knew*, the facts and figures of social disorganization, corrective action would inevitably follow. A horrified citizenry would rise up to demand and ensure action. Implicit, too, was the belief that the reformers had the solution to the problems in hand. All that was needed in the way of research was documentation of the extent and distribution of the problem. Then enlightened citizens would adopt their solution and see that it was enacted into law.

With the 1950s and early 1960s, two new strands were added to the still largely implicit argument. Research managers in foundations and government agencies and social scientists concerned about the political consequences of their work still tended to assume that funding and doing relevant research were all that mattered. Once people realized the situation, the nature of deliberations would almost inevitably change and more appropriate decisions would emerge from government. But the identity of actors who would power the change underwent a shift. Now it was assumed that the staffs of government agencies, rather than an aroused citizenry, would initiate action. Officials in the post-New Deal state were expected to be interested, responsive to need, and ready to move on the basis of research evidence. After all, that was what the New Deal, the Fair Deal, and successor administrations had been about—to put in place professionally staffed agencies that would deal professionally and with humanitarian intent with problems of employment, education, health, mental health, and the like.

The second shift in assumption was that contemporary problems were more complicated than those facing earlier reformers. Many of the most flagrant abuses and gaps in service had been overcome in the 1930s and 1940s. As the Great Society proceeded to enact the stockpile of social programs that reformers had unsuccessfully been advocating for decades (e.g., Medicare, federal aid to education, civil rights, etc.), the easy problems were increasingly coming under control. Now it was the intransigent problems that demanded attention, not the least of which was making the new agencies and programs work in the way that they were expected to work. Therefore, social science had to go beyond descriptive surveys of misery and need. Research was needed that provided direction for policy changes. Studies had to analyze the causes of social problems so that those causes could be addressed and removed. Large numbers of studies fused "basic" and "applied" concerns in the search for better *understanding* of problems that would serve as a basis for better intervention strategies.

In the late 1960s, evaluation research came to the fore. This was a mode of policy research that was expected to have direct and immediate application to government decisions. Evaluation research was designed to find out how well programs were meeting their intended goals. With those data in hand, government officials could continue and expand successful programs, modify and improve those programs that were achieving some but not all of their purposes or achieving them at only modest levels of effectiveness, and terminate the real duds. Every major social program undertaken during the War on Poverty was accompanied by a requirement—and funds—for evaluation of its effectiveness in fulfilling its official goals. This procedure, like the planning, programming, and budgeting system (PPBS) that came into government at about the same time, was expected to lead to a surge in responsiveness and efficiency.

Somewhere around 1970, the optimistic climate that had surrounded efforts to apply social science research to policy-making began to erode. First came the stream of evaluation evidence showing that the social programs that had been launched with such great enthusiasm under the Great Society banner were achieving only fitful success in solving social problems. This finding laid open to question not only the programs but also the social science on which they were putatively (although more in rhetoric than in substance) based. Skepticism about the authoritativeness of social science theory and content as a basis for program planning began to surface in government circles. If community action, client participation, deinstitutionalization, and other concepts that seemed to have come from social scientists were providing no panaceas for social problems, something must be wrong with their knowledge base. Even economists, who had appeared so effective in taming the business cycle and "fine tuning" the economy, lost their aura of infallibility as inflation and business stagnation simultaneously took hold.

Evaluation research itself, the bearer of initial bad tidings, came in for its share of criticism. Officials gradually became aware that evaluation was not the antiseptic purveyor of universally accepted, objective data. Evaluation research, like all social science research, was suffused with values. As social scientists had long recognized, every stage of the research process—from the formulation of the initial question to the development of conclusions—was punctuated with choices, which were resolved by applying value judgments. Whether the values that prevailed were the "official" values embodied in legislation or government "work statements" for the study, the values of the researchers, or some mixture of both, evaluation results bore the imprint. Because evaluation was explicitly judging programs against some criterion of success, the operation of judgmental standards was particularly obvious.

Another factor that contributed to the deteriorating climate surrounding policy research was the realization that study results were not serving as the basis for program or policy change. The implications of explanatory studies and the recommendations from policy-oriented studies seemed to have little effect on either the day-to-day operations of program management or the long-term directions of public policy. Social scientists began writing diatribes about the neglect of policy research in public decision making, often based on disappointment when their own research went unheeded.

For a while in the 1970s, a new burst of hope emerged when government agencies sponsored several large-scale, carefully designed social experiments. Long-term studies were developed to test the effects of proposed innovative social policies—guaranteed annual income, housing allowances, health insurance, educational vouchers. The designs were scientifically reputable, and the approach was prospective (to find out about good and bad consequences before a new policy went into effect nationwide); well qualified social scientists undertook the work with relatively generous funding. Here was a new opportunity to demonstrate that good social science research could be done for policy purposes and that it would provide valuable guidance for policy.

Although the story of the social experiments is not over, indications are that they did not fuel the major policy shifts that were envisioned. They took time, and much of the enthusiasm for new directions had evaporated by the time results were ready. In one case, the new policy thrust was incorporated into legislation on a limited basis (Section 8 Housing) long before the study had any data to report. When results appeared, they reported both good and bad consequences, and partisans could use those pieces of the report that supported their own positions. It was widely acknowledged that the experiments contributed valuable information, but they seemed relatively powerless to affect the course of policymaking. The disillusionment with research as guide to policy ("speaking truth to power," in a phrase from Rexford Tugwell that Aaron Wildavsky used as the title of his recent book) intensified.

Yet the sense of defeatism that many social scientists have come to accept is based on an imagery of political decision making that is, in many crucial respects, unrealistic. Both the boundless hopes for research-driven policy change and the disenchantment with the effects of research to date rest on assumptions, largely unexamined, about the relationship between "knowledge" and "action." As social scientists turned from pontificating about what the proper relationship should be and began empirical investigations of the influence that research actually has, somewhat different formulations of the research-policy nexus began to emerge.

In the last few years, studies of the consequences of social science research have led to a reconceptualization of the role of research in the policy process.[1] These studies tend to affirm that immediate and direct linkages between study results and policy decisions are relatively rare. But research does seem to contribute a series of concepts, generalizations, and ideas that often come to permeate policy discussion. Policy actors say that they are influenced by social science research and, when pressed to give examples, often cite broad generalizations ("home care for the elderly does not avoid institutionalization") or social science concepts (supply-side economics, program implementation, loose coupling of educational institutions). Not single findings, one by one, but *ideas* from social science research appear to affect the development of the policy agenda. Social science research is one of the sources from which participants in the policy process derive their sense of how the world works. They draw on it to understand current conditions, the options available for coping with problems, and the limits of the attainable. When they act, they draw upon their whole stock of knowledge which includes, in some

[1]Cf. Nathan Caplan, Andrea Morrison, and Russell J. Stambaugh, *The Use of Social Science Knowledge in Policy Decisions at the National Level* (Ann Arbor, Mich.: Institute for Social Research, University of Michigan, 1975); Carol H. Weiss, ed., *Using Social Research in Public Policy Making* (Lexington, Mass.: Lexington-Heath, 1977); Mark R. Berg *et al.*, *Factors Affecting Utilization of Technology Assessment Studies in Policy-Making* (Ann Arbor, Mich.: Institute for Social Research, University of Michigan, 1978); Marvin L. Alkin, Richard Daillak, and Peter White, *Using Evaluations: Does Evaluation Make A Difference?* (Beverly Hills, Calif.: Sage Publications, Inc., 1979); Henry J. Aaron, *Politics and the Professors: The Great Society in Perspective* (Washington, D.C.: The Brookings Institution, 1978); and Carol H. Weiss with Michael J. Bucavalas, *Social Science Research and Decision-Making* (New York: Columbia University Press, 1980).

unmeasurable quantity, the research to which they have been exposed.

The percolation of ideas from research into the awareness of policy actors has been called "enlightenment"[2] or, a phrase I adapted from Deborah Shapley, "knowledge creep."[3] In many fields it has had important effects on the nature of policy deliberations. In urban policy, for example, problems once considered central (e.g., slum removal) have subsided into desuetude at least in part because of research, and new aspects of concern (e.g., neighborhood social control) have come to the fore.

The recognizition that research often makes significant conceptual contributions may reduce the sense of futility that has afflicted policy researchers, but it does not resolve the basic issue as they are wont to define it, namely, how to increase the use of research information to policymaking. The thesis of this paper is that such a definition of the question is likely to be unproductive *unless* competing sources of influence are taken into account. Information is only one basis upon which policy actors take their positions. Although there are occasions when information is critical, it is usually outweighed by two other factors that carry higher emotional loadings—ideology and interests. To ignore these influences, or to regard them as illegitimate or irrational components of "resistance" to the truth and beauty of research, is to misread the nature of democratic decision making.

[2]Elisabeth T. Crawford and Albert D. Biderman, eds., *Social Scientists and International Affairs* (New York: John Wiley & Sons, Inc., 1969); Morris Janowitz, *Political Conflict: Essays in Political Sociology* (Chicago: Quadrangle Books, 1970); and Carol H. Weiss, "Research for Policy's Sake: The Enlightenment Function of Social Science Research," *Policy Analysis*, 3 (1977), 531–45.

[3]Carol H. Weiss, "Knowledge Creep and Decision Accretion," *Knowledge: Creation, Diffusion, Utilization*, 1 (1980), 381–404.

IDEOLOGY, INTERESTS, AND INFORMATION

The premise that I want to develop is that the public policy positions taken by policy actors are the resultant of three sets of forces: their *ideologies,* their *interests* (e.g., in power, reputation, financial reward) and the *information* they have. Each of these three forces interacts with the others in determining the participants' stance in policymaking.

When different sets of actors engage in the discussions and bargaining to determine the shape of enacted policy, other forces come into play. Negotiations within organizations, across organizations, and in the political arena are affected by a host of structural and procedural influences: hierarchy, specialization and internal division of labor, fragmentation of issues, reliance on standard operating procedures, control of information sources, and so on.[4] But the *content* of each group's policy positions, as these are advanced initially and modified in the course of negotiations, is based on the interplay of ideology, interests, and information as the group interprets them.

Observers who expect the subcategory of information that is social science research to have immediate and independent power in the policy process, and who bitterly com-

---

[4]Graham T. Allison, *Essence of Decision: Explaining the Cuban Missile Crisis* (Boston: Little, Brown and Company, 1971); Morton Halperin, *Bureaucratic Politics and Foreign Policy* (Washington, D.C.: The Brookings Institution, 1974); Harold L. Wilensky, *Organizational Intelligence: Knowledge and Policy in Government and Industry* (New York: Basic Books, Inc., Publishers, 1967); Herbert A. Simon, *Administrative Behavior* (3rd ed.; New York: The Free Press, 1976); I. M. Destler, *Presidents, Bureaucrats, and Foreign Policy* (Princeton, N.J.: Princeton University Press, 1972); Alexander L. George *et al.,* "Towards a More Soundly Based Foreign Policy: Making Better Use of Information," in *Commission on the Organization of the Government for the Conduct of Foreign Policy,* II (Washington, D.C.: U.S. Government Printing Office, 1975), app. D; and Charles E. Lindblom, *The Policy-Making Process* (Englewood Cliffs, N.J.: Prentice-Hall, Inc., 1968).

plain about the intrusion of "politics" (i.e., interests and ideologies) into the use of research, implicitly hold a distorted view of how decisions are made. Moreover, their normative view—that research *should* have direct effects on policy—proposes an imagery of appropriate policymaking that I believe is untenable and (if it should ever be realized) dangerous.

The imperative of democratic decision making is to accommodate the interests and ideologies represented in the society. In the nature of the system, it is more important to negotiate decisions that are at least mimimally satisfactory to significant segments of the population than to reach some scientifically "best" solution that will provoke significant cleavages.[5] In a period like the present, when "consensus politics" has been displaced by a more ideological politics, that statement does not have the firm axiomatic ring that it has had for decades. But it is still true that compromises and tradeoffs have to be arranged on most issues to avoid losing the support of influential groups and large blocs of voters, and this is likely to become more apparent again in the future.

An emphasis on the representation of ideology and interests in decision making is not meant to suggest that information is unimportant, particularly if the information suggests that politically acceptable policies have counterproductive effects. Nor is it intended to say that the current share of research information in the I–I–I (ideology–interests–information) amalgam represents an optimal pattern. What I do

[5]One of the enduring "projects" of democratic societies is to ensure representation for interests that are poorly organized and historically inarticulate. Much of U.S. politics in the past twenty years has involved the mobilization and participation of successive waves of underrepresented groups, such as blacks, Hispanics, the welfare poor, women, homosexuals, the handicapped, native Americans, former mental patients, the aged. Unless all segments of the society have a voice in political decision making (whether or not they win out at any given time), the political system is falling short of the prevailing liberal ideal.

propose is that an understanding of the nature of political decision making is essential to an understanding of the place of research.

Definition of the Terms

Before launching into the interesting part of the discussion, let me define the terms. By participants in policymaking, I mean not only the legislators and top-level executive officials who have a direct and visible hand in the drafting and enactment of laws. I also intend to include the many other groups that have at least a modicum of influence on the shaping of bills, their passage, and their implementation. Among the most important of this collateral crowd are the upper and middle tiers of bureaucrats in the executive departments (whose work molds the specific content of new legislation and whose regulations and guidelines shape the manner in which enacted laws are implemented) and interest groups (whose demands and objections influence the positions of legislators and executive agencies with regard to policy proposals). Aides to high officials, such as the president's advisers and Congressional staffers, and aides in institutionalized form, like the Congressional Budget Office or the Office of Management and Budget, are frequently important participants. (In other countries, political party officials are highly significant policy actors as they develop party programs, but in the United States today, the party apparatus has declined from its previous position of little influence to virtual insignificance.) The citizens (as John and Jane Q. Public) have the ultimate weapon of the ballot, but they exert influence on policy only to the extent that they aggregate their desires through participation in interest-group formations. Nevertheless, on any particular issue, the occassional interloper—like Howard Jarvis or Ralph Nader—can come charging in from outside to activate and sway the policymaking process.

Ideology, in this discussion, encompasses a broad range: philosophy, principles, values, political orientation. It subsumes any relatively coherent political predisposition, from the comprehensive programs of (say) splinter-group New Leftists to such vague proclivities as "the country should do more for the poor" or "we've got to bring discipline and hard work back into American life." At its core are ethical and moral values: the sanctity of human life, integrity, patriotism, and the like. In the political setting, it incorporates values with general dispositions toward programs of action. In Robert E. Lane's terms, political ideology represents an "evaluative–descriptive–prescriptive account of the political world"[6] which is "normative, ethical, moral in tone and content."[7] People's ideologies are sometimes carefully constructed and internally consistent, but often they are haphazard and makeshift. However weakly integrated they may be, they provide an emotionally charged normative orientation that provides a basis for position taking.

Interests, here, are defined primarily in terms of self-interest. Legislators want to be reelected; they want to move into positions of greater authority. Appointed officials want to retain their posts and increase their influence. Bureaucrats have an interest in the survival and expansion of their bureaus, the size of their budgets, and their own career chances. Beneficiaries or potential beneficiaries of policy have an interest in obtaining and increasing benefits. Organized groups speaking for beneficiaries are concerned not only with representing their constituents' interests but also with maintaining their legitimacy and the perceived effectiveness of their organizations. Taxpayers have a stake in the size of their tax

[6]Robert E. Lane, *Political Man* (New York: The Free Press, 1962), pp. 173–174.
[7]Robert E. Lane, *Political Ideology: Why the Common Man Believes What He Does* (New York: The Free Press, 1962), p. 15.

bills, consumers with the rate of inflation; although these unorganized interests rarely have much clout, at times of widespread public dissatisfaction they may be mobilized through a variety of devices, like referendums, to make their voice heard.

The play of interests represents the drama of public policymaking. It often takes place on center stage in the limelight of media attention, but it also goes on backstage in the offices of the bureaus of urban mass transportation, vocational education, and employment security. Since it is the stuff of politics, it tends to dominate our imagery of policymaking.

But all policy actors act on the basis of some knowledge. They have a sense of the current state of affairs, the relative seriousness of problems, why things happen as they do, which strategies of intervention will help or hinder, and how much progress is possible. This is the category that I have called information. "Knowledge" might be a better label, but it often communicates a sense of accuracy, rightness, and validity (despite efforts by scholars like Fritz Machlup[8] to broaden its purview), whereas "information" has a tentative enough aura to contain the partial, biased, or invalid understandings that I want to subsume as well. Where ideology is basically normative, information is basically descriptive.

All policy action is based on factual assumptions, that is, information; but information does not exist, or have bearing for policy, in discrete chunks. It is embedded in an explanatory framework of some sort—that is, in a theoretical model indicating that changes in X (program, budget, statute, or whatever) will lead to changes in Y (crime, economic growth, or whatever other purposes the policy makers have in mind). The model may be more or less complex, dealing only with

---

[8]Fritz Machlup, *Knowledge and Knowledge Production*, in *Knowledge: Its Creation, Distribution, and Economic Significance*, I (Princeton, N.J.: Princeton University Press, 1980).

X and Y or also encompassing intervening and countervailing changes in T, U, V, and W, en route to changes in Y. The model may be supported by scientific research, experienced judgment, folk wisdom, or gut feeling. It may reflect the dynamics of the situation well or poorly and thus be a good or poor predictor of the outcomes of policy action. But it is impossible to conceive of policy actions devoid of explicit or implicit assumptions about the relationships between what policymakers propose to do and the outcome of their action.

Research contributes information "bits" that can help in the calculation of the direction and slope of change from X to Y. It has more profound effects by altering the explanatory framework within which the whole problem is considered. Through research (as well as through other modes of learning), some variables that once seemed of high salience are omitted and new variables are taken into account. In fact, the definition of which issues need policy attention often undergoes change as research sheds light on such matters as the components of inflation, school achievement of inner-city pupils, and the health care services used by the poor.[9]

Information comes from many sources. Much of it is the fruit of direct experience, and long immersion in the substance

[9]Martin Rein has suggested that all research knowledge is permeated with implicit policy prescriptions and that the policy prescription inevitably precedes and shapes the research ["Methodology for the Study of the Interplay between Social Science and Social Policy, *International Social Science Journal*, 32 (1980), pp. 361–8]. It is a provocative insight, with that flavor of the paradoxical that charms intellectuals. But I suspect that it applies to only a minority of well-developed policy issues. In most cases that I know about, researchers and government officials who have attempted to develop policy implications from a study or set of studies (i.e., from the mix of theories, concepts, and data that is social science research) have argued long and hard about the logical policy conclusion, with divergences that spanned an extreme spectrum. In fact, Paul F. Lazarsfeld and Jeffrey G. Reitz have written vividly about the "gap" between research data and recommendations and the non-research-based "leap" that is required to develop policy proposals from social sience research. [Cf. *An Introduction to Applied Sociology* (New York: Elsevier Publishing Co., Inc., 1975).]

and struggles of a policy arena provides particularly salient learning. Some information is craft lore, the product of education and training in a particular professional field and exposure to the codified wisdom of its practice, as represented, for example, in textbooks or professional rules of thumb. Secondary reports make up a sizable share of policy-relevant information. The media are an especially potent influence, because news reports reach not just one subaudience but almost everyone. What they report cannot be swept under the rug or (the bureaucratic equivalent) filed away in dormant files. The information is out in the open and must be confronted by all the participants engaged in decision making on a particular issue. The media have the advantage, too, of timeliness and *dailiness*. The long lag times that plague other information sources, like social science research, are not much of a problem.

Policymakers get information from their own organizations, both through formal channels (e.g., program records, reports, testimony) and through informal interaction with colleagues (meetings, conversations, the grapevine, etc.). Certain kinds of information are built into the organization's standard operating procedures. Rules, practices, and accustomed modes of operation embody the lessons of past failures and successes. The organizational structure itself provides informational signals: which units (and therefore which issues) are more or less important by virtue of size, budget, and hierarchical level, which offices (and therefore which issues) have direct access to the secretary of the department and first call upon his or her attention. And, of course, policy actors make use of a wide array of consultants, advisers, experts, trusted aides, friends, and neighbors. The quick phone call to an acknowledged (or perceived) expert is a frequent method of information gathering in policy circles. Policymakers often become members of informal networks of experts on, say, farm price supports or relations with Latin America.

Then there is the information that pours in unsolicited from outside. Organized interest groups make use of all available channels and techniques to provide not only advocacy statements but also the informational underlay for their positions. Letters from constituents, specialized newsletters, statistical series—the list goes on and on. No wonder that "information overload" often seems a more critical problem than information shortage.

Just to round out the picture, let us recognize that policy actors also share the ordinary knowledge, beliefs, and assumptions that accrue to all of us as members of the society. We take a lot of information for granted, as we take many of our values for granted, simply because we have absorbed the knowledge "in good currency" in the United States of America in this year of 1983.

Somewhere in this informational mélange fits social science research. Social scientists often talk as though policymakers were waiting in breathless anticipation for the information they provide. But in fact the results of social science research have to compete with a cacophony of information to get a hearing. Possibly the most significant point to underscore here is that research only occasionally reaches policy actors directly in the form of written reports or even executive summaries of reports. More frequent is the diffusion of research generalizations and ideas through other existing channels—the media, conferences and meetings, expert consultation, conversations with colleagues, and so on.

THE INTERACTION OF IDEOLOGY, INTERESTS,
AND INFORMATION

Every policy is the product of interplay among ideology, interests, and information. If I were to try to diagram the interaction, I'd come up with three heavily overlapping circles. It would make a more interesting chart to separate the three circles and add a batch of arrows: say, to put ideology first as setting the boundaries for policy, and to place arrows from ideology to interests to information as a way of indicating the course of development of policy proposals. *But that is not how I think it works.* On the contrary, the interaction is constant and iterative, and policymakers work out the specification of their ideologies and interests *in conjunction with* their processing of information.

Given the heavy overlay that I am positing, we can pick up analysis of the interaction at any point. But since we have been discussing the role of policy research, let us start there. The thesis is that information, including the particular subset of information that comes directly or indirectly from social science research, interacts with ideology and interests in affecting policy. Research sometimes reinforces existing constellations of ideology and interests, is sometimes neutral or irrelevant, and sometimes conflicts with or challenges them. How much effect research will have on policy, therefore, depends on three sets of interactions.

Research and Prior Information

First is the interaction between research results and other information. The extent to which research is compatible with knowledge from other sources is a significant factor. Policy actors, as we have noted, have large stores of prior knowledge and theories about conditions and cause-and-effect linkages. Research results that are totally out of line with their preexisting knowledge are likely to be regarded with skepticism. This is not necessarily because the research challenges their interests or ideologies, as social scientists are wont to assume (although this, of course, is sometimes the case), but often because it is not congruent with their understanding of how the world works. Under such circumstances, they often criticize, or find some expert to criticize, the methodology of the investigation. They *know* it is wrong because the methods of inquiry yield results that contravene their settled understanding. On the other hand, if they are assured that the study meets appropriate scientific canons, they can sometimes be persuaded to pay attention. In my study *Social Science Research and Decision-Making,* previously cited, this conclusion about the "truth tests" that decision makers apply to research emerges clearly from the data. Counterintuitive research—or, more aptly, research that contradicts the decision maker's current knowledge—has to prove itself on methodological grounds before it is given a hearing.

Research that merely repeats the obvious and accepted is also likely to make little dent. It has a "ho-hum" quality about it and seems to deserve little attention. It is in the middle ground between "what everyone knows" and "what can't be right" that research has the greatest possibility for expanding and extending policy actors' understanding of the issues.

One of the special advantages of policy research and social science generally is the rich conceptual apparatus it brings to bear. Concepts from the social sciences—such as externalities, community norms, social support networks, bureaucratic politics, and the like—seem to be readily picked up in policy discourse. Their success may be attributable to the fact that much of what policy makers know comes from disparate, unorganized, and inchoate experience. Social science concepts give form to this tacit knowledge and enable policymakers to manipulate and use it. Thus, the notions and concepts from social science often seem to have special leverage in structuring the policy debate. When the social sciences produce theories of similar cogency, even the kinds of partial and temporally bound theories that economists trade in, it seems likely that their explanatory potential will have equivalent impact. As Robert Axelrod notes, decision makers tend to think and talk in causal terms, so social science theories that support causal thinking are likely to be welcomed.[10] His work shows, too, that decision makers have more information than they can take into account in particular situations; hence theories that suggest the relative priority of variables can be useful.

In sum, the effects of policy research on policymaking depend in some measure on the match with prior information. When research contradicts existing knowledge that is firmly and unequivocally accepted, it is likely to be buffered from influence. If research helps to resolve anomalies or inconsistencies or make sense of fragments of information, it can permeate, illuminate, or displace prior assumptions. In some cases, it apparently is put on hold: coexisting side by side but not integrated with other knowledge until later events indicate its worth.

Research and Ideology

A second interaction is between research and ideology. Whether research results are compatible or incompatible, supportive or challenging, relevant or irrelevant to policymakers' basic policy predilections will affect the degree of influence that the research will have. Let me be clear. I do not mean to say that research which is incompatible with a person's philosophy or political orientation is automatically discarded. The interaction is far more subtle. Most people—even highly informed and experienced officials—do not have coherent, detailed, comprehensive ideologies. They have something more akin to general predispositions (e.g., the environment should be protected, government should not overregulate private enterprise) which do not cover all situations or give very ex-

---

[10]Robert Axelrod, ed., *Structure of Decision: The Cognitive Maps of Political Elites* (Princeton, N.J.: Princeton University Press, 1976).

plicit direction for those they do cover. Thus, people *work out* their ideological positions in dealing with immediate, concrete issues. Let us say that a person has a general predisposition not to "coddle" criminals, and a research study shows that lengthier prison terms are associated with higher recidivism rates. The person's reaction can span a large range—from ignoring the research to redefining "coddling" to seeking "tough" alternatives to long sentences.

Often people hold a number of conflicting ideological positions at the same time. They want to get tough with criminals; they don't want the state to spend more money (which would preclude building more prisons); they want order in the prisons. In some cases, for some people, research information can help to determine which of these several orientations gets the upper hand. Similarly, people almost always have multiple values or goals, which in particular cases are in competition with each other. As Charles L. Schultze[11] notes, we can be for rapid transportation and for highway safety. It is only in considering the tradeoffs that a particular policy (like a highway speed limit of 55 miles per hour) will entail that we figure out how much we value safety and how much we value speed. Research evidence on the number of highway deaths and injuries attributable to speeds of over 55 miles per hour and the economic costs of slowing transport can help us make that determination.

Ideologies tend to be partial and fluid. They are probably almost as susceptible to being influenced by research as they are to influence the response to research (acceptance or rejection, distortion, selective acceptance of compatible "bits")— at least up to a point. There are no doubt boundaries beyond which committed ideologues cannot be moved by evidence

[11]Charles L. Schultze, *The Politics and Economics of Public Spending* (Washington, D.C.: The Brookings Institution, 1968).

if the issue is salient to them. On the other hand, if research unambiguously demonstrates that no available strategies are able to achieve the values that policy actors hold (e.g., the movement of all adult welfare recipients to gainful employment), it takes conscious blinders to continue making that value the goal of their policy proposals. People do it, but perhaps more as an emotional rallying cry than as serious policy action.

Information and ideology interact in complex ways. Often only in the specific concrete case do people construct their ideological position through a balancing of the positive and negative consequences that a policy will likely have on multiple valued ends. The nation's President can be in favor of a balanced budget and low unemployment. But we live in a complicated, multivariate world full of dynamic interchanges. When economic research indicates that a reduction of federal outlays will increase unemployment, the President can (1) accept one or the other objective as paramount, at least for a time, and ignore the other, (2) try to strike a balance between government spending and unemployment somewhere along the spectrum short of a balanced budget, or (3) seek out different, more congenial research or different interpretations of existing research. It is impossible to predict presidential policy on the basis of ideological position—or research—alone.

There is another and quite different interaction between information and ideology that warrants attention. Although it is marginal to the argument I am developing here, it is central to the understanding of why the systematic collection and citation of information is pervasive in policymaking processes. Few ideological commitments in modern Western societies are stronger than the ideas of rationality and intelligent choice, and no institutions are more normatively committed to the application of information to decisions than bureaucratic organizations. In effect, they demonstrate their intelligence and the quality of their decisions (in situations where criteria for "intelligence" and "quality" are highly ambiguous) by appropriate performance of the rituals of information processing. As Feldman and March note:

> Command of information and information sources enhances perceived competence and inspires confidence. . . . A good decision maker is one who makes decisions in the way a good decision maker does, and decision makers and organizations establish their legitimacy by their use of information.[12]

Thus, there is high symbolic value in requesting information and justifying decisions on informational grounds. Even when the actual linkage between information input and decisional output is weak (e.g., when the decision is substantially made before the information is attended to), political actors signal their commitment to the ideology of rational choice by taking an appropriate information posture. And one of the possible consequences of such ritualistic posturing is that the proclamation of the value of information creates a dynamic by which information actually comes to affect actors' interpretations and actions. What started as symbolic and ritualistic behavior can in time be transformed into responsiveness to information.

Research and Interests

The third interaction that determines the role of research in policymaking is the interaction between research and interests. Almost all participants in policy formulation have a *stake* in the configuration that policy takes. Legislators care about the preferences of voters in their districts and the effects of their acts on their electoral chances, their relationships with

[12]Martha S. Feldman and James G. March, "Information in Organizations as Signal and Symbol," *Administrative Science Quarterly,* 26 (1981), pp. 177–8.

fellow legislators, the party leadership, the distribution of committee chairmanships and other rewards, and their standing with the President (thus also the likely allocation of contracts, judgeships, and invitations to White House functions). Federal bureaucrats, state and city officials, and interest groups have similar lists of wants for power, prestige, or concrete advantage.

But how policy actors define their interests depends in part on how they perceive the situation. New information can alter their definitions of both where their interests lie and the most judicious course for achieving them. Workers at Chrysler who used to define their interests in terms of higher pay have come, after being informed of Chrysler's financial condition, to see their interests in the survival of the company—even if survival should require accepting lower pay. President Reagan seems to have convinced large numbers of voters, by brandishing information (and economic theories) on inflation and government spending, to redefine their interests from the extension of government benefits to a reduction in government spending.

Similarly, research indicating that an agency's program is not working well can lead to a shift in the specification of its interests. Instead of maintaining its customary interests in the perpetuation of the program, the agency may realize that such a course will put it at risk of being tagged ineffective— with consequent threats to its budget, autonomy, and influence. It may decide that drastic revisions in program are more in line with its interests and may therefore proceed to radical redesign. In the case of legislators, public opinion polls showing public dissatisfaction with government energy policies may help them perceive the value for their own careers of promoting legislation for major reform.

Again, interests are rarely hard-and-fast single-position commitments. Public officials work out the specifications of their interests on any particular issue in light of the information they have. Whether to go with the status quo, work for incremental changes, or take more drastic steps is a decision that depends in part on how officials estimate the consequences of these courses for their own and their organization's well-being. Research that reduces uncertainty (e.g., about the likelihood of successful outcomes of a policy, about unanticipated consequences, about public responses) can lead to major reestimates of where their interests lie.

Much of the analysis done by political scientists over the past generation of scholarship has highlighted the salience of self-seeking behavior in government. "Bureaucratic politics" and the "electoral imperative" have become familiar concepts.[13] But important as they are for understanding government behavior, they have apparently misled many students of the political process to believe that, on any given subject, officials have their minds made up, their positions predetermined. In actuality, redefinition of interests goes on continually. Note the stance of many liberal senators on President Reagan's budget cuts. They apparently saw greater political reward through acceptance of cuts even in programs that their ideologies support than in outright opposition to budget cuts at a time of popular sentiment for retrenchment.

Therefore, research suggesting changes in policies, even policies near and dear to the hearts of public officials, can have an effect through reconstructing their notion of their own interests. It may cause them to ally their definition of self-interest with change rather than with "as is" continuation. It can lead them to disown old policies and strike out in radically different directions if it becomes apparent that the

[13]On the former, see Halperin, *Bureaucratic Politics;* on the latter, see David Mayhew, *Congress: The Electoral Connection* (New Haven, Conn.: Yale University Press, 1974).

old policies are generating ill will and the new directions promise kudos for innovation, dynamism, and leadership.

Ideology and Interests

Although peripheral to our discussion of research, there is also an interaction between ideology and interests, a familiar sociological proposition. People tend to formulate ideologies that accord with their self-interest. People who were radical and egalitarian in their youth and active in the fight for greater government aid to the poor often, later on, become homeowners and taxpayers who vote for Proposition 13 to implement the ideologies of fiscal integrity, fair return for effort, and a limit to the intrusiveness of government. A body of sociological work illustrates the tendency of people to espouse value positions that support the interests of their ethnic, class, or occupational status. These findings are summarized in the well-documented maxim "Where you stand depends upon where you sit."

It is often the case that, as their status changes, people change their ideological positions to adapt to their new environment; for example, business executives may become more pro-business as they ascend the corporate ladder. Sometimes outside conditions cause the shift, as when union officials who formerly supported free trade become protectionists in the face of competing imports of shoes or steel. However, the process also works the other way 'round: people may choose occupations and communities that fit their ideological positions. Selective recruitment into corporate life, the ministry, or alternative schools represents the adaptation of environments to suit preexisting ideologies. The parallel between interests and ideologies is so pervasive that social scientists have occasionally been piqued to study the deviant case (e.g., working-class Tories).

In the policy sphere, the alliance of ideologies and interests is most obvious in the bureaucracies. Staff in the bureau
responsible for mental health services favor the expansion of
mental health services, in part because expansion is good for
the welfare of their agency but also in large part because of
their convictions about the value of such services to people
in need. They chose the field and joined the bureau because
they believed in mental health services, and it is almost impossible to disentangle self-serving motives from altruistic
ones. Among legislators, the match is less coagulate. Except
among extremists, or on certain high-voltage issues, politicians are more inclined to negotiate and bargain. The sacrifice
of "principles" to "politics" is one of the hallmarks of the
legislative process. Although this kind of compromise is often
viewed pejoratively, legislators are *responsible* for reaching acceptable accommodations. And they know that policymaking
almost never produces once-and-for-all solutions—that issues
recur repeatedly. There is time next year to press again for
the enactment of policies that their ideologies support.

Let us conclude the discussion of policy research in the
political process. In effect, I suggest that research rarely affects
policymaking by shoving aside all other influences and im-
pinging directly on decisions. That kind of influence can occasionally be seen on smaller-scale matters than are usually
subsumed under the label of "policy"—issues of program
implementation and program management. At that level research results *can* sometimes provide a missing piece of
knowledge that will largely determine the choice to be made—
data on the numbers of handicapped children in a school
district, conclusions about the relative efficacy of alternative
modes of service delivery—although even there, interests and
ideologies usually intercede. In the "high game" of policymaking, the only instances I know where research results
have had direct effects have been cases where interests and

ideologies were stalemated. Opposing factions had fought the issue to a standstill, and a study coming along either tipped the balance in one direction or suggested a new way out of the impasse that was acceptable to both sides. But by and large, research influences the formation of policy through its effect on prior knowledge, ideologies, and definition of interests and through higher-order interactions with all three.

POWER

The kinds of policy changes in which research is implicated are generally subtle and slow-moving. The formulation I have offered depicts a situation which, if not static, is moving with glacial momentum. Below the surface, significant alterations in perspective may be taking place which, over time, can erupt into drastic shifts in course. By the time they do, the configurations of knowledge will be heavily admixed with other elements and their unique influence will be visible only to the sympathetic observer.

For marked changes in policy to occur, other forces are much more potent spurs than research. The most obvious is power. *The distribution of power determines WHOSE ideology, interests, and information will be dominant.* Shifts in power—dramatically through revolutionary overturn, more moderately through electoral change—bring new people into office who bring with them different constellations of ideology, interests, and information.

Power relationships alter gradually *within* an administration, as the normal processes of political life advance the fortunes of some units, interests, groups, and individuals and constrain the influence of others. Contention is rife between the Congress and the executive, between the "President's men" and the executive departments, among the departments (witness the endemic struggles between State and Defense for influence on national security issues), and within each department. Even the authority of the judiciary is not immune to check, as attested by current attempts to limit the courts' jurisidiction over such constitutional issues as school prayer and desegregation. These continual competitions are usually tied directly to policy positions (e.g., the struggle between the President and the House of Representatives over tax cuts), and therefore the wins and losses have immediate consequences for policy.

Within each public bureaucracy there are perennial contests among bureaus for policy turf, budgetary expansion, and access to the secretary. Such struggles may be linked to policy positions (e.g., one unit within the Department of Health and Human Services seeking to expand federal grants to local health care institutions, another unit trying to restrain the escalation of health care costs), but often policy differences are subordinate to the contest for resources and influence. Yet the relative advantage gained by some units has consequences for the basic policy positions that they espouse. More powerful units (by size, budget, hierarchical location) are more likely to influence the course of policy development.

Groups outside government that represent interest formations also vie for access and influence. Advocates for nuclear power, the handicapped, and aid to Third World countries, for example, seek to increase the weight of their ideologies, interests, and information in political decision making.

In all contests for power and influence, an information component is present. The information that is salient for the Democratic congressional leadership (e.g., the needs of the elderly for social security benefits) differs from the information salient to the Republican administration (the impending depletion of the social security trust fund). Changes in power elevate the set of information associated with one faction over the information central to other factions, just as changes re-order the rankings of ideologies and interests.

IMPLICATIONS OF THE I–I–I FRAMEWORK

In many respects the discussion of the interplay between ideology, interests, and information merely pours old wine into new bottles. But "organizing constructs," if they are soundly conceived, can have heuristic value. Does the formulation help to advance our analytic capability—in this context, our ability to understand policy research?

One obvious implication for policy researchers is: Be modest in your expectations of influence. Do not expect your study to catapult you into the position of adviser to the prince. However, I think that most of us have already learned that lesson through the painful pleasures of experience.

There is another moral, although this one, too, grows as much out of "ordinary knowledge" as it does from the analytic schema. One suggestion to those who propose, fund, and do policy-relevant research is not to spend a heavy share of research money and time on studies designed to answer immediate policy problems. To do such work usefully usually requires accepting the conceptual and practical constraints of government sponsors—that is, limiting research to the variables that the funding bureau has the authority to manipulate and adopting the premises that currently guide the agency's action. If, in fact, even such practically oriented research is likely to run into entanglements with interests and ideologies both inside and outside the bureau, we may serve government better by broadening the scope of the research we do and contributing more critical perspectives on agency activities. Although such research will not have immediate impact, it probably represents a wiser investment of social science resources. And when alignments of ideology and interests make the information relevant to policymaking, the contribution may prove to be significant.

The I–I–I framework may also be useful in looking at policy research itself. Researchers are not immune from the influence of prior knowledge, interests, and ideologies. While the use of previous theory and empirical conclusions as a basis for new research is excellent practice, some of the knowledge that we apply to research comes from less scientifically respectable sources, like ordinary experience and secondhand reports. When our data analyses lead to results that are incompatible with ordinary knowledge, it is not uncommon to run the data again in different ways until more congenial results appear. I do not think that is bad practice; in fact, it is usually all to the good. But we can be more candid in recognizing that we, much like policymakers, do it.

Policy researchers have their ideological convictions too. When we are not straitjacketed by sponsors' limits (and probably even when we are), our value dispositions enter into the dozens of choices we make in the course of a study: how to frame questions, whom to interview, how much weight to give particular variables, which set of conclusions to highlight. The most obvious entry point for ideology is in drawing implications from data. Some forthrightness about our value assumptions and how they influence our interpretations may be useful here as well.

Finally, there are the interests, often the dual interests, that policy researchers have in their work: (1) an interest in doing reputable scientific research that will be publishable in disciplinary journals and advance their reputations and careers and (2) an interest in satisfying their clients and (not uncommonly) in gaining a measure of influence in the making of policy. These interests sometimes pull us in different directions, although we usually hope that they are, at least serially, reconcilable. Whichever one is uppermost at any given time or whatever compromise we reach between them is likely to have consequences for the contour of our research. Social scientists should be self-critical enough to enjoy taking a hard look at this dimension of policy research too.

In the policy sphere, perhaps the most useful contribution that the I–I–I analysis can make is to serve as a *diagnostic scheme* for particular situations. We can draw on an understanding of ideology–interest–information linkages to develop hypotheses about the likely effects of social science research under different circumstances.[14] For example, if ideological commitments and strong interests are joined in a compelling way, they probably represent a combination too formidable to be overcome by an infusion of social science knowledge. If ideologies are weak or confused or if there are divisions in interest among key policy actors, then social science knowledge is likely to stand a better chance of consideration and even of action.

It would be possible to develop a formal set of hypotheses. Starting with policy situations in which ideological commitments are powerful, interests arrayed on one side of the issue, and existing knowledge supportive, we would hypothesize that new information incompatible with the current constellation would make little headway. As we move toward configurations with less internal consistency—for example, when ideologies and interests coincide but available information discloses severe problems in implementing the preferred policy or when available information is sparse or of doubtful validity—then new information is likely to receive a marginally more receptive hearing. When important policy actors have divergent ideologies and interests and existing information can be interpreted to support a variety of positions, then new information is likely to be used to strengthen

[14] I thank Janet A. Weiss for this suggestion.

one or another of the sides in contention. As ideologies and interests become less salient or conditions make old commitments untenable, we would hypothesize that information would have greater influence.

One situation in which new information seems to have potential for influence is when a group finds its ideology and interests in conflict. For example, progressive corrections officials have long been committed to the rehabilitation of prison inmates through institutional programs of therapy, counseling, and training. Existing information, largely evaluation data on the effectiveness of rehabilitation programs, suggests that inmates who have participated in such programs are no less likely to commit crimes after release than those who have not participated. The implication is that correctional institutions are failing in their mission. Since it is in the interest of correctional institutions to appear effective, commitment to a rehabilitative ideology conflicts with their interests. In such a situation, a disequilibrium among the elements produces an opportunity for movement—either a change in ideology, a change in the definition of self-interest, or a receptivity to new ideas and information that may help to recast the nature of the problem.

In fact, there appear to be changes of all these types churning through the corrections field. Some people are retreating from commitment to the rehabilitation ideal. Some are accepting the impossibility of "correcting" offenders within the environment of a basically custodial institution with the limited resources available, and they are ready to cede responsibility for rehabilitation to other agencies. They are coming to realize that their institutional interests will be better served if they are not held responsible for inmates' postrelease behavior. Many are open to new research. They are looking for studies that can perhaps identify subpopulations of offenders who are amenable to rehabilitation, test the effectiveness of strategies that divert offenders from imprisonment, or demonstrate the efficacy of "fairness" in sentencing (e.g. fixed and uniform terms) in lieu of efforts at rehabilitation.

In the day care field, there is an example of federal agencies with conflicting ideologies who used research to break a stalemate. For years a bitter wrangle went on over standards for federally supported day care. One group was intent on setting high standards as a means to improve the social and cognitive development of poor children and another group was concerned with keeping costs low in order to expand the availability of day care, particularly to enable welfare mothers to take jobs. The conflict focused explicitly on the ratio of caretakers to children. Child development advocates favored high staff ratios; advocates of low-cost day care wanted lower and thus less expensive ratios. The sides were loggerheaded until a research study indicated that staff/child ratios were less important to children's well-being than the number of children in a group. The information effectively broke the impasse. By enabling each side to maintain its own ideology and interests, it provided grounds for a mutually acceptable settlement.[15]

To predict with any assurance whether research will influence policy, either in the short term or through gradual redefinition of interests and ideologies, is a difficult and complex undertaking. What I propose is that future investigations that try to tackle the question give explicit attention to the configuration of ideologies, interests, and existing information. Unless these factors are taken into account, I doubt that we will gain much cumulative understanding of when and how research makes a difference.

[15]National Academy of Sciences, *Making Policies for Children: A Study of the Federal Process* (Washington, D.C.: National Academy Press, 1982).

III

DISCIPLINARY STANDARDS AND POLICY ANALYSIS

10

USE OF SOCIAL SCIENCE DATA FOR POLICY ANALYSIS AND POLICYMAKING

RUTH S. HANFT

Social science data, empirical research, and social theory have always been used in some form or another for public policy formulation. Theories and data describing the behavior of people, economic systems, and nations were used by the first social organizations to develop public policy. The oldest and still most basic social data bases comprises the census and vital statistics. The collection of census information is an ancient practice; the Old Testament (Exod. 30; Num. 1) documents its use. In the eighteenth century, the framers of the U.S. Constitution(Art. 1, Sec. 2) saw fit to provide for a regular decennial census. With the rapid development of the industrial revolution in the latter part of the last century and the early part of this century, observational data about the

RUTH S. HANFT □ Senior Research Associate, Association of Academic Health Centers, 11 Dupont Circle, Suite 210, Washington, D.C. 20036.

consequences of industrial development, population changes, and mortality were collected through the census, vital statistics, and *ad hoc* local studies. Social reform movements, state government, and ultimately the federal government used these data to develop measures such as workmen's compensation, child welfare laws, industrial safety, and even Prohibition.

With the advent of the New Deal, the federal government began to assume responsibilities for social welfare that had previously been the domain of local communities, states, and private philanthropy. Data from a number of sources were assembled, analyzed, and used as the basis for important legislation. President Roosevelt's special cabinet committee, known as the Committee on Economic Security, working through an advisory council of outside experts and a technical board, conducted a major review of data from the census and the states as well as *ad hoc* data from the Committee on the Costs of Medical Care to make recommendations for social programs of the 1930s and thereafter.

The great social welfare push of the thirties slowed during and after World War II. In the early sixties, however, there was a resurgence of interest, and over the next decade there was rapid development of a plethora of social programs. To measure the achievements of these programs and identify continuing and changing needs, the federal government gathered data, conducted research, and sponsored research and evaluation in the private sector on a broad scale. By 1980, there were several sizable organizations at the federal level devoted to the collection and analysis of social, economic, and demographic data: the Bureau of Labor Statistics; Office of Research and Statistics (Social Security Administration); National Center for Health Statistics; National Center for Educational Statistics, and Office of Research, Demonstrations, and Statistics (Health Care Financing Administration). In addition, there was support for extramural research and evaluation conducted by academic faculty from some of these organizations as well as from the National Science Foundation, the National Center for Health Services Research, and programs in specific categories.

Developments in computer technology, paralleling the development in social sciences, survey methodology, and regression analysis, have enhanced our ability to handle large masses of data and stimulated the development of further data sources. The rise of new social programs, new data, and new tools of the computer age have spawned a new industry of *policy analysis*. This industry includes numerous planning, evaluation, and policy analysis offices at all levels and parts of federal, state, and local government as well as profit and nonprofit consulting firms, foundations, and universities. In the 1960s the health policy analysts in Congress and the executive branch could be counted on one's fingers. Today the combination of federal, state, and private policy analysis capability constitutes an industry. While the growth in data sources and their careful use have improved policy analysis and government decision making, a whole series of issues related to the role of data and social research for policy analysis have arisen.

This essay will explore some of the issues and problems in the use of data and empirical research for policy analysis and decision making. Particular note will be made of these problems: (1) the imperfection of much data and consequent uncertainties about the effect of poliices, and (2) the identification and articulation of disciplinary assumptions and value judgments by researchers and policy analysts. Finally, the roles of the researcher, analyst, and decision maker in describing and using assumptions, research results, and gaps in information will be discussed.

ISSUES IN THE USE OF DATA FOR POLICY ANALYSIS

General Issues

In the health field, the government collects general-purpose data mainly through national probability samples, collects data related to specific programs like Medicare, and both funds and conducts health services research and technology assessment. It also draws upon numerous state and private data sources. These activities support and relate to the basic goals of health policy for the federal government—a policy to promote and protect the nation's health. Over the past twenty years, attainment of these goals has presumed a government obligation to assure financial and physical access to care through various policies and programs and through programs addressed to specific health problems. Through such intervention, the government has tried to respect a number of humane and democratic principles—sometimes explicitly, sometimes implicitly. These principles are aimed at doing good and avoiding harm, distributing goods and services equitably, recognizing the dignity and autonomy of each citizen, and respecting a pluralism of values held by different citizens and groups. In this last context, a mixed public and private system of financing and delivery of services is promoted. A *reliable* data base is a necessary political condition for determining needs of the population and assessing the consequences of intervention.

More recently, government has also recognized the *ethical* conditions upon which a data base must rest. Legislative, administrative, and judicial decisions have become sensitive to matters of confidentiality and informed consent in the collection of data as well as in their use. The research community faces the unhappy task—call it the "dilemma"—of yielding the certainty of greater statistical confidence in data for the uncertainty of greater social confidence in government or in research itself. But the necessity for a reliable data base, ethically derived, is undiminished.

Ethical problems in the *use* of social science and research data are not primarily problems of conscious or flagrant violations such as dishonesty of analysis, falsification of data, or individual venality. Two categories of problems involving subtle ethical conflicts are much more significant. The first concerns the nature and limitations of social science research itself: the implicit assumptions made in the design of studies, the methodological problems of measurement and weighting, and the assumptions used in imputing missing data and in modeling. The second category concerns the use of the data by policy analysts and policymakers. These problems involve the users' limited knowledge of the sources of data and the methodology followed to collect them as well as of the assumptions used by the analyst in interpreting the data. Policy analysts and policymakers are very busy, often moving from crisis to crisis without adequate time to learn the nuances of the data or assumptions of different analysts, statisticians, and researchers. The following examples will illustrate the problems presented by these two categories.

Problems of Assumptions

A classic example of the problem of "assumptions" is found in the debate between proponents of market competition and proponents of governmental regulation in health services. In what follows, this complex debate will be oversimplified for the purposes of illustration. There is a major political debate about the factors that cause health care inflation and the methods that might control escalating costs. The health care industry is complex and composed of many interrelated parts. It is a service industry that, unlike other service industries, faces choices related to life, death, and disability. The good produced is not merely an economic good but also involved fundamental issues of social justice. Yet most attention is paid the economic issues; debates on access to care, content of health services, and form of delivery of services are cast in economic terms. The two poles of opinion in the economic debate are the *competition* school and the *regulation* school.

Most social scientists who propose a competitive model to address the cost problems in health care assume that a free market approach will work in health care, that supply and demand will reach an equilibrium, that prices will respond to the actions and reactions of supply and demand, and that goods will be distributed equitably. This model also assumes the following conditions:

1. Consumers have enough information to make rational choices.
2. Suppliers have free entry into the economic market.
3. Most demand is created by consumers, and demand can be withheld or delayed.
4. Demand induced by providers can be reduced through economic incentives.
5. Prices will fall if demand falls or supply increases.
6. If consumers pay directly for services (rather than through third-party payers) they will act as rational purchasers—shopping for the best buy.
7. Supply will expand or contract in relation to demand.

The regulation school, on the other hand, assumes that a medical market cannot operate as a free economic market or ensure equitable distribution of services for the following reasons:

1. Consumers can never have sufficient technical information to make truly informed choices.

2. There is no free entry of suppliers into the economic market because of licensure and other constraints related to quality.
3. The life, death, and disability results of choice, combined with the need for highly technical information, require that the consumer have a representative—the physician.
4. Demand is often created by the agent, who has an economic stake in providing services.
5. Direct payment at time of use may influence demand marginally, but it has less than normal influence when the product is related to urgent health needs or pain.
6. Direct payment at time of use acts as a barrier to access for some groups, particularly low-income groups.

Scientists coming from different schools will approach the same policy problem, such as controlling hospital costs or assuring equitable distribution, quite differently depending on which of these sets of assumptions they use. Until recently there was little empirical data to support or challenge either set.

In 1977, the National Medical Care Expenditures Survey, a major study based on a national probability sample, was undertaken to address some of these problems.[1] These data are now being analyzed, and it will take several years to complete the assessment. In a preliminary analysis of "who initiates physicians' visits," the data are quite revealing. On average, physicians initiate about 36 percent of the visits. However, this percentage changes under differing circumstances:

---

[1]U.S. Department of Health and Human Services/Public Health Service, *National Health Care Expenditures Study: Data Preview (#3, October): Who Initiated a Physician's Visit?*, (National Center for Health Services Research, Department of Health and Human Services Pubn. No. 80-3278, 1980).

1. Physicians initiate a higher percentage of total visits when there is a higher-than-average physician-to-population ratio. Supply apparently creates demand.
2. Physicians initiate a higher percentage of visits where there is a higher proportion of third-party payments. Third-party payments apparently affects demand.
3. Physicians initiate a higher percentage of visits for the elderly and for pregnant women. Exogenous noneconomic factors apparently affect demand.

Neither school's assumptions can be entirely supported by the empirical data. For example, although physicians initiated a higher proportion of visits when there was a higher average physician-to-population ratio, the majority of visits were still patient-initiated. While third-party payment appears to influence demand, there are not sufficient data currenlty available to determine whether the demand equates the need for services or to what extent price acts as a barrier to service. It would be premature, given the preliminary nature of the data, to use them alone in making a major policy shift in regard to the supply of physicians in training or third-party coverage.

While the evidence from the study of expenditures raises policy questions, the data need to be combined with more sophisticated analysis. These data, however, in combination with other data, can help in the development or analysis of policy options. For example, in considering continued support of medical education, one of the issues raised is whether government should continue to require an expanding number of medical students. If supply does indeed create demand, then the policy of expansion can be questioned, although the question of whether or not current supply meets the need cannot be answered by these data.

The policy of expanding professional health personnel,

particularly physicians, evolved during the 1960s in response to two major factors. The first stemmed from data showing widely differing ratios of physicians to population across the country and perceptions on the part of the public that there was a shortage. The second factor was the concern during the Medicare–Medicaid debates that there would be an increase in demand for physicians' services once financial barriers to care had been removed. Data showed that the poor and the aged utilized fewer services than middle-and upper-income groups in the pre-Medicare period.

Data and research findings in social policy rarely account for all economic and behavioral variables. Launching large-scale social experiments is generally very costly and raises numerous legal constraints and ethical dilemmas surrounding human experimentation as well as many methodological issues. Conscious of the uncertain effects of changes in social policy, many analysts and decision makers tend to seek incremental rather than massive changes. There have been and continue to be periods like the mid-1930s, the 1960s, and the current period where large-scale social changes are proposed. These changes generally are the result of political consensus and, although data and research contribute to the changes, their contributions are not primary factors. The social and economic effects of these changes are not known with precision and may not be fully recognized or realized for a number of years.

Problems in the Use of Data

Once data are available, there are many problems in their use. We all use data every day for a variety of purposes but rarely question their source or the methodology used to collect, assemble, and analyze them. Although it may not make too much difference if the weather report is several degrees off the mark or if our monthly telephone bill has a minor error, it can make an enormous difference if the cost-of-living index used to adjust wages and pensions understates or overstates costs or fails to reflect local, individual cost differences. Rippling and multiplier effects have an exponentially stronger influence on the cost and operation of some programs than others.

Public policy decisions rely in part on data from a variety of sources. Often the data do not match precisely the need of the policymaker. Policy analysts and decision makers routinely quote different sets of data, argue mightily about accuracy, validity, and interpretation, and constantly deal with conflicting results and uncertainty.

Problems of data use arise at several levels. Users, be they policy analysts or decision makers, must be aware of the following:

1. *Methodology used to collect the data* (reliability of the sample, the nature of the questionnaire, response rates, etc.)
2. *Adjustment of the data* (explicit assumptions, imputation of missing values, nonduplication of counts, etc.)
3. *Assumptions made by the analyst in applying the data* (the analyst's knowledge of similar data from other sources)

The following, illustrating some of the problems, occurred in 1979, when the Carter administration proposed a national health plan. Key pieces of data from which this plan was formulated were counts of

1. The currently uninsured and who they are
2. Those who would benefit and those who would lose under different types of plans
3. Currently available types of insurance coverage
4. The cost of the government, employer, and consumer of different plans

Three basic surveys provided data on the uninsured: the Health Interview Survey[2] based on a sample of household responses; the Survey of Income and Education,[3] where insurance was a supplementary question; and the preliminary data from the National Medical Care Expenditures Survey (NMCES).[4] Adjustments were needed in all survey results to account for coverage other than private health insurance (such as veterans' benefits and other public programs), to eliminate duplicate counts, to adjust for nonresponse, and in this case to "age" the data from 1976–1977 to 1980.

Analyses were conducted on the data bases from the preceding surveys by the assistant secretary for Planning and Evaluation; the Office of Health Research, Statistics, and Technology; and the Congressional Budget Office. The number of uninsured was estimated at 21 to 22 million, 26 million, and 11 to 18 million respectively. The administration used figures ranging from 19 to 21 million in preparing its cost estimate, legislative briefing material, and so on.

Why were the numbers different? The Congressional Budget Office adjusted private insurance counts to attribute the same extent of undercount of private insurance as in Medicare (those beneficiaries who fail to report coverage on surveys and a projection of growth in private coverage from 1976 to 1981).[5] There were also differences in accounting for people covered by public programs. In the case of the two depart-

---

[2]U.S. Department of Health, Education, and Welfare, *Health Interview Survey* (Washington, D.C.: National Center for Health Statistics, 1976 and 1977).

[3]U.S. Department of Commercie, Bureau of the Census, *Survey of Income and Education* (Washington, D.C.: Government Printing Office, 1976).

[4]U.S. Department of Health and Human Services, *National Medical Care Expenditures Survey: Preliminary Data* (Washington, D.C.: National Center for Health Services Research, 1977).

[5]U.S. Congressional Budget Office, *Profile of Health Care Coverage: The Haves and Have Nots* (Washington, D.C.: Government Printing Office, March, 1979).

mental numbers, there was a fundamental difference in the basic methodology of the surveys and some differences in calculating the population covered by programs such as Medicaid, veterans' benefits, and so on. The Health Interview Survey and the Survey of Income and Education estimates were based on whether or not there had been private insurance, Medicare, veterans' benefits, or Medicaid benefits *at any time during the year.* The NMCES survey asked the question of coverage at six different points in time, and the results are based on estimates of coverage for *a full year*—not just any point in time.

Differences in the estimates were also due to different assumptions about public program coverage of the population. Do you use Medicaid's counts from the states, or household surveys or surveys where the respondent shows a Medicaid card, or only data validated by actual payment for the services? Whom do you count as covered by veterans benefits—those currently using services, those technically eligible, or all three categories of eligibility? Do you count those as covered by private insurance with "dread disease" (e.g., cancer) policies but with no other policies?

Different choices in each of these areas have major implications for proposed beneficiaries, costs of the program, effect on employees, administrative complexity, those remaining uninsured, and design of the plan itself. A difference of a million in the count of the uninsured can mean a difference of $1 to $2 billion in cost, depending on the benefit structure. Such differences can influence political decisions and have a major effect on the lives of individuals, viability of small employers, and so forth.

How do policy analysts handle these differences in methodology, assumptions, and findings? Their role in this instance is to explain differences in the assumptions and data and to describe what these differences mean in terms of specific policy options. Analysts are not machines. They have philosophical and disciplinary views. A good analyst tries to make these views known, usually in debates with the policymakers about the options.

The source of the data also must be considered. Do you view a survey conducted by the Health Insurance Association in the same way you view a similar survey conducted by the AFL–CIO or the American Hospital Association? Not that any of these groups skew their results, but the assumptions made in interpretations and projections will be different depending on perspectives—the values underlying the "what ifs."

What then does the decision maker do, particularly one not highly skilled in social science research? A number of policymakers will turn to more than one source of policy analysis and will sometimes use the technique of adversarial dialogue. Obviously, policymakers will assimilate information and be influenced by their own value systems.

Inadequate Data

A number of problems arise when data are inadequate or not pertinent for policy purposes. There will never be enough relevant data on a specific issue to satisfy a competent policy analyst. Nevertheless, there will often be a need to act—to make political, social, and economic decisions—with or without complete and adequate data. Responsible policy analysts must (1) identify the gaps in data when presenting policy options, (2) specify the limitations and conflicts of data, and (3) describe assumptions used in imputing data and the judgments made in choosing among conflicting data or assumptions. They must be firm in confronting decision makers with the reality that complex estimates cannot be precise. Policy analysts and decision makers must also work closely with researchers to define what information is needed. Reciprocally, researchers must inform them as to their hypotheses and the availability, timeliness, and limitations of their data and research findings. In many instances, unless social experiments are undertaken well in advance of major policy decisions, the decisions ultimately will be based on fragmentatory data, unexamined or partially examined value judgments, parochial disciplinary theory about social or economic behavior, or small experiments that may be representative only of local or special experience.

Medicare and Medicaid are classic examples of major social decisions based on limited data and experience. Many of the results have confirmed the theoretical bases for the programs, but there have been many unintended consequences, consequences that resulted from policy decisions made to gain consensus, actions stemming from expedient decisions designed to solve immediate problems, or consequences that were results of actions in totally different social spheres.

It was assumed that providing financial access to care for the poor and the aged would lead to greater physical access, equity of utilization, and improved health status. In the case of *Medicare,* superficially, all three occurred. However, physical access for certain services is not equal and perhaps never can be equal. In the case of *Medicaid,* physical access remained a problem, spurring the development of programs like the National Health Service Corps and community health centers to fill gaps. Utilization is uniform across all income classes of the elderly, and health status has improved steadily. The actual use rates for physicians' services have shown that low-income groups make somewhat greater use of physicians' services than higher-income groups, a reversal of the situation in the pre-1966 period.[6] But there remains a race differential in health status, with improvement only partially attributable

[6]L. Aday, R. Andersen, and G. Fleming, *Haealth Care in the United States: Equitable for Whom?* (Beverly Hills, Calif.: Sage Publications, Inc., 1980).

to improved financial access to health services. During the same period there were major changes in other social programs—food stamps, housing subisdies—and major biomedical and life-style changes that may have affected health status.

An attempt was made at the end of the Carter administration to use the equalization data as a basis for a policy decision that more community health centers and the National Health Service Corps were really no longer necessary at the same level of investment. However, utilization data were one set of data which, if used alone, masked or ignored the following equally relevant data:

1. Lower-income groups were sicker than the higher-income groups by several health status measures. Their utilization rate, therefore, *should* be higher.
2. Lower-income groups were more likely to use emergency room and outpatient hospital care than "mainstream physicians' services." Mainstream medicine was a specific intent of Medicare and Medicaid.

The problem arose because the real purpose was to seek reductions in the federal budget and, rather than explicitly stating this, the analysts sought selected data for a predetermined conclusion.

The data available when Medicare and Medicaid were enacted could not be used to predict all of the consequences and changes stimulated by these programs. There were numerous unintended consequences of Medicare and Medicaid:

1. Cost escalation, in part attributable to increased demand from Medicare and Medicaid beneficiaries, inflation, and new technology
2. The development of a large nursing home industry and increased "warehousing" of the elderly (a value-loaded statement)

3. A substantial increase in certain surgical and medical treatment rates for the elderly and disabled—such as cataract surgery, renal dialysis, prostate surgery—often without adequate evidence of efficacy of the services or increased contribution to better health status or quality of life

In addition, other policy decisions were made in other programs that affected the Medicare and Medicaid programs and their beneficiaries in unanticipated ways.

The 1960 Census had undercounted the aged population by as much as 10 percent in some areas, seriously affecting cost estimates. There were few data on use of nursing homes or home health services and there was no empirical base for decision making, yet these services were included in the benefit package under the assumption that they would reduce the need for higher-cost hospitalization. Retrospective reasonable cost reimbursement of hospitals was used by very few insurance carriers in the mid-1960s. Most used charges or negotiated rates. However, without the decision to enact this form of payment for hospitals, the hospital industry probably would have opposed passage of Medicare.

At about the same period the government made a decision, based on very crude methodology, that there was a shortage of physicians; it therefore stimulated a doubling of enrollment in medical schools. There were a series of unanticipated technological breakthroughs in medicine, many not yet fully assessed, that had an effect on the volume of procedures and the cost of medical care—including coronary bypass surgery, lasers, and chemotherapy. Even in the "scientific" fields—clinical medicine and biostatistics—there is no agreement on what data, methodologies, and ethical values should be used to assess these technologies.

There were also data that convinced the public that government intervention in health service delivery was necessary to address the great disparities in access to care by age and income class, the substantial disparities in health status by race and income, and the inability of the aged to purchase private insurance because of lack of availability of insurance in some areas and high cost in others. Should there have been a decision not to launch a major program because data were incomplete? Who would have gained? Who would have lost? Would we now have national health insurance if we had waited? Would technology have been introduced more slowly? Would the costs have risen at a slower rate? Would health status have improved anyway?

There will always be uncertainty, even with adequate data. There will never be enough data or data that precisely answer a specific question. If we were to wait until every uncertainty were eliminated, we would make few public policy decisions. There would be social and political paralysis. Ultimately, decisions are made on political and philosophical grounds. Research and data are not designed to serve the purpose of proving or disproving positions, but they can clarify and sharpen the debates, provide new insights, and describe what is known and what is conjecture.

The Political Process

Concerns are frequently expressed that the political process interferes with the use of data. While this may occur from time to time, the more common problems have to do with selectivity in use of different data sources, the objectivity and validity of the data, and the differences in perspectives or the disciplinary school of the analyst or the political philosophy of the policymaker. I know of no instance of constraint on releasing the results of surveys, health services research findings, or technology assessments in the health care field. However, this does not mean that policymakers always use the data or apply them appropriately. When convictions or political philosophy are strong, the policymaker or policy advocate may seek other sources of data, rephrase the question, raise new issues, or ignore the findings.

Several years ago, a controlled experiment was conducted to determine whether day care and homemaker services were a substitute for nursing home care.[7] The researchers hypothesized that these services would be a lower-cost substitute. The findings, to the surprise of the researchers, were that rather than being a substitute, these were in fact additive services and the total costs of care were higher. There appeared to be no evidence that morbidity, mortality, or functional indicators were better for the noninstitutionalized than the institutionalized population. In fact, the homemaker and day care group had higher hospitalization rates. How have these findings been used by policymakers and program advocates?

Some, who are truly convinced that it is better to be out of an institution that in one, criticized the sample and the methodology. (Both had been rigorously peer-reviewed, as had the study design and findings.) Some policymakers concluded that there was no need for public support of homemaking or day care services.

One view of the findings is that day care and homemaker services may well be valuable, but not as health services or as a substitute for nursing home care in the near term. There may be a long-term difference, but there are no longitudinal data to support or contradict the initial findings. Instead, the issue may be one of quality of life, which could not be an-

[7]William Weissert, *Effects and Costs of Day Care and Homemaker Services for the Chronically Ill: A Randomized Experiment* (Washington, D.C.: National Center for Health Services Research, Public Health Service Pubn. No. 79-3258, February, 1980).

swered by a study addressed to substitution of services and cost.

A major attack on this study has now been launched by numerous groups and some researchers—the kind of dispute that always rages around social research. However, some of the attacks are clearly related to the policy perspectives or interests of advocates for these services rather than to the study or findings. Some of the criticism is also related to the life-style–quality-of-life issue, which was not the issue addressed by the study.

The Analyst and Uncertainties

How then does the analyst deal with uncertainty, missing values, different theoretical constructs? There is no cookbook solution, and the analyst's handling of uncertainties will be influenced inevitably by his or her social philosophy or disciplinary bias. The analyst is usually not the decision maker; but through explication of the options and discussion of the missing data, projections, and so on, he or she does guide the decision maker.

For example, in the competition versus regulation debate, there is insufficient empirical evidence to support either position in its totality; however, there is some evidence to support certain positions at either pole. If, for example, the issue is to encourage increased cost sharing at the time of purchase of service to increase cost consciousness (and lower cost), the analyst would take the following steps:

1. Explore the number of empirical studies on the effects of cost sharing.
2. Explore what the effects might be for subpopulation groups and specific services (e.g., the nonpoor versus poor, hospital versus ambulatory), not merely on average.

3. Seek any available health status data.
4. Look at long-term effects if available.
5. Explore the role of the supply side, not merely the demand side of the equation, to determine who initiates services.
6. Explore the institutional problems in changing policy.
7. Look at the administrative effects.
8. Determine the views of key political groups—labor, management, physicians, and so on. In the case of cost-sharing changes, this would involve collective bargaining contracts between management and labor and would have a ripple effect on wages and other fringe benefits.

My own conclusion is that seeking utilization and cost control through increased cost sharing now would not be effective and could harm low-income people. It would be part of my role as the analyst not only to advise the decision makers as to my own conclusion but also to inform them of evidence and views other than my own.

While the analyst often can be and is an advocate, it is important for the analyst to clearly differentiate his or her personal views from the evidence or lack of evidence, since the analyst is also the broker or translator between the researcher and decision makers.

Responsible Research, Analysis, and Decision Making

There are several responsibilities the scientific community should more actively assume in the area of public policy. The first is to increase the synthesis and dissemination of reserach findings in everyday language. The second is to state hypotheses and assumptions more clearly and explicity. The third is to be more responsive to public policy priorities. And fourth, there is a responsibility to examine critically the use of the data, and to challenge the analyst and decision maker when the data are misquoted or misapplied or where conclusions go beyond those justified by the research. Often, researchers and statisticians are inward-looking, concerned primarily with their specific activity as well as with peer contact and approval. They regard policymakers and decision makers as incapable of understanding the nuance of their trade and fear that their findings will be used beyond their scientific validity. They are also reluctant to respond to the specific policy questions of decision makers.

Policy analysts who would walk the middle ground as the brokers between scientists and policymakers must know the sources of data, assure consideration of the full range of options, challenge assumptions of scientists and policymakers, and make known their own philosophic and value perspectives. They must also not be so paralyzed by their sesitivity to limitations of data that they fail to exploit available information to the fullest extent possible to inform policy decisions.

Policymakers are often mystified by the technicians, unfamiliar with the professional jargon, and frustrated that they cannot be given quick, definitive answers to very specific questions. They need to talk with researchers, learn some of the basic questions to ask about the sources and validity of the data, and know the assumptions and adjustments made in relation to the raw data. The adversarial process sometimes used by decision makers with policy analysts can be useful in eliciting value differences or disputes about reserach and data findings as well as in assuring consideration of multiple options.

The public must also become aware that most decisions made are based on the interaction of political and social values with data. There will never be enough evidence to address all questions or to make perfect projections. Improved data sources, methodology, and techniques of analysis and projection will provide a basis at least for better elucidation of the issues for informed debate if not for better decisions. Political discourse in a democratic society ideally requires knowledge and an understanding of the nature and limitations of information. It also requires understanding of the social, political, and moral values underlying the positions of the policymaker. Policy analysts in their roles as brokers between the researcher and policymaker have a responsibility, through analysis of the issues and presentation of options, to increase the breadth and improve the quality of political discourse. In the final analysis, political consensus will develop from the combination of information with political, social, and moral values and from the charisma of the leadership.

11

SOCIAL SCIENCE AND POLICY ANALYSIS
Some Fundamental Differences

MARK H. MOORE

It always seemed that social scientists could contribute a great deal to policymakers. Since policymakers needed information about the likely consequences of policy choices and social scientists were trained to reason and collect information about social processes in careful, rigorous ways, social scientists could reduce the uncertainty about the outcomes of policy choices. This simple syllogism stimulated the development of a large social science establishment and thickened the bonds between policymakers and social scientists. In fact, policymaking processes now routinely incorporate social scientists and social science findings as part of the appartus that determines (and legitimates) policy choices.[1]

[1]For some general discussions of the role of social science in policymaking see: Laurence E. Lynn, Jr., ed., *Knowledge and Policy: The Uncertain Connection* (Washington, D.C.: National Academy of Sciences, 1978); Henry J. Aaron, *Politics and the Professors* (Washington, D.C.: The Brookings Instituition, 1978); Charles E. Lindblom and David K. Cohen, *Usable Knowledge: Social Science and Social Problem Solving* (New Haven, Conn.: Yale University Press, 1979); and Seymour J. Deitchman, *The Best Laid Schemes: A Tale of Social Research and Bureaucracy* (Cambridge, Mass.: The M.I.T. Press, 1976).

MARK H. MOORE ☐ John F. Kennedy School of Government, Harvard University, Cambridge, Massachusetts 02138.

Despite the apparent compatibility, however, the marriage between policymaking and social science has not been happy. To some, the union seemed corrupt from the start: it threatened to shift social values and impoverish the political process by giving the "experts" and their arcane language too influential a role.[2] But even those in the process who consorted with one another most avidly have become somewhat disillusioned. The policymakers are increasingly frustrated by the inability of social scientists to produce compelling information in the form they need at the time they need it and are tired of being accused of acting in ignorance by any expert whose advice was ignored. For their part, the social scientists feel that their scientific virtue is under constant attack and that their important findings and cautions are cavalierly brushed aside by policymakers. So a certain prickliness has appeared in what promised to be a friendly relationship.

My contention is that this tension is created by fundamental differences between the tasks of providing information useful in making policy choices (the tasks of policy analysis) and the task of studying social processes in general (the tasks of social science). We have been confused about this difference because personnel and methods for the different enterprises overlap significantly. In fact, most policy analysis is still done by people who think of themselves as social scientists and bring the professional virtues of social scientists to the task of policy analysis. The prickliness we observe exists because the professional virtues of social scientists fail to mesh neatly with the task of policy analysis, and this leads to disappointment and mutual suspicion on both sides. The condition will persist until the professional virtues of policy analysis are distinguished from those of social science and accepted

---

[2]Edward Banfield, "Policy-Science as Metaphysical Madness" in *Bureaucrats, Policy Analysts, Statesmen: Who Leads,* ed. by Robert A. Goldwin (Washington, D.C.: American Enterprise Institute, 1980).

by those social scientists and others who find themselves doing policy analysis. The purpose of this essay is to explore the differences in the goals, professional standards, claims, and relationship of the government to social science on the one hand and policy analysis on the other.

DIFFERENT GOALS

The goal of social science is to enhance our knowledge of human behavior—to help us understand why people and social institutions behave the way they do.[3] The agenda of inquiry is largely established by the internal logic of existing disciplines. The normal activities of social scientists are to test, extend, and elaborate the theories that constitute the core of the disciplines.[4] One "succeeds" by developing original propositions which bear specifiable relationships to previously established propositions and concerns and showing—through rigorous logic, empirical evidence, or both—that the propositions are true or false. To a degree, of course, the agenda of social science is tempered by the "relevance" of an inquiry to current social issues and by the availability of data, instrumentation, and methods that make some questions easier to investigate than others. But still, achievement in the enterprise of social science is largely defined in terms of contributions to the core concepts and ideas of the discipline.

The goal of policy analysis is quite different: it is to inform policymakers about the likely consequences of alternative policy choices. Thus, the agenda of inquiry is set not by the internal logic of an academic discipline but by the set of issues and questions raised by some contemplated use of govern-

[3]Abraham Kaplan, *The Conduct of Inquiry* (New York: Harper & Row, Publishers, Incorporated, 1964).
[4]Thomas S. Kuhn, *The Structure of Scientific Revolutions* (Chicago: University of Chicago Press, 1970).

mental authority or resources. Each imagined use of governmental authority carries with it some conceivable consequences—both intended and unintended. The basic goal of policy analysis is to make as precise predictions as possible about the important, likely results of policy interventions. A piece of policy analysis is completed when the choice has been given a structure, including alternative actions and relevant possible consequences, and when estimates of the consequences have been made by tracing the causal links between the alternative actions and the consequences.[5] Thus, the goal is to inform a particular, complex choice—not to establish a truth or elaborate a discipline that is reaching for a general understanding of social processes.

Of course, substantial overlaps exist in both the subjects and methods of social science and policy analysis. With respect to *subjects,* for example, macroeconomic theory is quite closely related to macroeconomic policy, criminology quite closely linked to crime control policies, and Freudian theory intimately intertwined with the practice of psychoanalysis. Similarly, with respect to *methods,* both policy analysis and social science are concerned with developing true statements about empirical relationships in the world. Criminology seeks to know what factors affect the incidence of crime, and policy analysts concerned with crime control want to know how increased imprisonment might affect the level of crime. In seeking to develop such statements, both social scientists and policy analysts are bound by the same rules of evidence and inference. Finally, in presenting their conclusions, social scientists and policy analysts must both adhere to the principle of full specification of methods, assumptions, and data to ensure that others may replicate their observations and cal-

[5]Edith Stokey and Richard J. Zeckhauser, *A Primer for Policy Analyses* (New York: W. W. Norton & Company, Inc., 1978).

culations. Otherwise, any claims are suspect. Since social science findings often seem to be very important parts of policy analysis and policy analysis seems to accept many of the same methodological disciplines as social science, the two enterprises often appear to be so closely related as to be indistinguishable.

In my view, these similarities create confusion by obscuring much more fundamental differences. The differences concern both the form and substance of propositions that emerge from social science and policy analysis. Social science seeks to produce general descriptive propositions of the form "If X occurs, then it is likely that Y will also occur." Moreover, in choosing the X's and Y's, social science is guided by theoretical issues current in the discipline. Policy analysis, on the other hand, is interested in producing conditionally prescriptive propositions of the form "If one's purposes are to produce X, Y, and Z and one imagines alternatives A, B, and C, then our current knowledge of the world suggests that one should choose action A because that is likely to produce more of what is desired than either B or C." Moreover, in defining the relevant variables (i.e., the sets of relevant consequences and imagined actions), the policy analyst is guided not by social science theory but by concerns and questions raised by some contemplated use of governmental authority and resources.

Note also that the variables selected for investigation in the two different enterprises are likely to be very different. Because social science is interested in *general* explanations, the social scientist is likely to focus on a few "structural" variables. This focus on structural variables is consistent with the desire to develop a parsimonious general theory. Moreover, this focus is convenient in terms of allowing the maximum use of available empirical information and statistical methods to produce significant conclusions. The policy analyst, on the other hand, will focus on variables that can plausibly be affected by discrete policy instruments. Typically, these variables will be smaller and more precisely defined than the variables relied on in social science investigation. An example may be helpful.

If one were interested in developing general propositions about the role that guns played in determining the level and character of criminal attacks, it would be natural to think of a general variable called a "gun availability" and to measure its relationships to observed levels of criminal attacks.[6] On the other hand, if one were facing the policy issue of whether gun-control efforts should focus on depleting the general stock of handguns, on preventing new purchases, on keeping guns from proscribed persons, or on preventing the illegal carrying of handguns, one might well need a more refined notion of "gun availability" that distinguished among kinds of individuals and degrees of availability.[7] Typically, then, the variables of interest to policy analysts will be more particular and idiosyncratic than the variables interesting to social scientists. This implies that the *actual* substantive overlap between social science and policy analysis need not be very great.

The difference in form is also significant. The conditionally prescriptive statements of the policy analyst contain empirical propositions (those that link possible actions to relevant consequences). But they contain more than this. They include an implicit normative judgment in the identification of the relevant consequences. They include an implicit political and

---

[6]For an excellent example of this sort of theory, see Philip J. Cook, "The Effect of Gun Availability on Robbery and Robbery Murder: A Cross-section Study of Fifty Cities," in *Policy Studies Review Annual*, ed. by Robert H. Hauman and B. Bruce Zellner, III (Beverly Hills, Calif.: Sage Publications, Inc., 1979).

[7]Mark H. Moore, "Managing the Effective Price of Handguns." (Mimeographed; available from author.)

bureaucratic judgment in defining a plausible set of alternative actions. And behind the conclusion that one option is preferred to another is a more or less crude optimizing logic that builds from the empirical statement. Thus, propositions of interest to policy analysts contain a great deal more than straight empirical propositions.

These differences may seem insignificant and easily transcended. In my view, however, the gulf is much wider than commonly discerned. Perhaps the gap between policy analysis and social science can be illustrated by two characteristic things that happen when social scientists try to be helpful to policymakers.

Consider, first, the question of how a social scientist might proceed when asked about a given empirical relationship of some significance to policy—say, for example, the relationship between drug abuse and crime. In all likelihood, he or she will begin by assessing what is now known or believed about the relationship, going back to "the literature" and discussing existing theories and evidence. Attention will be focused on what is known or disputed and what could conveniently be discovered. This will take most of the social scientist's time. A policy analyst, on the other hand, would be inclined to ask first what he or she needs to know about this relationship in order to answer some plausibly interesting policy question. In searching the literature, then, the analyst—rather than being guided by the history of theorizing in this area or the desire to say exactly what is now known—will focus on what is known about the issues he or she needs to know in order to answer the policy question.[8] One reads

[8]These observations are based on personal experience with a major study to review what was known of the relationship of drug abuse and crime. For the early result, see *Report of the Panel on Drug Use and Criminal Behavior: Preliminary Draft* (Research Triangle, N.C.: Research Triangle Institute, June, 1976).

the literature much differently when the purpose is to establish what is known with confidence than when it is to find out what is known about an issue on which a policy decision turns.

Consider, next, the typical effort to develop "policy implications" from social science findings. In the typical social science publication, elaborate efforts are made to establish a causal relationship among some variables—say, again, drug abuse and crime. The discussion of the data and methods of investigation are careful and restrained. The current investigation is placed in the context of other theories and findings. All this is consistent with the desire to build firm structures of knowledge slowly and carefully. Once the author has painstakingly established the existence (or nonexistence) of a relationship, however, he or she turns to the "policy implications" of the finding. At this moment all the caution that characterized the analysis is often abandoned as the author rushes toward conditionally prescriptive propositions at a pace that would make a serious policy analyst blush. Suddenly, goals are being suggested and governmental action conditionally prescribed all on the basis of *one* more or less firmly established empirical finding.[9] The policy analyst would ask why the goals suggested by the social scientist were the "right" ones for considering policy and whether the stated goals were presented as a relatively complete statement of society's stakes in the area. Other obvious questions would be what set of policy alternatives had been considered and how the empirical finding proudly displayed by the social scientist might shed light on the likely consequences of governmental action. Typically, the social scientist would be silent on this point and

[9]For an example of this, see M. Harvey Brenner, "Drug Abuse Trends in National Economy and Crime Policy Report: (Baltimore, Md: Johns Hopkins University, School of Public Health, 1977.)

explain that he or she was merely suggesting some possible implications—not insisting on conclusions. The policy analyst, left with the problem of developing conditionally prescriptive conclusions for governmental action, might properly feel that the social scientist had left a substantial piece of work to be done. The analyst had still to develop the conception of the goals, conceive of plausible policy actions, and trace the empirical connections between governmental actions and consequences. In this, the finding of the social scientist might be helpful but far from sufficient for conditionally prescriptive statements about the advisability of governmental action.

In sum, then, social scientists and policy analysts have different goals. While they both seek to develop reliable and useful information about social processes, they do so for different "masters" and with different aims. For social science, the agenda of inquiry is established by academic disciplines seeking ever more powerful and more extensive generalizations about human behavior. For policy analysis, the agenda is set by contemplated uses of governmental authority to accomplish given purposes. Moreover, in the end, they are interested in developing different kinds of propositions. Social science is interested in developing general descriptive statements about social process. Policy analysis is interested in developing particular prescriptive statements about the advisability of governmental actions assuming certain goals.

PROFESSIONAL STANDARDS

The different goals of social science and policy analysis have important implications for standards of completed, high-quality work. Arguably, the first virtue of a piece of social science research is its definitiveness. Of course, the importance of the conclusion, the elegance of the study, and its originality may also affect professional assessment of a piece of social science research. But definitiveness is a very important virtue aggressively pursued by social scientists.

The first virtue of a piece of policy analysis, on the other hand, may be its relevance and usefulness in informing a choice. Definitiveness may also be a virtue. And if definitiveness can be pursued without paying a price in terms of relevance, a policy analyst may be duty bound to pursue it. But the interesting situation occurs when the pursuit of definitiveness costs the policy analyst something in terms of relevance. At this moment, a tension appears in his or her commitment to the virtues of social science on the one hand and to policy analysis on the other. In my experience, this tension appears not rarely but routinely. Moreover, the issue is confronted and resolved not in the late stages of an inquiry but right at the beginning, when "the problem" to be investigated is first defined.[10]

Recall that the aim of policy analysis is to produce conditionally prescriptive propositions with a high degree of confidence (e.g., if you want to achieve X and you are choosing from actions A, B, and C, choose A because it is most likely to produce what you want). Such statements are essentially optimizing statements that depend on a *combination of empirical* statements (describing links between actions and consequences) and an analytic logic that yields the optimal choice based on weights assigned to the different consequences of the actions. To meet the social science standard of definitiveness, the conditionally optimizing statements generated by policy analysis must be rigorously developed and defended. This means that the empirical statements must be verified (or plausibly assumed) and the analytic logic explicitly laid out.

[10]Mark H. Moore, "The Anatomy of the Heroin Problem: An Exercise in Problem Definition," *Policy Analysis*, 2 (Fall, 1976), 639–62.

This is what makes the calculation reproducible and verifiable by others. In addition to the requirement for internal consistency, however, the propositions developed by the policy analysis must meet a test of *external* validity as well. The terms of the calculation must correspond to the terms of the situation as the policymaker confronts it.

Now, tension always exists between the standards of convenient empirical investigation, internal consistency, and external validation. The messy particulars of the world yield easily neither to elegant theoretical formulation nor to convenient measurement. Some verisimilitude must be sacrificed to allow for parsimonious theories whose internal logic can be fully and easily specified and which can be tested across a wide variety of situations. Professionals in both social science and policy analysis seeking to do quality work need to know how to strike this balance between verisimilitude and abstraction. Where to strike this balance, however, is a key issue. For social scientists, the standard is fairly clear: prefer parsimony and generality over verisimilitude. This is consistent with the goal of developing powerful general theories.

It is far from clear, however, that this should be the standard for policy analysts. After all, policy analysts justify their activities by being helpful to policymakers facing particular choices. Arguably, in formulating *their* problems (i.e., in defining relevant consequences, in conceiving of plausible government actions, and in estimating the likely consequences of actions), they should strike a different balance between elegance and solvability on the one hand and a close correspondence to the details of the particular world on the other. Because much of immediate practical significance turns on the particular way a policy problem is defined, it seems plausible that policy analysts should expand their definition of the problem until it corresponds closely to what is immediately possible and at stake in the world, even if that expansion implies sacrificing rigor and certainty in the internal parts of the calculation. Thus, the desirability of parsimony, generality, and elegance against the demands of verisimilitude may be less strong for policy analysis than for social science.

If it is accepted that, to accommodate important particulars, the definitions of policy problems must be complex, it follows that the standards for "completeness" must be relaxed. Implicit in most policy analyses are scores of empirical assertions, which may or may not be fully validated. There is also an optimizing logic that grows increasingly complex as terms are added to the analysis. If the calculation becomes too complex and many empirical propositions are buried in it, it becomes impossible to meet the test of internal completeness and validity: the conclusion about the appropriate action simply does not emerge from a reproducible calculation. The clear implication is that if policy analysis is to be useful, we cannot insist on the same standard of completeness. We must understand the analysis as something that informs but does not strictly force a decision. Great room is left for disagreement and judgment.

This applies to the empirical assertions contained in the policy analysis as well as the overall conclusions. In fact, this is the area of greatest tension between the standards of policy analysis and the standards of social science. As noted above, a policy analysis is often built on a series of empirical statements about causal relationships in the world (e.g., the presence of guns in assault situations increases the probability of death; therefore, if one could remove guns from assault situations and everything else remained unchanged, the homicide rate would fall). The empirical relationships (and the methods for confirming that they exist) are at the heart of social science. For this reason, social science treats them with great respect. Nothing should be reported or believed about empirical relationships (and certainly no action should be based on beliefs about relationships) unless one is confident in this knowledge. Policy analysts, on the other hand, have a much more voracious appetite for information. They are quite happy if a piece of information makes one hypothesis only a little more likely than another; they do not insist on 95 percent confidence that one hypothesis is true. The only imperatives are to use as much information as is available, to be disciplined in letting this information shape one's beliefs about the relative likelihood of a variety of alternative hypotheses being true, and to be careful in designing policies to hedge against the likelihood that the current most likely hypothesis will be wrong.[11] This apparently cavalier attitude toward empirical relationships—the willingness to use imperfect information and act on the basis of uncertainty about the relationships—stimulates indignation among social scientists, who feel that something important and solemn is being sacrificed when their painstaking conservatism in accepting information is brushed aside in favor of a less restrictive approach. It is important to understand, however, that while the approach may be less *restrictive* in terms of what kinds of information can properly be used and how certain one must be to begin talking about empirical relations, policy analysis is no less rigorous nor less faithful to the idea that we should form our views about causal relationships by looking at facts. Instead, it says that we will let available facts shape our views of which empirical statements are likely to be true and that we will act happily in situations where we cannot be sure that one hypothesis is true by hedging our actions against the possibility that alternative hypotheses will turn out to be true.

If empirical standards and requirements for completeness in the internal logic are relaxed, it also follows that no sig-

[11]Howard Raiffa, *Decision Analysis* (Reading, Mass.: Addison Wesley Publishing Co., Inc., 1968).

nificant threshold need be surmounted to do a useful bit of policy analysis. Since the purpose of policy analysis is to structure and inform choices, and since it is always possible to make some progress in performing this function and little prospect that one can fully complete it, one can work at the enterprise in good conscience no matter how much time is available. Back-of-the-envelope calculations, month-long inquiries that allow deeper searches for documented experience, the exploitation of natural experiments that may have occurred, and multiyear studies that allow explicit experimentation all have value within the enterprise of policy analysis. Since the professional goal is always to use whatever time one has available to inform a choice as effectively as possible, no great prejudice is attached to studes that are "quick and dirty." Indeed, if time is short, they may have great value. This tolerance of hasty work is fortunate, of course, since it is often difficult to predict in advance when information of certain kinds will be needed, and it is reassuring to know that we need not have to give several years to pieces of policy analysis before they have any use.

In sum, then, policy analysis and social science strike much different balances as they seek to understand the world. Policy analysis seeks a close embrace with the particular terms and conditions of the world as it is affected by a contemplated use of governmental authority. For this close embrace, it is willing to sacrifice something in terms of confidence in empirical statements and internal completeness of the logic that produces conditional, prescriptive propositions. Moreover, there appears to be no minimum amount of time or effort necessary to quality a piece of policy analysis as useful. It all depends on how helpful observations, reflection, and lines or argument turn out to be in revealing what is plausibly at stake in policy choices. Social science operates with much different standards—particularly with respect to the tradeoffs between parsimony and verisimilitude and thresholds for accepting pieces of empirical information as useful. The differences predictably create tensions between policy analysts and social scientists and within the same person switching from task to task without noticing that he or she is doing so.

PUBLIC CLAIMS

If the conclusions of a piece of policy analysis do not emerge unambiguously and definitively from a reproducible calculation, the claims it can make on public credibility are less than policy analysts sometimes suppose. As noted above, it can inform a policy choice but cannot dictate by force of logic. Substantial room is left for more or less idiosyncratic judgments. The relative importance of different objectives can be altered. New objectives and alternatives can be created. Pieces of information bearing on beliefs about causal relationships can be interpreted somewhat differently. And different attitudes towards uncertainty and time can affect the "calculation" of which course of action is most appealing. The power of a piece of policy analysis, then, depends on how helpful its structure and accumulated information is in illuminating a choice and how persuasive its line of argument is in defense of a given policy. To the extent that it reflects and stretches the concerns of those who must decide, putting before them information and reasoning that increases their capacity to discover the likely results of alternative choices, it can be helpful and even influential, but it can rarely command fealty.[12]

This loss of determinacy and the weakening of the claims of policy analysis is often seen as the price policy analysts

---

[12]Charles E. Lindblom, *The Policy Making Process* (Englewood Cliffs, N.J.: Prentice-Hall, Inc., 1968).

pay for sacrificing the rigorous standards of social science. If
the analysts had hewn more closely to the requirements for
internal logical consistency and verification of empirical assertions, if they were not so undiscriminating in their use of
information, and if they were patient enough for truth to be
established, they could claim much more for their work. As
it is now, their pandering to the concerns of politicians and
their casual use of the powerful tools of social science tend
to give all science a bad name.

The problem with this perspective, of course, is its presupposition that a properly "scientific" approach to the design
of policies could make greater claims than policy analysis now
can. In principle this is true. One can imagine a full specification of the choice confronting a policymaker that met all
tests for internal consistency and external validation where
the only indeterminacy was in the values to be assigned to
given objectives. In such a situation, the conditionally prescriptive propositions of policy analysis would be powerful
indeed. But in the real world, this is *not* true, and it is unlikely
to become true (except in a few areas) over the next decades.
Thus, it seems to me misguided to hope that a greater commitment to scientific principles would produce more powerful
policy analyses.

In fact, I think it is likely that the commitment to more
science and more powerful claims for policy analysis will not
only fail to produce better policy analysis but lead to distor-
tions in what well-trained, conscientious people do when they
try to inform policy choices. For one thing, to assume that no
ultimate tension exists between social science and policy analysis will cause social scientists to misallocate their efforts as
they confront policy problems. They will seek to advance the
science of solving that particular problem. That, in turn, will
lead them to forget that their first loyalty is to define the
problem in appropriate terms; they will shrink the terms of

the problem to make it more amenable to solution. Having reduced the problem and solved it, they will then think that their solution has more status than it deserves. It will be science demanding allegiance from intuition and judgment. Any failure to honor the claims of science will be treated as ignorance or corruption. And the tensions and mutual suspicion that now mark the relationship between policymakers and social scientists who are doing policy analysis will be exacerbated.

This conclusion that policy analyses cannot claim the definitiveness of social science findings is treated as bad news in many circles—so bad, in fact, that it is stubbornly resisted. The resistance seems based on a reluctance to surrender an elevated and special status. If one has the special skills required to produce truth and if others need truth, then one is in a powerful position. It is disappointing to find that a social scientist's status in confronting policy problems is reduced first by accepting the influence of mere policymakers in setting one's agenda and, second, by the discovery that one's tools harnessed to this task will fail to produce an undeniable truth. Some of the privileged status of social scientists is stripped away. They can still be scientists, of course. But they are denied the *dual* status of scientist and policy influential. In the conception of policy analysis presented here, the role of the scientifically trained policy influential becomes a more modest one, measured more by a capacity to be helpful than by exclusive access to truth and enlightenment.

Many social scientists, disappointed to discover that they could spend several years working carefully and imaginatively on a policy problem only to produce "conclusions" that are at best helpful in guiding policy for a few years, will decide that the returns are hardly worth the effort—particularly when contrasted with the hope of immortality through a significant contribution to a scientific discipline. But for many who decide this way, it is a wrong decision. Their talents could frequently have greater social value if they turned their attention to policy problems and away from the marginal contributions that can be made to the disciplines. There is plenty of scope for ambition, skill, intelligence, and imagination in seriously confronting particular policy problems as well as in elaborating a discipline. In fact, I would argue that the people trained in social science methods are now very badly allocated in society, with far too many working on basic research elaborating existing disciplines and far too few using their skills to illuminate the stakes of policy decisions. At any rate, I think it is undeniable that even the most gifted social scientists applying themselves to a policy problem will produce pieces of anlaysis that leave plenty of room for disagreement. Hence, the claims of both policy analysis and social science as they confront policy problems must be modest, and they must take guidance from the terms and conditions of the particular situations as they appear to policymakers.

Relationships to Politics and Government

Throughout this essay, I have suggested that a crucial difference between policy analysis and social science is their relationship to government. Like all sciences, the social sciences (as social science) should seek an arm's-length relationship to the government. The enterprise will need government subsidies, and current needs may reasonably influence research agendas on the margin. But social sciences should insist on their right to pursue lines of inquiry regardless of the political implications. Nothing else is consistent with our commitment to free inquiry.

Policy analysis, on the other hand, is inevitably closely intertwined with governmental actions and concerns. In fact, contemplated uses of government activity and resources are what define the issues to be addressed and resolved by policy analysis. Thus, the closer the relationship, the better. This observation is sometimes taken to imply that the government should (or will) subordinate policy analysts. Two threats to intellectual integrity are of particular concern. One is that policy analysts working for the government will be influenced to abandon their critical and imaginative perspective. They will accept the terms in which the government defines the problems rather than altering the terms to incorporate different objectives or new alternatives. As a result, potentially attractive alternatives will be lost and important stakes overlooked. The second threat is that the analysts will be biased in the way they report or interpret information. The bias will run to supporting current government programs. Both threats together will cause policy analysis to become a bastion for the status quo rather than an engine for innovation and change.

That such pressures exist, I have no doubt. Moreover, I am sure they are maximized for policy analysts employed by agencies within the government. Still, it seems possible that policy analysts could develop a professional norm resistant to such pressures. I think the government is best served by policy analysts who are aggressive and take initiative in defining policy problems, always going slightly beyond the strict terms of their assignment to see what other alternatives might exist and what unanticipated consequences might occur. Moreover, I think policymakers are best served (and know that they are) when analysts report and interpret information as objectively as they can. This does not mean that advocacy should not or could not ever appear in policy analysis. But it does mean that policy analysts should retain a substantial degree of intellectual independence in defining the problem and in collecting, reporting, and interpreting information. The close relationship with government does not mean that policy analysts should abandon their intellect or training. It means that they should put their skills to use in an effort to be helpful to the government.

CONCLUSIONS

The tools and methods of the social sciences are increasingly important to government as it faces a wide variety of complex, substantive choices. In addressing these choices, we must depend on careful definitions of the problems and careful observation and close reasoning to foresee the important results. People trained in social science often have the skills, patience, interests, and intelligence to perform this task well.

Unfortunately, social scientists bring with them some attitudes and expectations that are disabling as well as enabling. They often think that their most fundamental objective is to develop a discipline or establish a truth rather than to inform a policy choice. They resent the influence the government has in shaping the issues they are asked to address. They alter the terms of reference in the policy problems they confront to make them solvable, in the mistaken belief that solving a narrowed version of the problem is more important than defining the problem accurately. They dismiss imperfect information and are reluctant to propose action without certainty about key empirical relationships.

It would be valuable to develop a group of people well trained in social science methods who understood that their main professional responsibility was not to elaborate disciplines or establish truths but to structure and inform particular policy choices. In doing this, it would be important that they maintain some detachment from the political process—enough to allow them to go beyond the definitions of problems as they were presented and to prevent bias in their collection, reporting, and interpretation of available information. But they should also understand that in an important sense they are part of the political process. Their agendas will be shaped by government action. And their advice, while influential, could not be expected to command governmental choices. They would have to be comfortable with problems that were too messy to be neatly solved and would have to become disciplined in using imperfect information appropriately. Such changes in orientation are extremely difficult. And the only reward is the possibility of being appropriately influential over a short period of time on a policy choice. But in our current world, this seems a high calling indeed.[13]

[13]I am indebted to Ken Prewitt, Bob Behn, Phil Cook, and Dean Gerstein for helpful comments on an earlier version of this paper.

12

SUBVERTING POLICY PREMISES

KENNETH PREWITT

The chapter by Mark Moore, which is the occasion for the present commentary, enters a very old discussion in a somewhat limited fashion. On its own terms, I have no quarrel with Moore's central point. Science does have a difficult time accomodating itself to the "policy space" within which the official normally must act. The policymaker—whether in the government, commercial, or educational sector—operates under a series of well-known constraints: existing policies, budgets, personnel limitations, tight schedules, and political pressures. It is pernicious to offer as advice a set of policy recommendations that ignore these limitations. Whether or not one agrees with Moore in all his specifics about the differing goals and standards of the social scientist and the policy analyst, his paper repeats and elaborates a now familiar theme which most observers generally share.

But Moore's argument is, I believe, so limited as to fail to uncover a more basic point about the interaction of social science and policy process. In these few pages I will approach the notion of policy space from a perspective quite different

KENNETH PREWITT □ President, Social Science Research Council, 605 Third Ave., New York, New York 10016.

from Moore's. Social science makes its most profound contribution to policymaking when it subverts rather than tries
to accomodate itself to preexisting policy premises. This subversion need not be deliberate and indeed probably works
best when it is accidental—the unanticipated outcome of a
meandering research process.

As background to arguing this point I remind the reader
that the close interaction between social science and the policy
process is certainly as old as empirical social science itself.
The earliest professional organization for the social sciences
in the United States, founded in 1865, was the American Social
Science Association. This organization was dedicated to the
effort of applying social knowledge to the then current social
problems. It drew its members from a social reform as well
as "scientific" tradition. The emergence of an empirical social
science was, to be sure, influenced by the likes of Benjamim
Pierce and Louis Agassiz, men dedicated to raising scientific
standards; but it was also influenced by its deeper roots in
moral philosophy. In the words of Dorothy Ross, who has
written some of the best history of this early period, "the men
who responded to the call of the ASSA and who sought to
develop in the colleges a more worldly and effective kind of
knowledge were particularly sensitive to the need for intelligent leadership and social order."[1] Ross notes that this call
for a more worldly knowledge quickly influenced teaching as
well as research. The early leaders of the social sciences took
advantage of the then innovative idea of electives to present
undergraduate courses that "were oriented toward social
problems and took students into the cities and institutions to
actually see the 'delinquent, defective and dependent classes.'"[2]

[1]Dorothy Ross, "The Development of the Social Science," in *The Organization
of Knowledge in Modern America, 1860–1920,* ed. by Alexandra Oleson and
John Voss (Baltimore: The Johns Hopkins Press, 1979), p. 112.
[2]Ibid., p. 110.

The earliest period of modern social science set a pattern. Disciplinary developments were to be influenced by trends internal to intellectual life; in the 1860s this was the weakening of religious authority and the challenge to philosophical approaches. But they were simultaneously to be influenced by trends in the society more generally: urbanization, industrialization, immigration. Nowhere is this better seen than in the topics chosen for the first attempts at an empirical sociology. Thus in the United States, as early as the depression of the 1870s, there were surveys of unemployment in Massachusetts, of the condition of the poor in New York, and of sanitation facilities and disease in northeastern cities. And of course the famous Booth surveys, published in seventeen volumes as *Life and Labour of the People in London* (1892–1897); the Rowntree's studies of the conditions of the working class in York, England (1901); and Bowley's surveys of working-class conditions in Reading were British counterparts in the early establishment of empirical sociology.[3] As Peter Rossi observed in his 1980 presidential address to the American Sociological Association, "our roots in applied concerns are old and very much alive. Our ranks always have been full of ministers and ex-ministers, radicals and ex-radicals, even a few conservatives and ex-conservatives, all of whom were attracted to sociology because our discipline appeared to have some relevance to social reform or its prevention."[4]

The roots of which Rossi speaks took deep hold during the Progressive era, when the utility of scientific research for social reform was widely (and, as we know in retrospect,

[3]For a useful summary, see Richard W. Boyd and Herbert H. Hyman, "Survey Research," in *Handbook of Political Science,* ed. by Fred I. Greenstein and Nelson W. Polsby, VII (Reading, Mass.: Addison-Wesley Publishing Co., 1975), pp. 268–70.

[4]Peter H. Rossi, "The Challenge and Opportunities of Applied Social Research," *American Sociological Review,* 45 (December 1980), 889.

somewhat wildly) promised. As perhaps best characterized in the career of Charles E. Merriam and the network of organizations he worked with or helped launch—the Brookings Institution, the National Bureau of Economic Research, the Social Science Research Council, the Laura Spelman Fund, and the Institute for Public Administration—the attempt to put social scientists at the disposal of the governing process was neither fully successful nor fully a failure.[5] A success story, *Recent Social Trends,* commissioned by President Herbert Hoover, brought together the nation's leading scientists to investigate the topics forced on the nation's agenda by the Depression and its after effects: social security, unemployment, internal migration, agricultural prices, and so on. This massive two-volume study stimulated a great deal of problem-focused research, research which, among other things, led to the social security system and to a reconception of the national statistics on work force behavior.

The linking of research and government policy has many more chapters. In the 1940s, not surprisingly, social scientists turned their concepts and methods to war-related issues: civilian morale; enemy propaganda; the recruitment, training, promotion, and eventual discharge of members of the armed forces; and the effects of strategic bombing on the civilian populations of Germany and Japan.

In the 1950s, as the prewar colonial empires disintegrated and the United States became strategically and economically involved with new nations around the world, the interdisciplinary field we now know as "area studies" was established. Area studies has much the same relationship to foreign policy as certain disciplinary research has had to domestic policy—an uneasy exchange of ideas, influence, and even personnel.

---

[5]See Barry D. Karl, *Charles E. Merriam and the Study of Politics* (Chicago: University of Chicago Press, 1974).

The 1960s saw the return to some topics that had motivated research and policy interest in the 1860s—urban problems, poverty, health care delivery, education—though of course the techniques had by now become far advanced over those available in the earlier period. It is largely the experience of the 1960s and 1970s that has motivated Mark Moore's argument. It seems to me, however, that to take full measure of his argument we must see the last decade or so in some historical perspective. I draw three general lessons from the historical record.

First, a large share of social scientific resources has always been directed to issues, problems, and questions suggested by the contemporary political–social agenda. What is on the mind of the society is, not surprisingly, what is on the mind of those who study the society. This has been true whether the funding is from private sources, as it was in the early years, or from public sources, as it increasingly has been in later decades. It has been true whether the research is conducted largely in universities or in specialized research institutes, and in recent years the mixture has tended to favor the latter. It has been true whether the research is labeled basic or applied, if indeed those labels offer us anything. And it has been true across quite a variety of social issues and of political judgments about how to respond to them. There is peace research, just as there is research designed to improve the military capacity of the state. There is research motivated by egalitarian ideologies and research focused on finding and rewarding excellence. There is research that presumes an expanding national authority and research into ways of limiting the public sphere. There is research that has helped the United States establish a dominant economic and political presence in nations around the world and research that points away from hegemony and toward greater sharing of the world's resources.

If we look back on a century of experience in the social

sciences, we will find it difficult to locate the dichotomy so pronounced in Moore's paper—the dichotomy between social science and policy research. The nation's actual political–social agenda so interpenetrates intellectual questions and approaches that there ~~there~~ is something forced about Moore's view of social science driven solely by disciplinary concerns. These disciplinary concerns have, very often, derived from the agenda with which the policymakers are trying to cope.

If the first lesson we draw from the historical record is probably uncontroversial, the second is no doubt more debatable. To sharpen the debate, I will state the lesson in its most unvarnished form as follows: "All science is, in the long run, applied science." Malinowski, in the opening paragraphs of his classic essay *Magic, Science and Religion*, opines:

> a moment's reflection is sufficient to show that no art or craft however primitive could have been invented or maintained, no organized form of hunting, fishing, tilling, or search for food could be carried out without the careful observation of natural process and a firm belief in its regularity, without the power of reasoning and without confidence in the power of reasons.[6]

That is, continues Malinowski, "without the rudiments of science." This is not to deny the claims of the sacred and the supernatural on people's beliefs and actions. It is, rather, to state the truism that reliable knowledge about the world is used by people trying to live in that world.

The principle that "all science is, in the long run, applied science" has particular relevance for the social sciences. The social sciences attempt to provide some of that reliable knowledge used by people who have to manage the modern insti-

---

[6]Bronislaw Malinowski, *Magic, Science and Religion* (Garden City, N.Y.: Doubleday & Company, Inc., 1955), p. 17. The essay was first published in 1925.

tutions—government, industrial, educational, scientific, commercial—which now organize much of the world's activity. In struggling with foreign policy issues, for example, not many officials would trade the knowledge we now have of other people's cultures and histories for the ignorance that characterized stereotypes about "foreign" people and "remote" places just a few decades ago. People trying to plan commercial investments or local government services appear to prefer the insights into population characteristics that derive from demographic projections over the shortsighted views about population dynamics which prevailed until very recently. In trying to manage a complex social-service-delivery state, only the arrogant seem willing to trade in the empirical intelligence based on a national statistical system for the guesses and hunches that had to serve the policy process before modern measurement and statistical developments occurred.

To claim, then, that all science is eventually applied science is to assert that as long as we live in a reasoning society, reasonable people will prefer to work with such knowledge as is available, however limited or flawed. This extends to those people who make policy. Obviously the policymaker will balance multiple political pressures and conflicting social goals. The process being described is not a deterministic one. Knowledge, especially the kind provided by social scientists, might help sort out some policy options; it is seldom determinative.

To make this obvious point even more obvious, we can distinguish between ignoring and ignorance. The policymaker may have compelling reasons for ignoring some forms of knowledge—information, insights, or interpretations—but it is hard to see why the policymaker would want to be kept ignorant of knowledge (except, of course, in the limiting case when the costs of acquisition outweigh the possible usefulness).

The third lesson I draw from the historical record returns us to a point made earlier in the paper. Mark Moore believes that social science can better serve the policymaking process if more of its practitioners accomodate themselves to the policy space within which those who frame policies necessarily live. My contrary argument is that social science makes its greatest contribution when its findings and methods stretch and even transform preexisting policy premises.

Compare what this society used to presume about the "Negro race" with what it now presumes. The eleventh edition of the *Encyclopedia Britannica*, published in 1911, purported to be a comprehensive summary of available knowledge and was so treated by most informed persons. This is what it had to say about "the Negro race":

> In certain . . . characteristics . . . the negro would appear to stand on a lower evolutionary plane than the white man, and to be more closely related to the highest anthropoids.. . .
>
> Mentally, the negro is inferior to the white. The remark of F. Manetta, made after a long study of the negro in America, may be taken as generally true of the whole race: "the negro children were sharp, intelligent, and full of vivacity, but on approaching the adult period a gradual change set it. The intellect seemed to become clouded, animation giving place to a sort of lethargy, briskness yielding to indolence. We must necessarily suppose that the development of the negro and the white proceeds on different lines." This explanation is reasonable and even probable as a contributing cause; but evidence is lacking on the subject and the arrest or even deterioration in mental development is no doubt very largely due to the fact that after puberty sexual matters take the first place in the negro's life and thoughts.

The most recent edition of the *Encyclopedia Britannica*, the fifteenth, published in 1974, also comments on racial differences in intelligence:

In studies of racial differences in intelligence in countries where white culture is dominant, it has been a very consistent finding that groups classified as Negro or black are likely to achieve lower scores on standard intelligence tests than do groups of whites or Caucasians. Yet, despite typically significant differences between the mean scores of the two so-called racial groups, the ranges (i.e., the spread between the lowest score and the highest score in each group) are usually found to be about the same, revealing extensive overlap in the score distributions of the two groups. Indeed, even in studies in which average scores strongly seemed to favour whites, considerable numbers of black subjects achieved higher scores than those of the average white.

Thus, while it has been argued that IQ data constitute support for those theories of genetic racial inferiority, it seems more likely that the differences reflect persistent social and economic discrimination. Under legal or de facto segregation in many countries, educational facilities for blacks rarely have been equal to those provided for whites (e.g., South Africa, Angola). There is considerable evidence that the growth of intelligence, as reflected in the IQ, is influenced significantly by the quality of available educational resources regardless of race. For example, lower class whites also show lower average IQ scores than do middle class whites in European and North American countries.

A lot happened in the first three-quarters of the twentieth century to transform common explanations for differential achievements of various racial groups. Social science research was a significant part of this transformation. The early studies of Klineberg and colleagues laid the basis for an interpretation of differential achievements that stressed unequal opportunities and environments, a set of research findings that greatly expanded the policy space—dramatically revealed when the Supreme Court, in *Brown* v. *Board of Education of Topeka, Kansas*, referenced a number of social science studies. There was also Gunnar Myrdal's enormously influential study *An Amer-*

ican Dilemma, not designed, of course, as a policy study but identifying those social conditions which it was neither moral nor practical for policymakers to ignore. Since these early social science studies there has been an avalanche of research reports and books—all generally pointing away from "inherent racial inferiority" and toward patterns of institutional racism and discrimination as causes of differential levels of achievement. If the eleventh edition of the *Encyclopeida Britannica* stated the premise for racial policy at the start of the century, the fifteenth edition states the premise for racial policy at the end of the century. In between was lots of work by social scientists.

There is, in this example, a larger familiar point to be made. As so eloquently stated by Edwin H. Land:

> Each stage of human civilization is defined by our mental structures: the concepts we create and then project upon the universe. They not only redescribe the universe but also in so doing modify it, both for our own time and for subsequent generations. This process—the revision of old cortical structures and the formulation of new cortical structures whereby the universe is defined—is carried on in science and art by the most creative and talented minds in each generation.[7]

Creating concepts and projecting them on the universe is one of the things which social science is very much about. This activity powerfully affects the making of policies in this and other societies. Our policy language is full of terms whose meaning has either started in the social sciences or has moved from ordinary language to the social sciences and then returned to policy discussions bearing the added meaning fixed upon them by research: *GNP, standard of living, juvenile delin-*

[7]From his comments at the groundbreaking ceremony on April 2, 1979, for the House of the American Academy of Arts and Sciences, as reproduced in the Bicentennial Program of the Academy, May 15–16, 1981.

quency, stagflation, nuclear family, span of control, human capital, externalities, unemployment. These terms are interpretive constructs. They identify and thereby make accessible dimensions of social life which have to be labeled if they are to be accessed by a policy effort.

Consider the last term on the list, unemployment. John Milton used it in Paradies Lost: "Other Creatures all day long Rove idel unimploid.. . ." in a fashion that imputed idleness and moral weakness. Unemployment was a personal choice, not the consequence of market failure—or so was the conventional wisdom during the frequent economic depressions of the nineteenth and early twentieth centuries. Social science research corrected this conventional wisdom when it began to use the term in connection with the characteristics of business cycles and labor markets, treating unemployment as a social condition. It is difficult to imagine the Full Employment Act of 1946 except in a policy context provided by several decades of social and economic research. Contemporary research on the "hidden economy," a seemingly permanent informal labor market and system of production in the United States, may have equally far-reaching consequences for economic policymaking.

The capacity to locate and label phenomena such as the hidden economy—or the changing family structure or the baby boom or white flight—gives to social science a powerful role in the policy process. Often the conventional policy space comes equipped with blinders that screen out social conditions and opportunities. These conditions and opportunities can become known as a consequence of the research discoveries of social science.

Social science and the policy process, thus, are each open-ended activities, feeding each other and transforming each other. So it has been for at least one hundred years. The results are mixed, but I doubt that Moore's advice, if resolutely followed, would much improve things. Indeed, if social scientists were to package themselves as policy analysts and squeeze themselves into the policy space as described by Moore, we might lose more than we would gain. In my judgment, society is best served if the research enterprise has ample room to challenge and subvert one generation's conventional wisdom on behalf of an expanded understanding for the next generation.

13

PARTIAL KNOWLEDGE

THOMAS H. MURRAY

Perfect knowledge is a chimera; imperfect knowledge our timeless condition. Still, there are vast differences in degree of imperfection, since we can build bridges, confident that they will not fall, and construct chemical plants, confident that they will produce the compounds intended; yet we are unable to design a program for the alleviation of poverty with any confidence that it will reach the goal we set.

It will not do to say that the difference between the bridge and chemical plant on the one hand and the antipoverty program on the other is that we have a clear consensus on the goals of the former and disagreement on those of the latter. That is certainly true, and an important problem in its own right, but there is a separable problem here. Even if we could agree on our goals (as in many instances of social policy I believe we can, at least as well as many of those drawing on the physical sciences), what role does and can social knowledge play in reaching those goals?

This is how I will take the problem of imperfect social

THOMAS H. MURRAY □ Associate for Social and Behavioral Studies, The Hastings Center, Institute of Society, Ethics and the Life Sciences, 360 Broadway, Hastings-on-Hudson, New York 10706.

knowledge and social policy. Questions about the goals of policy—who should choose them and how they should be chosen—are crucial. But I must bracket them temporarily and get to the other fundamental questions about how to deal with imperfect knowledge whatever the goals, however they were fixed.[1] It would require an awesome display of self-control and dissociation—well beyond my abilities—to completely avoid any discussion of goals here. But I will try to keep it to a minimum.

[1]In another paper in this volume ("Social Science as Practical Reason"), Robert N. Bellah argues for the moral primacy of what he calls "practical social science" over the more common "technological social science." The purpose of this note cannot be to evaluate the whole of Bellah's argument, which is a major statement for a program for which I have deep sympathy, but merely to place this modest article in relation to Bellah's position and to the larger issues at their intersection.

As I understand Bellah, practical social science gains its moral primacy from three factors: (a) it relies, in its practice, on a moral relationship between the studier and the studied; (b) it contains a moral vision—in Bellah's case, of a dialogic, democratic society; and (c) it is conscious of its own moral force, of the impact it has on society.

Technological social science, on the other hand, lends itself to manipulation and even despotism because (a) it concerns itself with means and techniques, irrespective of the ends to which such means might be put and (b) it often refuses to acknowledge its own moral force, either in its process (the relationship of scientist and subject) or its product (the tools and techniques it provides to change society).

What Bellah has done is to sketch out a method (the dialogue), a political–moral theory (democratic mutuality), and a means of change (self-knowledge) that are compatible and are threatened by the hallmarks of technological social science, manipulation, and self-deception (about the moral force of one's work).

One could, of course, imagine a practical social science revolving around a different political–moral theory but that otherwise looks formally like Bellah's democratic-dialogic one. For example, Machiavelli's *Prince* is a marvel of practical wisdom to which the best of contemporary practical social scientists might aspire. Its moral vision is undoubtedly one that many of us would find repulsive, but no one could deny that it was deeply

THE PROBLEM

The one point of agreement I find among purveyors of social knowledge and their potential consumers—policy-makers—is that the relationship between social knowledge and social policy is unsatisfactory. Intelligent use of the best social knowledge is a rarity if it exists at all. Whatever use is made is often inappropriate, based on poor examples of the genre and sure to become a matter of considerably dispute.

Diagnoses of the etiology of this unsatisfactory relationship are legion. At first I thought I might array the various diagnoses on a continuum of cynicism. I quickly discovered, though, that there was not much variation among the positions; each had its thoroughly cynical representatives. Instead, imagine a continuum of diagnoses where, at one end, the nature of social science itself is blamed, while at the other the problem is taken to be simply the failure, thus far, to find reliable social facts, though they are attainable in principle.

---

conscious of its moral impact and conveyed its power through persuasion of its readers. My point is really a set of questions: Do we call only those works that embody Bellah's particular conception of justice and political morality "practical social science"? If so, what do we do with Plato's *Republic*, Machiavelli's *Prince*, or any contemporary work with a distinctly different vision? If not, then Bellah's particular conception of justice is not intrinsic to practical social science even if the general feature—a commitment to a political–moral vision—is. And if the latter is true, then there is only a thin line between practical social science and that technical social science which itself has a vision.

In any case, Bellah does not foreswear technical social science entirely, in part because it could not be ripped from the social fabric without much travail and in part because, informed by the moral vision of practical social science, it might be of some use. Perhaps Bellah implicitly acknowledges here that insight alone is rarely enough to effect change and that the techniques discovered and developed by technical social science might be useful in the pursuit of good and just ends.

But then, the question of ends is not as easily resolved for either practical or technical social science.

Like most typologies, this one will be crude and will allow of overlap. Moreover, some of the people I assign to the various positions will feel themselves misrepresented. As my purpose is to characterize general trends rather than specific individuals' positions, I have opted to be provocative rather than definitive.

Social Knowledge Is Reliable and Relevant

Adherents of the first position, and I have in mind two opposed variations on it, believe that there *is* reliable social knowledge and that it is directly, or with some modest adaptation, relevant to social policy. The first variant sees the problem as that policymakers are either fools, knaves, or both. That is, the fault lies entirely with the policymaker who fails to appreciate or, worse, cynically disregards the social knowledge available for policymaking. A critic of this view could describe it as a version of "blaming the victim," although since the victim in this case is a powerful political figure, a more appropriate label might be "blaming the villain."

The other side of the view that social knowledge is ready and able to aid public policy claims that the problem lies with social scientists and would-be policy analysts who fail to present the information they have in a timely and intelligible fashion to the appropriate policymakers. Again, the knowledge is presumed to be there and readily usable. The fault lies with the analysts, whose failings in political acuity, communication abilities, and perhaps a dab of professional snobbery and insecurity lead them to present the information at the wrong time in the wrong form to the wrong person.

In both these variations it is assumed that reliable social knowledge exists and that it is relevant for policy. I can think of no pure representatives of the fools/knaves position, though I suspect it describes fairly well a large number of social scientists who have only a passing familiarity with policymaking. Arnold Meltsner approaches the communication problem position in his book *Policy Analysts in the Bureaucracy*.[2]

Social Knowledge Exists but Is Not Relevant

The second major position holds that there is reliable social knowledge, but that some aspect of its form or of the relation between basic knowledge and policy severely mitigates its usefulness. Gouldner represents the version that emphasizes the gap between basic research and the knowledge there produced and the production of knowledge suitable for application, including policy applications. Gouldner, like others, emphasizes the distinction between basic and applied research including differences in the settings in which data are gathered, in the variables deemed important, and in theories and conceptual models.[3]

Policymakers are not typically interested in nuanced studies of the interplay between social structure and social character; they want to know what causes what and especially what the pressure points in a system are—that is, where can they exert pressure to force change. They want to know how actual—not ideal—systems operate and where they can effectively intervene in those *in vitro* systems to produce the desired effects.

Gouldner and others, who stress the lack of fit between the internal needs of a discipline and the pragmatic and outward focus of those who would influence policy, urge that applied fields establish themselves as quasi-independent professions, drawing on the parent disciplines but insisting on the special requirements of applied research, including

[2]Arnold Meltsner, *Policy Analysts in the Bureaucracy* (Berkeley, Calif.: University of California Press, 1976).

[3]Alvin Gouldner, "Explorations in Applied Social Science," *Social Problems*, 3 (1956) 169–81, also "Theoretical Requirements of the Applied Social Sciences," *American Sociological Review*, 22 (1957), 92–102.

special methods and theories. Applied researchers, in his view, should receive specialized training to avoid being seduced into the standard disciplinary values of elegant theory apart from utility.[4]

The other variant here admits that social knowledge does exist but argues that in many circumstances it *should not* have much impact on public policy! Lindblom and Cohen approach this at times in their book *Usable Knowledge,* where they praise interactive problem solving, ordinary knowledge, and casual analysis.[5] They argue that better resolutions would often emerge from interactions (e.g., voting and bargaining) than from formal data gathering and analysis. Under what conditions interactive solutions are preferable to knowledge-based ones they do not precisely say. Does their deemphasis of knowledge-based solutions rest on some fundamental flaw in those kinds of solutions or on the current poor state of social knowledge? At times they seem to favor one or the other. They use the example of a coin-flip to decide which fork to take at a totally unfamiliar intersection. Flipping the coin certainly "solves" the problem in that a choice has been made. But it is only a rational solution when we have no other grounds, no other information on which to base our choice. If we knew that the roads were equidistant from our goal but that one was infested with villains and predators and the other was peaceful, flipping a coin would made no sense.

My supposition is that Lindblom's and Cohen's relegation of professional social inquiry to a minor role in policymaking is a distillation of years of experience dealing with policy and policymakers. It is the wisdom of the artisan who says not to promise what cannot be done well and that it is prudent to concentrate on what one does best. Their sugges-

[4]Ibid.
[5]Charles E. Lindblom and David K. Cohen (New Haven, Conn.: Yale University Press, 1979).

tions embody the wisdom that ambiguous scientific facts pale in importance before political realities.

Social Knowledge Is neither Reliable nor Useful

The third major position—the one that poses the greatest challenge to social policy analysis—claims that there is little or no social knowledge that is reliable or useful. One version of this position holds that reliable, useful social knowledge is unattainable in principle, that all social knowledge is radically historical, and that the very notion of transhistorical social knowledge is incoherent. Kenneth Gergen, a social psychologist, takes this position, believing that he bases it on the work of people like Peter Winch.[6] This would not prevent individuals from gathering social facts or speculating on how society functions; however, this would not be a social *science* but some other form of inquiry.

I think this position is mistaken. It is often the conclusion of an attack on a radically ahistorical and clumsy variant of positivism. While the attack is fully deserved, the conclusion is too much of an antithesis and not enough of a synthesis. That is, the alternative to rigid positivism need not be a disavowal of *all* theoretical generalizations; it can be a more modest view of their attainability.

Other variants on the "social knowledge cannot be reliable or useful" position fix on what they see as logical encumbrances to the establishment of social science laws. For example, some critics emphasize *reflexivity* (i.e., the human capacity to comprehend and respond to description and prediction in confounding ways). Self-fulfilling prophecies are cases where people act to fulfill predictions while all sorts of contrary responses work to frustrate predictions. While re-

[6]Kenneth J. Gergen, "Social Psychology as History," *Journal of Personality and Social Psychology*, 26 (1973), 309–20; Peter Winch, *The Idea of a Social Science* (New York: Humanities Press, 1958).

flexivity may act to frustrate *some* kinds of predictions (face to face) and may act generally to shorten the half-life of scientific theories (by inducing people to modify their reactions), practically speaking I doubt that it has much effect on the general relevance of social science to social policy.

I have saved the most significant variant for last. This holds that there are contingent obstacles to social knowledge which are extremely powerful. Chief among them is the sheer complexity of human individual and social life.

The extent to which these complexities create practical difficulties in producing reliable, useful knowledge depends upon many factors. For example, can we be satisfied with the aggregate probabilities (e.g., much economic behavior) or must we have relatively certain predictions of individual behavior (the dangerousness of a psychiatric outpatient) and is it crucial to anticipate side effects?

To put it more bluntly, I think that social knowledge does not translate easily into social policy because, for the most part, it is unreliable and hence cannot be useful. By "unreliable" I mean that you cannot construct a social program on the basis of some social theory with secure confidence that you will achieve the results you intend and with no adverse side effects. To put it another way, social science does not generally have useful advice as to where and how to intervene in social systems to achieve desired ends effectively and directly. It is unreliable not because social scientists are less gifted or lazier than their natural science counterparts but because the questions posed to them, given the inherent complexities of human social life, are fundamentally more difficult and less tractable than typical questions in the natural sciences. This is difficult to prove, although our experience so far in this century certainly suggests that, while the social sciences have influenced our understanding of the social world, they have not been especially useful in the more narrow sense. Many commentators share this judgment.

The philosopher of science Jerome Ravetz has written,

> For some decades, psychology has been an impor-
> tant folk-science in America, generating an enormous
> handbook literature on all aspects of the art of living.
> Economics is doubtless the folk-science of all those com-
> mitted to an economy planned to any degree; in spite of
> the vacuity or irrelevance of most of its theory, and the
> patent unreliability of its statistical information, it ranks
> as the queen of the sciences in the formation of national
> policy.[7]

Folk science, by the way, is according to Ravetz "part of a
general world-view, or ideology, which is given special articulation so that it may provide comfort and reassurance in the
face of the crucial uncertainties of the world of experience."[8]

Referring to the relevance of laboratory research for behavior outside the laboratory, the eminent cognitive psychologist Michael Cole has written:

> Laboratory models preclude the operation of principles
> essential to the organization of behavior in non-labora-
> tory environment. . . . Theories and data derived from
> the laboratory cannot be used as a basis for predictions
> about the behavior of individuals once they leave the
> laboratory.[9]

The list could go on, but I think the point is made: for
many observers of the scene, including many with a vested
interest in promoting social science, reliable knowledge about
the external world is meager at best. W. H. Auden wryly
anticipated this judgment in a passage from "Under which
Lyre":

---

[7]Jerome R. Ravetz, *Scientific Knowledge and Its Social Problems* (New York:
Oxford University Press, 1971).
[8]Ibid.
[9]Cited in Seymour B. Sarason, "Bias in Mental Testing," *Transaction/Society*,
November/December 1980, 86–8.

> Thou shalt not answer questionnaires
> Or quizzes upon world-affairs
>   Nor with compliance
> Take any test. Thou shalt not sit
> With statisticians nor commit
> A social science.[10]

But this is still prologue to the question: What should one do with imperfect knowledge in the making of policy? Indeed, one thing ignored by the sweeping criticisms of social science are the enormous variations within and among disciplines in what is known and what can be done. Even if social scientists have a hard time creating elegant and invariant theories, they have an increasingly sophisticated tool kit for gaining much useful information. The next step must be a finer-grained analysis of types of knowledge within the social sciences and the ways in which knowledge can be relevant to policy.

WAYS KNOWLEDGE MAY BE RELEVANT TO POLICY

I'll begin with the latter—the ways knowledge must be relevant to policy. Here a simple typology will do. There are at least four ways knowledge may be relevant to the creation and implementation of policy. It may serve to:

1. Identify a problem (Discovery)
2. Propose and compare possible interventions (Intervention)
3. Aid in the effective management of an intervention (Management)
4. Evaluate the intervention (Evaluation)

---

[10]From "Under Which Lyre" by W. H. Auden in *Selected Poems*, ed. by Edward Mendelson (New York: Random House, Inc., 1979). Reprinted by permission of the publisher.

Identifying the Problem: Discovery

Michael Harrington's book *The Other America* has been described as the "discovery" of poverty in the United States.[11] Of course, one does not discover poverty in the same way one discovers an Indian burial mound or Boyle's law. The poverty Harrington described existed long before, but Harrington's discovery was twofold: he artfully brought to public attention the pervasive existence of terrible poverty in a supposedly affluent nation and he succeeded in getting this poverty defined as a social problem. Before Harrington, it might have been possible to speak of the "deserving poor"—that is, the poor who deserved their poverty; and it might have been possible to assume that voluntary charity was adequate to assuage the deepest suffering of the poor. But Harrington presented evidence that appeared to point to the poor being poor as a result of circumstances rather than deserts and to the failure of private charities to reach the worst off.

Comparing Possible Interventions

Probably the function most commonly ascribed to policy analysts is the description and analysis of policy options. Many trees have sacrificed their pulp so that policy analysts could urge their fellows to keep the options they investigate pragmatic ones. It matters little that I have knock-down data proving that policy X would solve the drug problem if policy X stands not a chance of being adopted. More to the point here, though, is the fact that social knowledge rarely if ever is sound enough to provide a really solid prediction of what to expect. This is especially so when the purveyor of social knowledge is asked not merely for descriptions of some phenomena but

---

[11]Michael Harrington, *The Other America: Poverty in the United States* (New York: The Macmillan Company, 1962).

also for advice as to how and where to intervene with greatest impact. Comparing interventions normally requires having some theory of what causes what (e.g., tax cuts increase investments). But this is precisely the failure of the social sciences—a failure in which I believe social policy analysts share. They have failed to produce potent theory, that is, theory which is well-established and which travels well from the circumstances of its inception to the actual real-world phenomena it purports to describe.

Managing Interventions

There is a profitable branch of the applied social sciences which advises on organizational structure and management style, all in the name of productivity and morale. It goes under a variety of names—organizational behavior, management training, and so on—but in all cases it includes a hefty proportion of social science findings. This conglomerate of subdisciplines appear to meet Gouldner's criteria for an applied discipline in that they have adapted traditional techniques and theories for their own use and, especially, they have achieved an independent power base.

I mention this category, not because I believe it has any great importance for this study but because I suspect that when policymakers acknowledge having used social knowledge, they usually mean either this sort or the very simple descriptive methods used in discovery.

Evaluating the Intervention

An entire profession—evaluation research—has recently grown up around the problem of assessing social programs. Practitioners use the methodological tools of the social sciences, most especially the extraordinarily sophisticated statistical ones, to describe the effects of an intervention.

The most heartening consequence of this nascent field is

that in it the most methodologically advanced and rigorous tools of the social sciences are confronted with the heretofore intractably complicated real social world. The collision can only be salutary. A worrisome consequence, though, is that the most technologically sophisticated are unfortunately also often those fascinated by their tools and therefore less attentive to the ethical ambiguities present in all evaluations. The timing of an evaluation, the design, the variables chosen to be measured, and the operational definitions are all likely to carry moral freight, irrespective of the cleanness of the scientific design and analysis. The Westinghouse Evaluation of Head Start is a good example of this. It was done early in the evolution of the program, did not accommodate the gross variation in goals and competence among different centers, and concentrated on cognitive variables, which may be the most difficult in which to detect change.

An official research committee composed of Urie Bronfenbrenner, Edmund Gordon, and Edward Zigler opposed the study. Bronfenbrenner describes the reasons for their opposition:

> The proposed design was an overly mechanical and mindless plan for massive computer analysis of data regarding changes in intellectual development of Head Start children, obtained for noncomparable groups of children under noncomparable program conditions. The most predictable result of the proposed analysis given this particular design, which left many significant variables uncontrolled, would be the finding of no differences, whether or not differences in fact existed. Moreover, this evaluation was based upon the results of objective measures primarily restricted to the domain of cognitive development, without regard to other goals of Head Start in the areas of health, motivation, and social development. Nor was any attention being paid to the children's parents or the communities in which the parents lived,

in our view all equally important targets of the program.[12]

So much for the ways in which social knowledge may be relevant to policy. I will say nothing further about the third category—the management of innovation. But categories one and four, discovery and evaluation, are similar, and in their similarity distinctly different from category two, comparing possible interventions. The former rely mostly on the craft tools of the social sciences—descriptive and inferential statistics and on theory mostly in the sense of the theory of methods (i.e., theory which elaborates and justifies statistical tools and design procedures). The latter, predicting the impacts of alternative interventions, relies much more heavily on substantive theory, and especially theory cast in the language of cause and effect. To this issue—the role played by theory-ladenness in rendering social knowledge more or less reliable and useful—I now turn.

THEORY-LADENNESS INFLUENCES THE USEFULNESS OF SOCIAL KNOWLEDGE

This may be a case of trying to explain the indefinable with the ineluctable, but it seems worth the attempt. The background of the argument is simple: lumping all forms of social knowledge together obscures vast differences in the reliability and hence potential usefulness of subtypes of social knowledge. The problem is to describe the subtypes and identify that which discriminates among them.

First, it is essential to distinguish between a scientist's tool kit of methods and instruments and the theories offered

---

[12]Urie Bronfenbrenner. "Head Start, A Retrospective View: The Founders," in *Project Head Start: A Legacy of the War on Poverty* ed. by Edward Zigler and Jeannette Valentine (New York: The Free Press, 1979).

in explanation of the observations made with those tools. It is the difference between instruments and procedures for measuring temperature and pressure (tools) and Charles's law (a theory relating the observations made with the tools). Others have noted that the objects of study—concepts such as temperature and pressure in physics, self-concept and social learning in psychology—are always theory-laden. That is, they can only be measured and given meaning in the context of a theoretical understanding of what temperature, for example, is and does. If you'll excuse the pun, temperature does not exist in a vacuum. Tools can never be given substantive application without some theoretical context to explain the significance of measuring or varying this thing in just this way. At this time, the social scientist's tool kit includes innumerable statistical procedures, techniques for designing studies, measurement instruments, and the like.

It is important to recognize the primacy of tools. Good scientific theory is almost impossible to imagine without good tools, whereas good tools do not necessarily lead directly to good theory. Every observation is potentially prey to any number of pitfalls which would render it inaccurate and misleading.[13] Increasingly sophisticated tools eventually minimize the most likely pitfalls, so that observations may be made reliably. Creating good—that is, accurate and powerful—theory in the absence of reliable observations would require a combination of brilliance and terrific luck. But even having reliable observations does not guarantee that good theory will inevitably follow, though it certainly increases the chances.

My claim is that categories 1 and 4—discovery and evaluation—are closely tied to tool use with a minimum of constructive theory, while category 2—comparing interventions—draws mostly on theory. Those social facts which are

---

[13]Ravetz, *Scientific Knowledge.*

largely the product of well-understood, reliable tools are close to "brute" facts—facts that are not likely to be vitiated by pitfalls.

The difficulties social theory encounters are due mostly to the complexity of the interrelations among the many variables in real-world social phenomena. It is at least plausible that, compared with typical problems in the natural sciences, social science problems involve more variables in more interactions with each other and in more complex (higher-order) interactions. And certainly, the reflexivity of social knowledge makes its pursuit more complex and difficult. Nothing like the force table, with its neat additions of forces adjusted by vectors, exists in the social sciences. Nor do we have anything with the clarity and predictive accuracy of shadow diagrams for simple optical phenomena. (Of course, the shadow diagrams, with their implication that light may be treated as particles, fail to account for phenomena such as diffraction patterns. But this reminder that simple physical theories are often supplanted by more sophisticated ones alerts us to how much worse is the situation in the social sciences, where we do not even have a degree of accuracy comparable to shadow casting.) Generally speaking there is a set of "facts" in the natural sciences, facts that have survived pitfalls in the original tools and transformations in the meanings given the central concepts of the theory. I do not believe there exists a comparable set of facts in the social sciences, at least not facts of relevance to policymakers. Some attribute this lack to the alleged youth of the social sciences, others (usually natural scientists) to the intellectual inferiority of social scientists. I find neither explanation convincing. The sweeping simplifications we must make in doing science have been more successful in the natural sciences than in the social sciences. For the purpose of calculating the acceleration of an object, regarding it as a point mass is an acceptable simplification—

acceptable being defined as a simplification that does not interfere substantially with accurate description and prediction. Assuming that all persons are rational maximizers of satisfaction, as does the theory of consumer behavior, creates as many complications as it solves and indeed does not result in adequate descriptions of either individual *or* aggregate economic behavior of many kinds.

What makes a fact a "brute" one is in part the ease and certainty with which it can be determined and in part in the incontestability of its conceptual base. For example, the actual number of votes cast for each candidate in a presidential election is a very brute fact. But although it is of great importance to a citizen, it is relatively meaningless to a social scientist who wants to analyze the election. The next step could be to determine how various groups voted in that election. We could look at carefully selected wards and at comparisons among districts to estimate how different racial, ethnic, class, income, and party groups voted. While these are estimates and not as reliable or precise as the actual vote count (which itself was subject to fraud and error), these estimates of group preferences are still a very brute fact—a sophisticated form of counting, but counting nonetheless.

The art of social science is to explain *why* these groups voted as they did—to offer a theoretical explanation for the observed patterns. Potential explanations are numerous and often incompatible. We could try to construct explanations in terms of economic interests, the relatively more effective manipulation of political symbols by one candidate, religious or racial antagonisms, or even principled and rational judgments. These are all clearly explanations of the facts and not facts themselves.

Another sort of fact is the income distribution of the United States. It is more difficult to determine than a vote count, since people may disguise or not even know their income, some kinds of economic gain are difficult to discover or attach a price to, and so on. So although it is not nearly as brute a fact as the vote count, it is much more of one than that required by a closely related question: What is the extent of poverty in the United States? Obviously, this depends upon how we define *poverty*. As a certain amount of money income? As a percentile of the national income distribution? Do we adjust for size and type of household? For region, community, or special needs? The number and distribution of poor people in this country is still a "fact" of sorts, begging for explanation (and action!). But it is clearly more contestable for conceptual reasons than a vote count or income count.

The questions asked of the social scientist are simply more complex. The degree of difficulty in solving a problem probably varies as some power of the increase in complexity of the phenomenon. But while all this certainly hinders the growth of robust social theory, it does not render it logically unattainable. It should engender modesty, not despair.

THE RELATION OF QUALITATIVE TO QUANTITATIVE RESEARCH

One of the long-standing debates within the social sciences is over the apparent incongruity between qualitative research—whether it is called interpretive, narrative, or *Verstehen*—and quantitative research, with its emphasis on precise measurement and generalization.[14] That debate has too many ramifications to encompass here, but one perspective on it is informed by what I have just said about the intractability of social theory and the complexity of the social world.

Imagine the social landscape one wishes to map as extraordinarily irregular, even convoluted; imagine also that the

---

[14]For an interesting recent view of the narrative tradition, see Clifford Geertz, "Blurred Genres," *American Scholar*, 49 (1980), 165–79.

terrain varies enormously from region to region, so that the major impediments to travel in one area are minor in another nearby and give way to an entirely different set of obstacles. Finally, imagine that the would-be cartographers of this terrain—a rapidly changing territory of jungle, mountain, swamp, desert, prairie, and metropolis—draw their maps by taking an aerial photograph, trying to copy a few of its features in a sandbox kept for this purpose, and then loosing a mouse to run its way from point to point. By observing the mouse— or a college undergraduate if they have enough money to build a large enough box—they will identify and describe the major features of the terrain. This, I submit, is approximately the situation of the experimental social scientist and very nearly that of the survey researcher.

One major pitfall is blatantly obvious: in modeling a complex terrain simply and from one perspective (which obliterates some important features), the cartographers cum social scientists are very likely to miss the most important local features. So while one may develop a fairly abstract science of map drawing and obstacle traversing, the specific maps drawn are unlikely to be of much use to the traveler who wants to know what route options there are for getting from here to there. The maps are especially useless, even counterproductive, when they are drawn in one region and projected to quite another. They might inspire a false confidence in the traveler.

The most useful information for our traveler will come, not from the elegant cartographer but from the person who has spent much time nosing around in the neighborhood— who has personally looked into a variety of routes and who has personally encountered many of the obstacles. This observer, immersed in the particularity of the region, is much more likely to be able to identify the most significant features in that area. Our observer is, of course, the qualitative social scientist.

Now it may be that our laboratory cartographer, having done numerous studies on the most effective maps to traverse a certain kind of obstacle, could provide the traveler with this sort of information much more accurately than the local observer. The laboratory scientist can examine much more sensitively than the local observer the effects of systematic variations in approaches to each sort of obstacle. But again, such knowledge is of no use until you know just what obstacles you will encounter.

This prolonged metaphor is meant to illustrate what I take to be a complementarity between qualitative and quantitative reserach—one that I know has been mentioned in other contexts but not, I think, in relation to policy research. This is ironic, for it is precisely in policy-relevant research that one most wants to be certain that the important features of the local terrain are included in the map.

What social theory, for example, would have predicted that the survivors of the Buffalo Creek disaster would suffer great anxiety from the sound of rain on the roofs of their government-supplied trailers because it would remind them of the terrible night of the flood? It took qualitative work like Kai Erikson's to bring this to light.[15]

One lesson to be drawn from this analysis of the imperfection of social knowledge, then, is that qualitative work is grossly underrated for policy purposes—not for quasi-mystical or romantically humanistic reasons but for the hard-nosed practical admission that social scientists often do not know what the most important features of a situation are without first taking a very close and detailed look at it in all its messy particularities.

---

[15]Kai T. Erikson, *Everything in its Path: Destruction of Community in the Buffalo Creek Flood* (New York: Simon & Schuster, Inc. 1976).

I think it is appropriate here to sum up my major points thus far:

1. While all knowledge is imperfect, social knowledge is generally much more so than other scientific knowledge.
2. Diagnoses of the failure of social knowledge to play a more important and constructive role in social policy can be described according to their assessment of the reliability and usefulness of social knowledge.
3. The several ways in which social knowledge may be relevant to social policy call on knowledges of varying reliability.
4. Variance in reliability is due in part to the extent to which the knowledge is directly tied to the sophisticated tools of the social scientist, as opposed to less reliable theoretical statements.
5. Qualitative and quantitative methods are complementary in making social knowledge useful for social policy.

With all this said, I have one task remaining: to elucidate rules, moral and otherwise, for using imperfect social knowledge in forging social policy.

PARTIAL KNOWLEDGE

Social scientists who despair of finding the proper ends of policy might seek consolation in the thought that at least the knowledge they provide is ethically neutral. But their solace is illusory. Their contribution to the understanding of an issue must be partial both in the sense of being *incomplete* and of being *nonneutral* as between policy options. Why is this so? We can understand increases in scientific knowledge as either holograms or paintings. The metaphors are worth considering more carefully.

Holograms and Paintings

The two remarkable things about a hologram are first, that when properly projected, it preserves the scene in three-dimensional detail and, second, that the entire scene is present in every piece of the hologram—so that even a small corner of it will reveal the full scene—although it will be a grainier and less perfect representation. One could view social knowledge as a corner of the hologram: an undistorted, un-subjective representation of the scene, however grainy and cloudy. Increases in social knowledge would represent more pieces of the hologram, so that the image would grow steadily clearer and more vivid. But we must remember that even the smallest fragment of the hologram contains the undistorted image, however fuzzy. If you wanted to rearrange the items in the scene using the hologram as a guide (or choose social policy based on the social knowledge), you could be assured that at least what was clear in the image was just as it is in reality. Fuzzy portions, if you had to change them, would require some guesswork, but you could be assured that things were just as they appeared to be.

Paintings are very different. Like maps, they always involve the selective interpretation of the creator. A particular interpretive school may guide the artist's selections. Kandinsky, Klee, and Cropsey would paint the same scene very differently, according to their interpretive principles. The artist's task is to capture something essentially true about the scene, even if it be the artist's own response to it. Therefore the artist must select certain features for emphasis and neglect others. No one would claim that a painting is a complete and undistorted record of what the artist saw. Distortion is a misleading word here, for rather than an intentional misrepresentation—as the word implies—the painter gives us a carefully selected, novel representation of what, according to his or her principles, is the deeper and truer meaning of the scene. This new vision is not random and chaotic; it is the creative reconstruction of reality according to a principled understanding of it. If you wanted to understand the scene in order to change it, you would have to use a painting carefully. Paintings lend themselves to some uses much more readily than others. Paintings done by artists of different schools contain vastly divergent images of the scene, and there could be no question of their adding to our understanding in a simple, cumulative manner. Increased understanding will come not through the gradual emergence of clarity, as in a slide coming into focus, but through the artful play of insight against conflicting insight.

If social knowledge is like a hologram, such that every additional piece adds to the clarity of the overall image, then more knowledge is always better than less (assuming that our ends are morally worthwhile). But if social knowledge is more like a series of paintings, more knowledge is *not* always better than less, especially in cases where the paintings all come from the same school and all miss morally relevant features of the scene. I believe social knowledge is more like paintings than like holograms and that partial knowledge is therefore always liable to be morally dangerous.

Take the case of the World War I Army Alpha test, an early mass administration of an IQ measure, on which certain immigrant groups scored well below the average. What social policy implications would we draw from such knowledge? Now, you may argue that, for moral reasons, we should never make policy distinctions on the basis of presumed or demonstrated inferiority of groups—that justice forbids such invidious distinctions. This is not the place for that discussion. The fact is that the Army came to use the results of tests like these to sort individuals into what were deemed appropriate classifications; your score could nominate you for O.C.S., the Quartermaster Corps, or cannon fodder. The Army was simply trying to make the most efficient use of its human resources; if certain groups were more likely to end up in the trenches, well, that is just because that was a better use of their talents (or rather their lack of talents).

What was wrong with choosing men's fates this way? We might complain that the test was poor science—as indeed it was. But the science of the past almost invariably looks poor and naive from the perspective of the present. Let us assume it was the best knowledge of its time and that, so far as the scientists of the day knew, it was sound procedure. We could also point to the motivations of the scientists: we could mention that some of them were in the forefront of the eugenics movement and, as nativists, fervently opposed the immigration of southern Europeans and other "less intelligent" ethnic stocks.[16] But attributing the entire problem to the evil intentions of a few individuals would offer us false reassurance. Even if the scientists were all good and honest men with the right moral learnings, problems remain.

Even if the scientists were well intentioned and the knowledge reliable, there would still remain a residual moral problem. This is that knowledge which is partial, in the sense of incomplete, is also always partial in the sense of carrying an intrinsic moral bias or, better, a lack of moral balance. Incomplete knowledge is also always morally imbalanced. (It may also be morally irrelevant, but that is never the case when knowledge is being used to make social policy, where considerations of justice and dignity are prominent.)

---

[16]Franz Samelson, "World War I Intelligence Testings and the Development of Psychology," *Journal of the History of the Behavioral Sciences*, 13 (1977), 274–82.

The Army Alpha test was one bit of knowledge relevant to the policy question: How do we assign men to make the optimal use of their talents? It was a bit of knowledge that emphasized individual differences of a specific kind—a kind that at best could have only a tenuous relation to performance as an officer. Alternative kinds of knowledge could have been used to select officer candidates. Early sociometric techniques might have been used to make a systematic search for men with natural leadership qualities. This would probably have resulted in the selection of many more members of those groups excluded by the Alpha tests. A similar judgment is embodied in the recent court decisions requiring that any test used in job classification have a clear relationship to performance in the job. Task-relevant tests are much less likely to discriminate against racial minorities than are IQ tests. The specific point here is that differences in individual abilities can be scientifically described in a wide variety of ways and that each of these ways can have the same claim to scientific validity. However, since each bit of knowledge is itself only a part of the picture and each bit lends itself to one or the other social policy with accompanying ethical features, each bit of partial or incomplete knowledge is intrinsically leaning in a direction with specific moral force. If I want to study the "problem of the black ghetto," the policy implications, and hence the moral leanings of my prescription, will be very different if I focus *à la* Moynihan on the "pathology of the black family" than if I focus on corporate and financial policies that sustain the existence of racial ghettoes.

It is the nature of imperfect knowledge which is policy-relevant to be partial in the dual senses I have outlined. And no social scientist can take refuge behind an appeal to scientific objectivity. Even if the scientist is utterly fair and conscientious, as long as the knowledge produced is imperfect, it will be morally imbalanced. We do not have to impute bias to the researcher; we merely have to recognize the interplay of fact and theory in moral argument and that social policy choices are always also moral choices.

The fact that imperfect knowledge is always morally imbalanced should not lead to cynicism or despair. So far, I have merely described the relation. What is the appropriate prescription for policy analysis? Every psychoanalyst knows that enlightenment itself does not cure; cure comes only with the difficult working through of insights to ways of incorporating new awareness into everyday life. So it must be for the policy analyst with partial knowledge. A vague awareness that imperfect knowledge is also morally partial is not enough. Policy analysts must invent ways to incorporate that awareness into professional practice. The identification of sources and directions of moral imbalance in types of social knowledge should become part of the routine of policy analysts.

It is time to stop and draw whatever conclusions we can. I will put them in terms of two moral duties for social policy analysts and three imperatives for the profession.

First, duties for individual practitioners:

1. Avoid misrepresenting the completeness, reliability, and relevance of the social knowledge introduced into the policy process. This is not only morally desirable but, in the long run, prudent. Eventually, sloppy data and faulty predictions will catch up with one, especially if the profession develops the sort of quality control measures suggested below.

2. Policy analysts should educate policymakers and perhaps the public to sources of moral imbalance in social knowledge. It is probably unrealistic to exhort analysts to see and publicize moral imbalances in their own position, but they can certainly be critical of such imbalance in others. Again, the successful identification and publication of moral imbalance in social knowl-

edge will be a cumulative social enterprise and will rest on developing and nurturing institutions to nourish it.

Finally, imperatives for the profession:

1. Foster the development of canons of quality in policy research. Just because policy research must often be done quickly is no reason not to have standards distinguishing *good* quick research from *poor* quick research. The standards developed are likely to resemble those for the parent disciplines but will have to be adapted to the special circumstances of the analyst's tasks, particularly, the demands for relevancy and speed.

2. Support the development of an etiquette, if not an ethic, of dispute. Lively disagreement is part of a vital profession. But unless informal rules evolve to distinguish good argument from poor and fair argument from irrelevant, dispute will not serve to sharpen the skills of the profession but will merely make it more fractious.

3. Last, the profession must provide for the examination of both the tools of the profession and examples of actual analyses. Further, the profession must provide rewards sufficiently strong to move the analysts themselves—and not merely academic teachers of analytic technique—to lay open their own work for dissection and criticism, perhaps on the model of medical grand rounds.

Ultimately, it is up to the profession to support the kinds of internal critical networks which will lead to the development of those craft skills and wisdom that make a profession worthy of the title.

IV

TOWARD ETHICAL GUIDELINES

14

TOWARD ETHICAL GUIDELINES FOR SOCIAL SCIENCE RESEARCH IN PUBLIC POLICY

DONALD P. WARWICK AND
THOMAS F. PETTIGREW

Front-page newspaper headlines about economic indicators, voting analyses, national scores on school achievement tests, and a myriad of other topics tell the story. Social science is now taken seriously in public policy. No longer are social science findings and theories of great interest only to those in the discipline. Such work now has the potential to affect the lives of citizens.

This development of just the past two decades raises important ethical issues for both social science and society. The rapid growth of this nexus with public policy has worked against careful reflection about its ethical dimensions. But the time has surely arrived when these issues should be faced directly.

DONALD P. WARWICK □ Institute Fellow, Harvard Institute for International Development, Harvard University, Cambridge, Massachusetts 02138. THOMAS F. PETTIGREW □ Department of Psychology, University of California, Santa Cruz, California 95064.

This paper will (1) **pinpoint** key ethical problems raised by the relationships **between** social science and public policy and (2) present suggestions for needed ethical guidelines. The focus will be on social science *research* that is consciously addressed to the formulation, design, implementation, or evaluation of public policy. We will not deal with such areas as psychoanalysis, the work of Piaget, or economic theory. These have had major effects on public policy in many countries, but tracing the trajectory of their influence would be a task of heroic proportions. We shall focus instead on the newer phenomenon of social research applied immediately to public policy. We will do so from the perspective of the researcher, or "knowledge generator," rather than that of the consumer, or "knowledge broker."

THE NEW RELATIONSHIP

Of course, policymakers did not totally ignore social science before the 1960s. In addition to the pervasive indirect influence of Freud, Piaget, and Keynes, one political scientist, Woodrow Wilson, even became President. The U.S. Census has been an instrument of government since the early days of the republic. Rural sociologists helped to shape farm programs. Social psychologists were witnesses in the early school desegregation cases. Economists were part of President Franklin D. Roosevelt's "brain trust" of the 1930s. And though it causes extremely negative criticism from the white South, the U.S. Supreme Court cited social science sources in the famous footnote 11 of its 1954 opinion on public school desegregation.

It was not until the mid-1960s, however, that social research began to be used systematically in the policy process. Three publicized events marked the transition. In 1965, President Lyndon Johnson explicity cited the research and advice of the University of Minnesota economist Walter Heller in advocating a major income tax cut. In 1966, the U.S. Office of Education released *The Equal Educational Opportunity Survey.*[1] Headed by the sociologist James Coleman, this massive study of over 600,000 public school children throughout the nation had been mandated by Congress in Title IV of the 1964 Civil Rights Act. Also building momentum throughout the 1960s was what came to be called the Knowledge–Attitude–Practice (KAP) survey. This species of survey research attempted to assess the existing and future demand for family planning services, especially in the developing countries.

The cautious, even skeptical acceptance of these social science contributions highlights their uniqueness at that point. Just before seeking Congressional approval of the tax cut, President Johnson is reported to have said ominously to Heller, "Professor, it better damn well work!" And when the "Coleman report" was initially released, less than a half-dozen reporters appeared at the press conference. Only when the report's relevance for educational policy became the subject of controversy did the mass media begin to focus attention on it. KAP surveys had a similar history.

Soon, however, social science research became a routine element in the policy process. Congress specified evaluation studies as an intrinsic part of social programs, and it established its own budget analysis office headed by Alice Rivlin, an economist. Comparable evaluation efforts were often mounted for social programs in the developing countries. Federal agencies shifted monies from university-based grant research to more specified, policy-oriented contract research increasingly conducted by large contract research firms (e.g., Abt Associates, American Institutes of Research, Stanford Re-

---

[1] J. S. Coleman *et al., Equality of Educational Opportunity* (Washington, D.C.: Government Printing Office, 1966).

search Institute, System Development Corporation, The Rand Corporation). And many politicians leanred to cite social research and data as never before.

This sweeping change in the relationships between social science and public policy raised an array of new issues and problems, not the least of which concerned ethical standards in research. The swiftness of this change left little time for either the social sciences or government to develop suitable ethical guidelines for policy-related research. But time was not the only barrier to the confrontation of ethical questions within the social sciences. These disciplines have been ill equipped and ill motivated to deal with the ethics of research in any systematic way (though we shall note a recent exception in the American Sociological Association). In fields built on the foundations of logical positivism, there is a lingering sense that the entire domain of ethics is soft and subjective and therefore suspect. Even among social scientists who grant the existence of ethical problems, discussion has been hampered by the absence of a hospitable forum for dialogue, by the plurality of disciplines and methodological traditions involved, and by the lack of a suitable idiom for discourse. The recent backlash against institutional review boards, entities perceived by many as the organizational manifestation of ethics, has exacerbated the problem.

This situation has major implications for our present task. First, there is an urgent need to begin work on ethical guidelines. For the past twenty years, social scientists could claim that they had neither the time nor the experience to propose ethical standards for policy research. We now have the experience and, with the arrival of the Reagan administration, social scientists may have more time. Second, given the newness of these interactions, a modest, tentative approach is appropriate. When breaking new ground, an evolutionary, learn-as-you-go strategy seems more realistic than a detailed, top-down, enforced code. This is why we will speak throughout this paper of ethical guidelines rather than an ethical code. We also worry that an enforced code of ethics would make social scientists reluctant to debate and discuss ethical questions about policy research and would thus prove counterproductive.

Third, the development of widely accepted and actually observed ethical guidelines is best done with concrete cases of past practice. But to be fruitful, the analysis of such cases must seek generic issues of ethics rather than personal recriminations for the behavior of particular social scientists. Both the present writers have been critical of particular work in the past, and our interest in ethical questions derives in good part from that experience. However, our aim here is not to reopen old controversies but to move ahead toward new guidelines.

KEY ETHICAL ISSUES IN POLICY RESEARCH

There are distinctive ethical problems that arise in policy research. To be sure, most if not all the ethical issues that routinely arise in social research of any type confront policy work as well. But there are classes of ethical concerns that particularly characterize policy research. Some of these are more critical forms of the standard research issues and some are unique to policy research. In his paper "Politics, Ethics and Evaluation Research," Gideon Sjoberg observes that:

> The more one delves into the massive literature on evaluation research, the more cognizant one becomes of the deep-seated ethical and political implications of the social scientist's efforts, whether direct or indirect, to evaluate the performance of individuals or the programs of ongoing organizations. The political and ethical dilemmas

are especially troublesome in the evaluation of experimental programs.[2]

Not surprisingly, then, in virtually every major sphere of public policy in which social research has entered, there has been intense debate about the work. The most publicized cases involve public education—as with achievement testing, the Coleman report, school desegregation, and the Head Start Program. But bitter exchanges have occurred in other realms, too. Project Camelot, a U.S. Army attempt to use social science to measure and and forecast revolutions and insurgency, was abruptly canceled once it received heated opposition from around the world.[3] And critics have charged that the KAP survey is biased toward obtaining the kinds of information sought for policy purposes by its promoters.[4] Although "politics" is the usual charge, at root these controversies typically focus on the posture that social scientists *should* take in the policy arena—an ethical question.

Why should these social science efforts appear intrinsically more controversial than those of the natural sciences when applied to public policy?[5] Though sharply divided in their views on environmental protection issues, for instance, natural scientists have shown more consensus about the

[2]G. Sjoberg, "Politics, Ethics, and Evaluation Research," in *Handbook of Evaluation*, ed. by E. Struening and M. Gutentag (Beverly Hills, Calif: Sage Publications, 1975). p. 29.

[3]I. L. Horowitz, "Life and Death of Project Camelot," *Trans-Action*, 3 (November–December, 1965) 3–7, 44–47.

[4]For an especially thorough critique of the entire KAP approach, see A. Marino, "KAP Surveys and the Politics of Family Planning," *Concerned Demography*, 3 (1971), 36–75.

[5]Of course, the physical sciences vary considerably among themselves on these matters. Occasionally, publicized cases arise that resemble social science controversies. Consider seismology and the sweeping earthquake predictions of Brian Brady, a mathematician with the U.S. Bureau of Mines. With unusual specificity, Brady predicted that a quake of 8.0 Richter mag-

meaning of science and basic concepts than sociologists have in debating "white flight" or psychologists in debating test scores. There are at least five reasons for this differential propensity of the social sciences to polarize on issues of public policy:

1. The social sciences entertain a greater range of permissible, even conflicting conceptualizations because there are few widely accepted theoretical models.
2. They also allow a greater range of permissible research designs and methods.
3. Weaker ethical guidelines exist in the social sciences.
4. There is also a weaker "norm of skepticism."
5. There is far greater difficulty in achieving true empirical replication that can act as an effective peer review mechanism.[6]

The cumulative operation of these characteristics of the social sciences leads to eight specific areas where ethical problems arise when social research is applied to public policy. A review of these areas will shape our later discussion of suggested ethical guidelines.

---

nitude would hit near Lima, Peru, on or about June 28, 1981, followed by a 9.2 quake on or about August 10 and culminating in a massive 9.9 disaster on September 16. This third earthquake would be the largest ever recorded by modern instruments. At first, these forecasts were supported by William Spence, a geophysicist of the U.S. Geological Survey. But as understandable concern arose in Peru and a special Evaluation Council rejected the predictions, Spence and others withdrew their support and sharp controversy ensued. "Quake Prediction Rattles Peru, Scientists Disagree," *San Francisco Chronicle*, June 29, 1981, p. 10.

[6]For further discussion on these points, see T. F. Pettigrew, "Race, Ethics, and the Social Responsibility of Social Scientists," *Hastings Center Report*, 9 (October, 1979), 15–18.

STATEMENT AND CONCEPTUALIZATION OF THE RESEARCH
PROBLEM

Given the loose structure of conceptualization in social
science, ethical issues often arise in policy reserach with the
initial statement of the problem. Sometimes the very language
used implies conclusions and introduces values. *White flight*
and *racial gap in achievement*, for example, prejudge the cause
as racial and interject a conservative bias. Typically the conceptualization bias is more subtly interwoven into the theoretical fabric of the research. Large-scale, often mathematically
elegant econometric models, for instance, are shaped by their
base assumptions, and these assumptions, though often un-
stated and untestable, significantly mold the policy conclusions that are drawn from such models.

Frequently social scientists unquestioningly accept a conceptual bias from the policy sponsor. Irving Horowitz emphasizes that the U.S. Army's conceptualization of Project
Camelot grew out of the Army's hostility to all revolution and
insurgency without consideration of the desirability of successful revolutions under certain conditions.[7] The New Jersey–Pennsylvania Income Maintenance Experiment has been
criticized, too, as slanted toward the interests of its sponsor
to the detriment of other concerned parties.[8] A study of the
effects of shift work would also have to be considered biased
if it focused only on such harmful effects as ulcers and marital

[7]Horowitz, 3–7, 44–47.
[8]P. H. Rossi, M. Boechmann, and R. Berk, "Some Ethical Implications of
the New Jersey–Pennsylvania Income Maintenance Experiment," and D.
Warwick, "Ethical Guidelines for Social Experiments," in *The Ethics of Social
Intervention*, ed. by G. Bermant, H. Kelman and D. Warwick (Washington,
D.C.: Hemisphere, 1978), pp. 245–88.

difficulties and neglected the potential advantages of night-time hours.[9]

But no study can collect data on all relevant conceptual possibilities. The key ethical question is how far the social scientist must go to avoid conceptual bias. This problem exists for all social research, of course. But nonpolicy research usually enjoys a longer time perspective, and at some later point corrective research, derived from a rival conceptualization, is likely to redress the balance. The time span in policy research is generally too tight for such a leisurely corrective process to take place. Hence, conceptualization bias is a far more serious concern for policy research.

Choice of Research Method

Method preferences reflect many factors, including personal talents and professional socialization. Ethical concerns enter when the choice of research method forecloses the gathering of certain types of data needed for a rounded policy decision or requires the collection of data that are at best dubious. Serious ethical problems arise, for example, when researchers know that a significant percentage of respondents will not understand the KAP survey or that questions on it are biased toward particular results. More subtle are the limited perspectives that flow from particular methods. For example, the rebirth of the race and IQ debate in recent years requires a rigid partitioning of hereditary and environmental causations, a partitioning that modern genetics long ago found untenable. Yet a few psychologists and an electrical engineer keep this issue alive by utilizing statistical models that minimize the

[9]P. Mott *et al., Shift Work: The Social Psychological and Physical Consequences* (Ann Arbor, Mich.: University of Michigan Press, 1965).

interaction of nature and nurture. Their unquestioned statistical assumptions thus shape their conclusions.

Similarly, the repeated preference of some federal agencies to fund policy-oriented research with one type of method—large-scale sample surveys in cross-sectional designs—limits what we learn.[10] The typical questions are: Did the program work? What was the program's total effect? The inappropriateness of these questions becomes apparent when one considers the varied nature of such nationwide programs as Head Start and public school desegregation. There was no single Head Start Program; the enormous variation across sites meant that there were virtually as many Head Start programs as there were individual projects.

The "total effect" fallacy, embedded in the choice of research method of many national studies, ensures that few significant results of nationwide social programs will be uncovered. Instead of this unrealistic search for total effects, evaluation studies could more usefully be asking: Which types of individual projects succeeded on a range of pertinent dependent variables? Which failed? And what are the differences between the two? This approach to evaluation research implies a diversity of methods applied to a variety of sites—what Donald Campbell has called "the cottage-industry model" of evaluation research. This shift in methods would lead to a greater diversity of policy-relevant findings. And, not incidentally, it would mitigate many of the ethical problems raised by the repeated use of a single methodological approach.

Once again, the ethical problems here are not unique to but are exacerbated in policy research. Nonpolicy work, through its diversity across time and numerous sites, more naturally resembles the cottage-industry model. The biases and limi-

---

[10] T. F. Pettigrew, "Competing Evaluating Models: The ESAA Evaluation," *Journal of Educational Statistics*, 3 (Spring, 1978), 99–106.

tations of one method are usually corrected by the applications of rival methods. But the greater centralization of policy research funding, as well as its restricted time span, have not generally allowed this corrective process to operate in a similar manner. The cottage-industry approach using a multiplicity of investigators, methods, and sites would have to be consciously built into funding procedures for policy work.

Research Design and Outcome Measures

Within any methodological tradition, social scientists have considerable discretion is choosing a research design and outcome measures. Problems are created when the most powerful research designs available are not employed and when outcome measures are styled to fit the desired conclusion. Often the biasing effects here are subtle and highly technical and hence are of little interest to policymakers and the public. But these effects may cast serious doubt over the policy implications that can be drawn from the results. Consequently, these factors have often been the focal points of contention in social science debates surrounding policy research.

Can, for example, white families be said to be "fleeing" racial desegregation in a research design that neither asked them about their motivations nor placed its school enrollment data in a larger demographic perspective?[11] Critics thought not,[12] but the mass media coverage of the white flight research did not find such points compelling.

[11] The critical literature on the white-flight research is now so voluminous that we cannot attempt to review it here. We recommend as an entry into this literature an early review of the entire episode and a more recent demographic article: T. F. Pettigrew and R. L. Green, "School Desegregation in Large Cities: A Critique of the Coleman White Flight Thesis," *Harvard Educational Review*, 46 (1976), 1–53; and D. L. Sly and L. G. Pol, "The Demographic Context of School Segregation and Desegregation," *Social Forces*, 56 (June, 1978), 1072–86.

[12] Pettigrew and Green.

More technical issues involve evaluation studies that compare groups which differ sharply on such critical variables as social class. The controversial Westinghouse–Ohio University evaluation of Head Start illustrates the problem.[13] By law, Head Start programs selected children who were unusually disadvantaged members of economically deprived households. Children used as nontreatment comparisons were therefore necessarily more advantaged. The Westinghouse–Ohio University investigation attempted a statistical correction for this difference in socioeconomic status between its experimental and control groups. Thus, the study "adjusted" for the difference by utilizing socioeconomic status as a covariate in its analysis of covariance. But this procedure undercorrects for the class difference between the groups.[14] The choice of research design in this study, one common to many programs designed specifically for the poor, systematically underestimates the effect of the program by undercorrecting for the crucial control variable. Indeed, as Campbell and Erlebacher show, this undercorrection for social class can even make beneficial programs such as Head Start appear harmful.[15] In reverse, the same research design can cause harmful

[13]V. Cicirelli et al., The Impact of Head Start: An Evaluation of the Effects of Head Start on Children's Cognitive and Affective Development. A report to the Office of Economic Opportunity pursuant to Contract B89-4536, June 1969. Westinghouse Learning Corporation and Ohio University. Distributed by Clearinghouse for Federal Scientific and Technical Information, U.S. Dept. of Commerce, National Bureau of Standards, Institute for Applied Technology, Washington, D.C.

[14]The inadequacy of this research design was known prior to the Head Start study. See, for example, F. M. Lord, "Large-scale Covariance Analysis when the Control Variable is Fallible," Journal of the American Statistical Association, 55 (1960), 307–21; and S. H. Evans and E. J. Anastasio, "Misuse of Analysis of Covariance when Treatment Effect and Covariate are Confounded," Psychological Bulletin, 69 (1968), pp. 225–34.

[15]D. T. Campbell and A. Erlebacher, "How Regression Artifacts in Quasi-experimental Evaluations can Mistakenly Make Compensatory Education Look Harmful," in Struening and Gutentag, pp. 597–617.

interventions to appear beneficial. This reverse evaluation result occurs when the treated experimental group ranks significantly higher on socioeconomic status than the untreated control group (as when only volunteers enter the program). Campbell and Erlebacher conclude:

> We academics are apt to assume that, when things go wrong in collaborations between the political and scholarly communities, the failure comes from the political process, in the form of a failure to make use of our more than adequate wisdom. In this instance, it was quite the reverse. . . . [T]he failure came from the inadequacies of the social science community (including education, psychology, economics, and sociology) which as a population was not ready for this task. . . . On using analysis of covariance to correct for pretreatment differences, the texts that treat the issue are either wrong or noncommittal. . . . The prestige of complex multivariate statistics and their associated computer programs will perpetuate such mistakes for years to come, under such terms as dummy variable analysis, multiple covariate analysis of covariance, step-wise multiple regression, and the like. The deep-rooted seat of the bias is probably the unexplicit trust that, although the assumptions of a given statistic are technically not met, the effects of the departures will be unsystematic. The reverse is, in fact, true. The more one needs the "controls" and "adjustments" which these statistics seem to offer, the more biased are their conclusions.[16]

Indeed, this pessimism has already been validated. Campbell[17] recently noted that the same research design problem has reappeared in the analysis of achievement scores of

---

[16]Ibid., pp. 612–13.
[17]D. T. Campbell, "Statement by Donald T. Campbell, approved for press release, on the draft report entitled "Public and Private Schools." Unpublished manuscript, University of Syracuse, April 6, 1981.

private and public school children.[18] Once again, large initial differences between the comparison groups meant that the covariates employed to "adjust" for crucial differences in family background, educational effects of peers, and intelligence seriously undercorrected for these factors. Campbell believes that this sytematic undercorrection could by itself produce the much-publicized higher achievement scores for private school pupils. "Certainly," he concludes, "these differences should *not* at this stage be interpreted as due to school effects."[19] Predictably, Campbell's press release on this point received scant media attention in comparison to the nationwide coverage provided the release of the initial findings.

More generally, the strength of the research design appears to affect evaluation research differently across various fields. In pharmacology, for example, the more rigorous research designs show the least favorable effects of antidepressant drugs.[20] But in compensatory education studies, for reasons just discussed, the more rigorous designs provide the most significant gains on cognitive measures.[21] The policy implications likely to be drawn from weak research designs

[18]J. S. Coleman, T. Hoffer, and S. Kilgore, *Public and Private Schools* (Chicago: National Opinion Research Center, March, 1981).

[19]Campbell, p. 1. The same point, among other criticisms, has also been made by the economist Arthur Goldberger. Difficult as the problem is, Goldberger notes that "the approaches to statistical removal of such selectivity biases . . . are now routine in the econometric literature." A. S. Goldberger, "Coleman Goes Private (in Public)." Unpublished manuscript. University of Wisconsin, May, 1981, p. 8. Goldberger has himself contributed to this literature; see B. S. Barnow, G. G. Cain, and A. S. Goldberger, "Issues in the Analysis of Selectivity Bias," Madison, Wis., University of Wisconsin Institute for Research on Poverty, April, 1980, paper no. DP 600-80.

[20]A. Smith, E. Traganza, and G. Harrison, "Studies on the Effectiveness of Antidepressant Drugs," *Psychopharmacology Bulletin*, March, 1969, 1–53.

[21]E. L. McDill, M. S. McDill, and J. Sprehe, *Strategies for Success in Compensatory Education: An Appraisal of Evaluation Research.* (Baltimore, Md.: The Johns Hopkins University Press, 1969).

in these areas, then, are too favorable to antidepressant drugs and too unfavorable to educational interventions intended to benefit the children of the poor.

Striking examples abound of how the selection of outcome measures can determine policy conclusions. One generic form of this problem involves using "soft," easy-to-change attitudinal dependent variables instead of "hard," resistant-to-change behavioral dependent variables. Energy conservation programs appear successful when judged by survey data that show how Americans are becoming increasingly concerned about energy. But their effectiveness is often called into question when the outcome measure is actual use of energy.[22]

Similar problems occur in the evaluation of family planning programs. Researchers have used a range of plausible indicators of success.

- Changes in knowledge, attitudes, or interest related to birth control
- Changes in information that may be related to birth control
- Initial acceptance of some method of fertility control
- Continuation with a method of fertility control over a fixed time period, such as one year
- A reduction in fertility for the area covered by the program
- A reduction in fertility that can be attributed causally to the program's intervention[23]

---

[22]T. F. Pettigrew, D. Archer, and E. Aronson, "Recurrent Problems in Evaluation Studies of Energy Conservation Programs," unpublished manuscript, University of California, Santa Cruz, August, 1981.

[23]For a detailed discussion of both research designs and outcome measures in this area, see E. T. Hilton and A. A. Lumsdaine, "Field Trial Designs in Gauging the Impact of Fertility Planning Programs," *Evaluation and Experiment*, ed. by C. A. Bennett and A. A. Lumsdaine (New York: Academic Press, 1975), pp. 319–400.

It is far easier to obtain "favorable" results with outcomes at the beginning than at the end of the list. People are more likely to report a change of attitude than a shift in behavior and to use contraceptives once than to continue them over an extended period. In Pakistan a few years ago, knowledge about contraceptives ran about 90%, but only about 5% of the relevant population used contraception. Similarly, it is easier to show a fertility decline in a program area than to show that the decline was caused by the family planning program. In many areas of the world, fertility has been declining without organized interventions; therefore the question becomes not whether fertility is declining but what proportion of this decline can be attributed to the intervention.

The tough ethical question is to what extent the social scientist has an obligation to use the most powerful research design available and the widest range of outcome measures. At the very least, social scientists should adopt a design and outcome variables that permit alternatives to be explored, making clear the rationale and limitations of these choices.

Policy-oriented researchers have stronger obligations along these lines than other researchers. We have noted how the shorter time span and greater centralization of policy research funding heighten these ethical concerns for policy research. Here we add two additional considerations. The consumers of policy research, unlike those of "basic" research, are less likely to be sophisticated about the technical aspects that bias and mold the results. If the investigators themselves do not warn policymakers and the public about the limitations of their own work, fragile but politically beneficial findings are likely to be engraved in stone as proven truths.

Finally, many of the ethical issues occasioned by particular choices of research design and outcome variables apply largely to studies that attempt to specify *causal* relationships. Thus, Campbell's strictures about the undercorrection for social class controls in the Head Start and private versus public school studies apply only when causal inference is involved. Many of these problems do not arise when, say, statistical forecasting is the object. But here again we have a difference between policy and nonpolicy social research. Policy interpretations almost invariably involve causal inference, and research put to policy uses is interpreted causally even if it is poorly designed for this purpose. By contrast, much nonpolicy research does not require causal inference.

Sampling

All research methods, quantitative or qualitative, historical or contemporaneous, involve sampling. In essence sampling is a systematic process of choosing some part of a larger body to represent the whole. And public policy cares about the whole, about the generalization of research findings to the entire domian in question. Here again problems raised in nonpolicy research are magnified in policy settings. The significance of any set of results for policy can be no greater than the accuracy of its sampling procedures. Yet policymakers and the public generally do not understand sampling theory and its importance. They are necessarily dependent on the honesty and competence of the investigator in this technical area.

One especially notorious case illustrates the point.[24] An educational psychologist without specialized training in survey research developed a speciality of aiding the defense in court cases on pornography. In repeated cases, he would conduct a citizen attitude survey on "community standards" styled to fit recent U.S. Supreme Court rulings on the subject.

[24] A. St. George and P. H. McNamara, " 'Filthy Pictures' or The Case of the Fraudulent Social Scientist: Unmasking the Phony Expert," *American Sociologist*, 14 (August, 1979), 142–9.

Together with biased questions and faulty analysis procedures, the psychologist claimed to be drawing "representative"samples of respondents, though apparently he simply
talked to anyone who would talk to him. And he successfully
got away with these procedures in case after case, though he
underwent cross-examination in each. Not until two other
social scientists became involved were the fraudulent methods exposed. This example highlights the vulnerability of even
the sharp adversary process of the courts to gross deception
on sampling.

More generally, three ethical questions concern sampling
in policy research. First, was any deliberate attempt made to
select samples likely to produce results congenial to a particular policy line? The gauge here would have to be the degree
of departure from acceptable principles of sampling. Second,
even if there were no intentions to distort the results, was
the sample adequately drawn to represent the population
about which the policy generalizations are made? Third, whatever the sampling procedures employed, did the investigators
release enough information for other scholars to replicate and
criticize the procedures? Straightforward as these questions
may seem, some of the sharpest points of debate over policy
research have centered around them.[25]

Data-Gathering Procedures

A major source of bias in social research involves how
the data are collected. And the ethical concerns occasioned
by this general problem are again sharpened by the importance and special qualities of policy research discussed earlier.
The literature on sources of bias at this research stage is voluminous. But we can illustrate the special relevance of these

---

[25]For one example, see Pettigrew and Green.

problems for policy research by reconsidering the KAP survey.

For persons who have no idea of what a household survey is supposed to be, who are unaccustomed to sharing their most intimate thoughts with total strangers, and who have no experience in compressing their thoughts into fixed response categories, this fleeting encounter is unlikely to elicit considered expressions of opinions. Yet among people accustomed to deference in the face of authority from the capital city, answers may be given and duly recorded. Often the answers will be projections of the respondent's view of what the interviewer wants to hear. Another limitation is that such surveys assume that the respondents have thought enough about the matters under investigation to have crystallized opinions about them. Yet many KAP surveys forced respondents to select a predetermined response without allowing for such realistic answers as "Don't know" or "Never thought about it." Ethical difficulties mount when such suspect survey data are adduced to support the case for widespread interest in family planning.

Other sources of bias in data collection include poorly trained interviewers and outright falsification. Untrained field interviewers may not probe for deeper levels of meaning and may simply accept instant platitudes. Usually such biases slant toward official views of reality and against critical analyses of public policies. Outright falsification does occur, not only in survey interviews but also in field reports written by individuals whose performance is judged by the attainment of numerical quotas. This problem is painfully analogous to the fictitious "body counts" reported in the Vietnam War by U.S. Army officers whose promotions depended on them. Social scientists using such information may not be able to prevent falsification, but they should try to limit it, assess it, and warn readers about it.

Analysis and Interpretation

Further ethical issues emerge with the analysis and interpretation of social science data. We have noted how causal inferences play a larger role in policy than in nonpolicy research. And it is precisely the enormous epistemological problems surrounding causal inferences that lead to the most complex ethical problems for social research. This stage conspicuously exposes these problems. But they are intertwined with the issues raised at each stage of the research process, from initial conceptualization of the problem through choices of methods and data gathering. Consequently, we have already listed examples of where causal analyses and interpretations were at the core of policy research debates about white flight, the Head Start Program, and private versus public schools.

A recurrent form of this problem involves causal interpretations that center on key variables neither directly measured nor compared. One much criticized study of school desegregation puported to show how "busing" had "failed" by comparing one group of desegregated black children with a "control" group in which most of the black children also attended desegregated schools![26] The "white flight" research was also widely cited as involving busing, though the study included no measure of school transportation whatsoever.[27]

The 1966 report of the Population Council to the government of Kenya provides another example.[28] In summarizing the results of KAP surveys in other countries, the Council's

[26]T. F. Pettigrew, *et al.*, "Busing: A Review of The Evidence," *Public Interest*, 30 (Winter, 1973), 88–118.

[27]Pettigrew and Green.

[28]Population Council of the U.S.A., *Family Planning in Kenya: A Report Submitted to the Republic of Kenay by an Advisory Mission of the Population Council of the United States of America* (Nairobi: The Kenya Ministry of Economic Planning and Development, 1966), p. 16.

mission asserted that the majority "would like to limit the size of their families and to space intervals between births of their children." This assertion was actually a composite inference from responses to such questions as:

- Do you want to have any (more) children? [If more] How many more do you want to have?
- Now suppose that you could start your married life all over again and choose to have just the number of children that you would want by the time you were 45 years old. How many children would you have?

Claims about interest in family planning were apparently based on reported discrepancies between an individual's ideal and actual family size, statements about the number of additional children wanted and those likely to be born without birth control, and stated approval for "doing something" to delay or prevent a pregnancy. Aside from the inherent problems of hypothetical and retrospective questions, the authors of the report went far beyond their data. The majority did *not* "state" that they would prefer to limit the size of their families. This assertion was an inference of the authors that went unchallenged at the time. Only later, when demand proved considerably less than expected, did other scholars take a close look at this reasoning.

Statements on Policy Implications

Expansive interpretations of research results flow naturally into expansive implications for policy drawn from social research. Here we encounter ethical problems truly distinctive for policy research. Consequently, there is even less consensus within social science about the ethical standards that should apply.

Two recent and highly publicized cases involving James Coleman illustrate the complexity of these issues. After studying white flight, Coleman drew policy implications that ranged from characterizing the federal courts as "the worst of all possible instruments for carrying out a very sensitive activity like integrating schools" to advocating "activities that encourage racial intermarriage."[29] But his research included neither court nor intermarriage measures. In his more recent work comparing achievement test scores among private and public school children, Coleman concludes that higher scores for private pupils constitute evidence in favor of an educational voucher system.[30]

Many social scientists, we suspect, would argue that Coleman is merely exercising his First Amendment rights as a citizen to advocate his favored public policy alternatives. In addition, this type of "bias" is not of the same character as those previously considered; here the public can more easily determine the appropriateness of the link between the research findings and the advocated policy position.

But these points do not address a difficult ethical problem, one unique to policy research. When social scientists report on the policy research, we believe that their advocacy position will often not be judged as if it were advocacy but rather represented "scientifically" derived results. Put differently, policy researchers will be viewed in their role as *social scientists* even when they are clearly advocating policy that goes far beyond their research findings. Indeed, the mass media show interest in their policy views precisely because they are social scientists and not just random citizens on the street.

The ethical issue is thus tightly drawn. On the one hand, policy researchers, like other citizens, have every right to

[29]Pettigrew and Green.
[30]For a spirited attack on Coleman's policy preference which is being drawn from this research, see Goldberger.

express their policy opinions forcefully. But, on the other hand, these views need to be sharply separated from their research findings and their role as "experts" and "social scientists"—not an easy thing for someone as well known as Coleman.

Publication, Publicity, and Public Debate

Further ethical issues unique to policy research emerge with the release of the research findings and their implications. How are they released? And at what level is any ensuing controversy conducted?

These questions got a thorough, if heated, hearing in the white flight debate. Critics were unhappy that Coleman did not provide the interested social scientific community with written copies of his report for four months following a much publicized speech on the research in Washington, D.C. Coleman later commented that it was "unfortunate that the full report was not available earlier."[31] And critics, noting Coleman's many television appearances and "many dozens" of separate press interviews, charged him with conducting a nationwide mass media "campaign" to advance his views against racial desegregation of the public schools under the guise of reporting on his study. This charge Coleman flatly denied: "By no means have I sought out the media, much less engaged in [a] mass-media campaign."[32]

However, despite the argument over the facts and characterization of the particular case, both sides were in agreement over the proper means of disseminating policy research. Coleman and his critics agreed that mass media campaigns

[31]Reply affidavit of James S. Coleman, *Morgan v. Kerrigan,* United States Court of Appeals for the First Circuit, August 28, 1975, p. 1.
[32]J. S. Coleman, "Response to Professors Pettigrew and Green," *Harvard Educational Review,* 46 (May, 1976), 223.

are inappropriate, even if they disagreed over the definition of such "campaigns." And both agreed that reports of policy research should be readily available.

We will push one step further and urge that the data be available at cost to those who wish to reanalyze them. If social scientists with conflicting policy preferences anlayzed the same data and obtained similar empirical results, the public and policymakers could place more reliance on them. Much of the debate in these policy research controversies has involved empirical claims that could have been at least partially settled by equal access to the same data sets.

Yet the timely availability of the data in question has not been the rule either in policy research or in social research in general. Some years ago, Wolins asked 37 researchers in psychology for the raw data used in recently published journal articles. Five of the investigators never replied to his requests.[33] Of the 32 who did reply, 21 claimed that their data were either misplaced, lost, or inadvertently destroyed. Wolins ultimately was able to reanalyze only 7 data sets out of the original 37 studies (19 percent); in 3 he found gross errors sufficient to alter the previously published conclusions.

To expect routinely to have your policy research reanalyzed would, we believe, act to upgrade standards. It would be a type of peer review for social science comparable to the tighter empirical replications generally possible in the physical sciences. But three qualifications are in order. First, such reanalyses would usually be unable to detect faulty data collection. Second, necessary safeguards of confidentiality would restrict access to some limited forms of data. Finally, some types of data—such as personal field notes—are not suitable for this

---

[33]L. Wolins, "Responsibility for Raw Data," *American Psychologist*, 17 (1962), 657–8. The authors wish to thank Prof. Sharon Herzberger of Trinity College for calling this significant reference to our attention.

practice. But these data types do not characterize the bulk of policy research conducted today.

The white flight controversy also highlights the role of the mass media as brokers for social science influence on public policy. This fact creates problems, because there is a dangerous lack of fit between the mass media and social science. On the media side, social scientific policy research has not been elevated to a specialized "beat." General reporters frequently force their policy research stories into "human interest" formats that concentrate on *ad hominem* attacks by opponents in a public debate, while they ignore the central issues of scientific and policy significance.

On the research side, few social scientists have had any experience in dealing with media personnel. And, as many observers have sourly observed, lecturing to captive audiences of students is not the best preparation. Social scientists, especially those interested in policy research, are generally flattered by media attention, do not wish to waste their rare moment in the spotlight, and frequently become uncharacteristically expansive. Many of the ethical problems that occur at this stage are, we suspect, more the result of momentum than intention.

The complexity of ethical issues is intensified by the Chinese box quality of cumulative ethical problems across each of the stages under discussion. Consider a study done before Medicare on the needs and resources of the aged in the United States.[34] After drawing a sample biased toward upper-income respondents and using leading questions, the authors concluded that nine out of ten older persons reported

---

[34]This case is described in full in L. D. Cain, Jr., "The AMA and the Gerontologists: Uses and Abuses of 'A Profile of the Aging: USA,' " *Ethics, Politics, and Social Research,* ed. by G. Sjoberg (Cambridge, Mass.: Schenkman Publishing Co., Inc., 1967 pp. 78–114.

they had no unfilled medical needs. A press release by one
of the authors drew this policy inference:

> Since all resources are limited . . . the recognition that
> the dependent and helpless in our aging population are
> limited in number will allow available resources to be
> applied with discrimination, with far greater hope of
> return to the society and its people.[35]

Shortly afterward, the President-elect of the American
Medical Association cited this study as evidence that most
persons over the age of sixty-five did not want a government
program of health care. The subject of wide ethical criticism,
this case aptly demonstrates the interlocking of problem conceptualization, value-laden policy inferences, and publicity
for a particular policy line.

TOWARD ETHICAL GUIDELINES FOR POLICY RESEARCH

We believe that the 1980s are an auspicious time within
social science to begin a collective dialogue about ethical issues
in policy research. In this spirit, we present the following
suggestions for ethical guidelines.

As we have noted, many of these guidelines also apply
to social research that has little or no apparent policy relevance. But guidelines for policy research should be the starting point for several reasons mentioned earlier. First, policy
research is more immediately (though perhaps not ultimately)
important in its potential for affecting the lives of citizens.
Second, the ethical problems that it shares with nonpolicy
research are typically heightened by four factors: a shorter
time span of influence, greater concentration of funding, less
sophisticated consumers, and the greater likelihood of employing difficult causal analyses. Third, there are some es-

---

[35]Ibid., p. 85.

pecially difficult ethical issues that are unique to policy research. We have noted how they occur at the final two stages of the research process, drawing policy implications from the results and disseminating the results and interpretations.

Fortunately, we have a comparison for our efforts. Recently a special committee of the American Sociological Association completed a draft code of ethics for sociologists.[36] Interestingly, the ASA's efforts began with a modest code of ethics drawn up in the early 1960s. But the membership voted down this initial effort. Later a code was adopted, but it had little to say of direct relevance to policy research. However, the latest code does give attention to the special concerns addressed in this paper. It also delves into many important ethical questions that are not treated in this paper, such as the rights of research populations, authorship, the review process, and teaching.

We find in the ASA efforts evidence for our contention concerning the auspicious timing of ethical guidelines at this point. And we have been influenced by the many discussions that have taken place around this effort. The proposed ASA code and our suggestions are not independent endeavors, however. The first author served on the committee that drew them up, and the second author serves on the ASA council that amended and approved them for membership vote.

Statement and Conceptualization of the Research Problem

1. The key concepts used in social scientific research on public policy should not be emotionally loaded or biased toward the interests of any partisan group.

2. The conceptualization of the research problem should not prejudge the direction of causality or, through persuasive

---

[36]Ethics Committee of the American Sociological Association, *Code of Ethics: May 1981 Revision for Consideration by the ASA Council*. Washington, D.C.: American Sociological Association, May 3, 1981.

definition, suggest an outcome that may or may not be sustained by the research findings.

3. In research explicity concerned with exploring or testing particular public policies, the conceptualization of the investigation should be as fair as possible to the interests of all major groups involved with these policies.

Choice of Research Method

1. The most powerful research methods appropriate to the problem should be chosen within the limits of available resources. Methods should not be chosen because they are more likely to produce results congenial to the investigator's or the research sponsor's biases and interests.

2. Multiple rather than single research methods should be employed in complex areas of policy or where public debate about the research findings is likely to occur. If the resources are not available for multiple research methods, such critical work should not be attempted.[37]

The proposed ASA Code of Ethics does not speak directly to problems of conceptualization, but it does address these issues of methods:

> Sociologists should strive to maintain objectivity and integrity in the conduct of sociological and research practice. 1. Sociologists should adhere to the highest possible

[37]In discussion at the Hastings Center on this point, Mark Moore raised an interesting objection to this flat exclusion of single-method research in complex areas. He feared it might act to drive out reasonably competent if not fully adequate work in favor of less competent, "quick-and-dirty" work. Setting the standard too high, Moore argued, will simply force policy analysts to rely on even cruder work than that which the guidelines seek to upgrade. Though not without merit, we find this argument unpersuasive. Moore assumes the perspective of the policymaker and "knowledge broker." Our guidelines apply to "knowledge generators." And we focus on the *legitimization* function of research that bears the imprimatur of social science. It is precisely at such points that the two perspectives clash.

technical standards in their research. *Especially when findings may have direct implications for public policy or for the well-being of subjects, research should not be undertaken unless the requisite skills and resources are available to accomplish the research at the highest possible level of excellence.* 2. Since individual sociologists vary in their research modes, skills and experience, sociologists should always set forth *ex ante* the disciplinary and personal limitations that condition whether or not a research project can be successfully completed and condition the validity of the findings.[38]

Research Design and Outcome Measures

1. The most powerful research designs appropriate to the problem should be chosen within the limits of available resources and the situational context. Specifically, where causal attributions are the focus, the study design must be suitable to this difficult task and permit the testing of a range of alternative causes and explanations.
2. A range of outcome measures should be chosen on scientific grounds alone and be appropriate and fair to the complexities of the problem. In program evaluation work in particular, multiple outcome measures that cover a range from attitudes to behavior should be used whenever possible.
3. In reporting the results of policy research, the investigator should discuss the scope and limitations of the basic research design and the outcome measures employed. Such information should be presented in such a fashion that informed readers can judge the relative power of the design and measures for causal attribution.

The proposed ASA code's most relevant section to these considerations reads:

[38]Ibid., pp. 2–3 (italics added).

Regardless of work settings, sociologists are obligated to report findings fully and without omission of significant data. Sociologists should also disclose details of their theories, methods and research designs that might bear upon interpretation of research findings.[39]

Sampling

1. Samples drawn for policy research, whether of individuals, households, communities, events, or other populations should be representative of the population about which generalizations will be made.
2. It is professionally unethical deliberately to bias a sample when such bias is not part of the research design, to omit cases falling within the sample, or to add cases falling outside the sample.
3. In reporting the research findings, the investigator should provide detailed information about the sampling procedures and make clear the limitations these procedures place on the policy relevance of the findings.

Data-Gathering Procedures

1. Investigators should ensure that the basic procedures of data collection are adequately understood by the subjects or respondents of the study. Where there is reason to suspect that this condition does not hold, the investigators should not proceed.
2. The items of questionnaires and interview guides should not be leading, loaded, or otherwise contribute to response bias.
3. The questioning process should have the depth necessary to address the policy-related concerns of the study. Where it is possible within the research design to obtain infor-

[39]Ibid., p. 3.

mation on central questions of causality, such information should be collected and not left to inference later.

4. Persons involved in data collection should have the training and supervision necessary to obtain data of quality sufficient for the policy purposes of the study. Quality control measures are especially necessary in situations where the risks of falsification or distortion are high.

Analysis and Interpretaion

1. Policy researchers should avoid known or suspected sources of bias in causal attribution (e.g., regression artifacts) both in designing their studies and in analyzing their data. Where such sources of bias cannot be avoided in the research design, investigators should make every effort to limit the bias in their analyses, discuss the problem openly in their reporting of the research, and restrict their interpretations accordingly.

2. Attributions of causality should be made only when: (a) plausible links have been established in a robust reserach design between the hypothesized explanatory factor(s) and the outcome of interest and (b) plausible rival explanations of the same outcome have been seriously considered and persuasively ruled out.

3. Special efforts should be made to establish the validity of items that are critical to the policy content and based on self-report or other interview data. Specifically, the investigator should attempt to establish the consistency of such items with other information and should seek behavioral indications of validity whenever available. Findings should not be reported as if their validity is unquestionable when there is a high probability that a key response has been influenced by various types of distortion.

4. The empirical conclusions and inferences drawn from research data should be faithful to those data and their com-

plexity. Thus, unqualified statements about the population should not be made from sampled data, and significant variations and nuances of the findings should not be compressed into oversimplified summaries. Particular care should be taken against overstated conclusions and simplifications of data patterns when these can be misused in subsequent debates about public policy.

5. While high standards of analysis and interpretation should be observed in all social science research, special care should be taken with those parts of the analysis likely to have the greatest influence, stir the sharpest debate, or be most open to misinterpretation in the policy arena. For instance, especially stringent consistency checks should be made of any information based on coding and checks for programming errors made for computer-assisted statistical analyses. In general, the greater the chances of use or abuse in policy discussions, the greater the care that should be exercised in analysis and interpretation.

Statements on Policy Implications

1. In offering policy recommendations based on social science research, investigators should draw a clear distinction between the empirical and normative bases of their recommendations and show how they are connected. The personal, social, and political values that invariably lie behind policy recommendations should be stated honestly and openly rather than being denied or buried in language connoting a purely scientific basis for such recommendations.

2. Where policy recommendations are based on empirical assumptions about the operation of government or the political system, such as assumptions about the likely course of policy implementation, these central assumptions should be made explicit.

Publication, Publicity, and Public Debate

1. At the time of the initial public release of policy-relevant research findings, investigators should (a) have available for general distribution complete reports of the research with full details of methods, (b) disclose all sources of financial support for the research and any special relationship with the sponsor, and (c) offer to provide promptly the data sets at cost to interested social scientists (except where necessary confidentiality would be violated by doing so).

The proposed ASA Code of Ethics extends these considerations as follows:

> Consistent with the spirit of full disclosure of method and analysis, sociologists should make their data available to other social scientists, at reasonable cost, after they have completed their own analyses, except in cases where confidentiality necessarily would be violated in doing so. *The timeliness of this obligation is especially critical when the research is perceived to have policy implications.* Sociologists should not accept grants, contracts, or research assignments that appear likely to require violation of the principles above, and should disassociate themselves from research when they discover a violation and are unable to achieve its correction.[40]

We close with three further suggestions for guidelines along these lines:

2. Social scientists should not engage in publicity campaigns for their policy preferences as part of disseminating their research results. The problem to be avoided here lies not with the publicity *per se* but with the social science legitimization of the policy preference rendered by the campaign.

3. When dealing with the mass media, social scientists should be careful to present an accurate summary of their research

[40]Ibid., p. 4 (italics added).

findings and to emphasize their limitations. Effort should be exerted by policy researchers to make the public aware of the distinction between their stance as scientists and their stance as citizens and policy advocates. Typically such effort should include a candid statement of the investigator's values.

4. Public policy debate among social scientists should be conducted in a civil manner, free of *ad hominem* attacks. Reasoned discussion should focus directly on the social scientific and policy points at issue. Such discussion is enhanced by separating empirical and normative issues as much as possible and by avoiding policy conclusions that extend well beyond the data presented.

A FINAL WORD

We have no illusions that such guidelines could win ready acceptance throughout the social sciences. Moreover, the level of generality at which these guidelines must be written allows for considerable disagreement over specific, operational definitions. The debate over what constitutes "a mass media campaign" in the white flight controversy highlights this limitation. Only heightened concern, discussion, and concrete cases over time can help to develop the necessary specificity.

But two of the principal sources of ethical difficulties are beyond the direct confines of social science itself—the sponsors of research and the mass media of communication. Repeatedly, our discussion has shown how these influences contribute to ethical problems in policy research. Social scientists can, of course, affect these external institutions in the way they deal with them. But social scientists are not likely to reconsider their relations with sponsors and the media until there is more concern about the ethics of policy research within social science itself. With our own house in better order, we will be in a stronger position to deal with others.

INDEX